CEREMONY OF THE SOUPS
And Other One-Act Plays

By

Douglas M. Young

Stonehouse Publishing

Stonehouse Publishing
2715 North Edison Street
Arlington, Va. 22207

Copyright 2001 by the author. All rights reserved. Except for brief passages quoted in a newspaper, magazine, radio or television reviews, no part of this book may be reproduced in any form, or by any means. Copies of the book may be obtained by writing Stonehouse Publishing, 2715 North Edison Street, Arlington, Va. 22207.

Groups wishing performance rights for any of the plays should contact the author directly at 207 St. George Street, Farmville, VA 23901, (804) 392-3476, or by e-mail dyoung@moonstar.com.

ISBN 0-9710201-0-8

TABLE OF CONTENTS

Preface 5

The Greensboro Trilogy:
The Ceremony of the Soups 9
Miss Doris Anderson 35
On the Morning of the First Day 65

On the Warpath 89

Relationships: White, Black and Gay
Three One-Act Plays:
The Lunch Hour 123
On Beech Street 139
Metamorphosis 163

About the Author 193

PREFACE

Some of the one-act plays in this book were written over a number of years and include a blend of historical events and my imagination. Others are more recent and are much smaller in scope and deal with different kinds of human encounters and relationships.

The first three plays in this volume were commissioned by the Greensboro (N.C.) Bicentennial Committee in the early 1970's. This was a few years after the famous Woolworth sit-ins by African-American college students from North Carolina A & T College in 1960. Thus, I made the theme of the plays the events associated with the efforts of African-Americans to achieve educational and social equality. Unfortunately, the Bicentennial Committee decided not to fund the project and thus never read the plays I had written for the commemoration.

In the mid-1960's in Greensboro, the movement to integrate restaurants and other public facilities took on a special significance for the country and for me personally. I was at the time a reporter for the *Greensboro Daily News*. The move by the Congress of Racial Equality (CORE) to integrate restaurant facilities in Greensboro was lagging and the picketing of facilities was generally being ignored. One night I witnessed a new figure I had never seen before leading the group of pickets as they headed up East Market Street to the downtown area. The new figure leading the pickets had a special quality about him. There was a "presence" about him. What was it? His walk? His demeanor? I couldn't say. I just knew that he was different and that suddenly the evening had become electrical. This was clearly a figure of strength who would lead this march and many to follow and achieve the goal, the integration of Greensboro's restaurants and public facilities. This new leader was Jesse Jackson and I was the first to see him in action in his very first appearance as the new leader.

Jackson and the four A &T students who sat in at Woolworth's in February 1960, willingly or unwillingly, changed the social attitudes toward race in Greensboro and beyond. Thus, I thought it fitting to write for the Committee a trilogy of plays that would reflect the racial attitudes in Greensboro and elsewhere for the celebration of the Greensboro Bicentennial. Perhaps that was not what was wanted. Since they never read the plays, it is difficult to say. However, one of the plays, *Miss Doris Anderson* was published in **Southern Theatre** magazine in 1974. This particular play is based on a racial incident in Baltimore as described in a column by Nicholas von Hoffman that appeared in the *Washington Post*. Mr. von Hoffman has granted me permission to use that incident as the foundation for this play.

The other one-act plays in this volume are based on relationships. *On the Warpath* concerns two soldiers from opposite camps who meet on the battlefield. The play is a satirical view of religious conflicts that have ruined so many possibilities for developing good human relationships. *The Lunch Hour* deals with a couple who have a chance encounter in a deli that whets their sexual appetite, while *On Beech Street* deals with a hostile, luckless couple who come together in adversity. *Metamorphosis* concerns a long-term gay relationship that proves, in the end, to be incomplete.

I hope you will enjoy this group of one-act plays as much as I enjoyed writing them and that they will be entertaining to you, the reader, in a thoughtful and, at times, amusing way.

My thanks go first to novelist John Ehle who felt that I had some talent in writing in the dramatic form while I was a graduate student at UNC-Chapel Hill. The late E. Roger Boyle was my mentor at the University of Virginia and the director of the two full-length plays that premiered there while I was the Shubert Playwriting Fellow. Roger Boyle was like a second father to me. His criticism and generosity went well beyond the normal teacher-student relationship.

My thanks also go to the late Arthur Greene at UVA, who was also generous and supportive in so many ways, and to David Weiss, who was Chair of the Department of Drama at UVA when I was a student there.

Others who have encouraged me and made a difference in my career as a writer are Nancy Haga, former Chair of the Department of Speech and Theatre where I taught Theatre for 27 years; my wife, Sarah, and son, Chris, who have endured my years at this avocation, and my daughter, Katherine and brother, Frederic, who are my severest critics.

Francis Wood, a well-known local writer, has been most helpful to me in putting together this anthology, and Ed Baker of nearby Keysville, who is a fine actor, has been an encouraging reader of my work. My thanks also to Dudley Sauve, director of the local community theatre, The Waterworks Players, who has offered both readings and a production of some of my full-length plays.

Douglas M. Young
Farmville, Virginia

THE GREENSBORO TRILOGY:

The Ceremony of the Soups
Miss Doris Anderson
On the Morning of the First Day

THE CEREMONY OF THE SOUPS

A Fantasy

Dedicated to the four students at North Carolina A & T University, Greensboro, North Carolina, who were the first to "sit-in" at the Woolworth's lunch counter, February 1, 1960

CHARACTERS
(in order of appearance)

THE GREAT WHITE CHEF
GEORGE WASHINGTONIO JONES
OLD BLACK JOSEPH
ABRAHAM LINCOLN-TURNER
FRANKLIN ROOSEVELT-ROCKEFELLER, (alias the ALMIGHTY-WHO)
1ST GREAT WHITE WAITRESS
2ND GREAT WHITE WAITRESS
1ST GREAT WHITE FATHER
2ND GREAT WHITE FATHER
THE GREAT WHITE WITCH
FOUR BLACK YOUTHS (non-speaking roles)
THE GREAT WHITE STORE MANAGER
THE GREAT WHITE YOUNG MEN (2 to 4 of them)
THE GREAT WHITE REPORTER (non-speaking role)
THE GREAT WHITE PHOTOGRAPHER (non-speaking role)
THE GREAT WHITE AUDIENCE MEMBER (Note: This character should not be listed on the program)
THE YOU-KNOW-WHO-IN-BLUE (non-speaking role)

NOTE: The Director may duplicate some roles.

THE SETTING

A giant soup bowl and spoon stage left. Later, a dime store lunch counter stage right. The time in this ceremony is February 1, 1960.

The Ceremony of the Soups

The HOUSE LIGHTS are up and the audience, upon entering, sees a huge soup bowl downstage left with a huge spoon poking out of it. Inside the bowl unseen are platforms and ladders leading to the top of the bowl. The time is February 1, 1960.

Enter the GREAT WHITE CHEF wearing the great white hat and great white apron. He carries a great silver ladle and a great silver kettle that is empty. He bangs the ladle against the kettle to get attention. The HOUSE LIGHTS dim out and cross fade to general STAGE LIGHTING.

GREAT WHITE CHEF: (to audience) Soups on, yawl come and get it. (He smiles a great white smile and exits).
GEORGE WASHINGTONIO JONES: (henceforth known as G.W. He is free (to a certain extent), black and 21. He pops up from inside the soup bowl) Soup's on, boys.

OLD BLACK JOSEPH (Henceforth known as JOE), ABRAHAM LINCOLN-TURNER (henceforth known as ABE), and FRANKLIN ROOSEVELT-ROCKEFELLER (henceforth known as ROCK, alias the ALMIGHTY WHO), all are free (to a certain extent), black and 21, pop up inside the soup bowl.

JOE: Soup's on.
ABE: The soup's on me. (He pulls a carrot from his pocket and drops it in the bowl).
ROCK: The soup's on us. (He holds up a turnip and drops it in the bowl).
G.W.: Don't wanna offend nobody.
OTHERS: No suh.
JOE: Don't wanna hurt nobody's feelins.
OTHERS: No indeed, suh.
ABE: Ain't polite to point out a little weakness or two.
ROCK: Or three.
G.W.: Or four.
JOE: I bid five.
ABE: I raise it to six.
ROCK: Pick up your night sticks.

ALL duck down in the bowl with the SOUND of a splash.

G.W.: (He comes up for air). Glub. Well, you know how it was, boys.
OTHERS: (They come up for air). Glub. Naw, how was it, boy?
G.W.: Well I come in on that great white bus with the blue trimmin'. You know, the one got the hound painted on it.

OTHERS: (They howl like hounds on the hunt). Yargle, yargle.
JOE: A-barkin' at the moon.
ABE: In January 'stead of June.
ROCK: At the moon, not a coon.
ALL: (They howl). Yargle, yargle.
G.W.: But sure wasn't in heat.
JOE: It bein' January and cold and awesome bleak.
ABE: Uh huh, January and Jack Frostie chunkin' ice on the sunny southland.
ROCK: Sorry, sonny of the sunny southland, but taint no heat in yon back of the bus.
G.W.: I had sat—that is to say—I had been placed, due to a priori conditions, placed myself, my own little body, I'm speakin' of …
JOE: Titter, titter.
ABE: My own little black body.
ROCK: No, *his* own little black body.
G.W.: at Z-row in the back of that little playhouse because—due to a priori conditions …
JOE: You done said that, man.
ABE: Erudition and education are said to be our sure salvation.
ALL: Rah! Rah! Rah!
ROCK: Thank you for them kind words, brother. Now let us move on and turn to the second chapter, the first verse according to—
G.W.: Up front in that hound it was as warm as a Mississippi swamp.
JOE: Ah! So maybe you tasted that, has you, brother?
ABE: It sure beat the soup.
ROCK: Oh yeah, it got a certain zing to it. It be 38 calibre.
JOE: If it ain't the bestest it be the fastest. The hound, brother?
G.W.: Well hound don't bite, but drivers sometimes do.
JOE: Would you, sir, be so good as to step to the back of the hound before I bites you?
ABE: Would you care for a pillow for your head?
ROCK: It made from our finest tombstone.
JOE: Sorry, we fresh out of black marble. It ain't the style no way.
G.W.: Got so cold I was combing ice curls out of my kinky hair.
JOE: Kinky-stinky-boo.
G.W.: So cold my black sweater froze to my black shirt which in turn froze to my black skin.
ABE: They didn't make black undies in them days, youngster-boy, so he didn't wear none.
ROCK: Oh I say!
JOE: Wasn't the style. Now where were you in the narrative, brother-boy?
G.W.: The name be G.W. Jones.
JOE: G.W.! I'll write that down.
ABE: you sure that ain't VW?

ROCK: G.W. Stand for George—
ALL: Washingtonio!
ABE: (A beat). Jones.
JOE: Jones?
ABE: Jones.
JOE: Oh well. So where was you in the narrative, boy?
G.W.: Well, suh, you might say I live a hound's tooth away from a big-little place called Greensboro, Nawth C'lina.
ROCK: Which is Nawth of Calhounsville, South C'lina.
ABE: Interposition and nullification ain't the way to sure salvation.
G.W.: See, this Greens-towns-ville, whatever, was the place where I was takin' my schoolin'.
ROCK: And what were the name of your school?
G.W.: A and Tee-tee.
JOE: Oh, I say!
G.W.: Actually by count, there is really only one Tee in the Tee-Tee which is A and T.
JOE: I am relieved to hear it.
G.W.: It bein' the Nawth C'lina Agricultural and Technical University of the Consolidated University of Nawth C'lina which was the corporate body which it was under, which made various and sundry unqualified schools and kindergartens and colleges into universities (which they wasn't) but was done to please and appease black folks and others to believe they was universities when they wasn't by no stretch of the imagination. So therefore, due to a priori conditions ... I is suddenly lost in my rhetoric.
JOE: I is ashamed to say that I did not follow all that wind, brother.
ROCK: It is clear you are politically-minded, brother, which I understand is a brain disease.
G.W.: I would surely be elected, brother, were it not for a priori conditions.
ABE: You have digressed from the narrative again, dear brother.
G.W.: But now I am consolidated, brother. As you know, we take our schoolin' amongst those who lives on the east side of town where the sun rises in the early mornin' in vain hopes of lightenin' up the coloring of the skin on that side of town. 'Twas in vain, though, as you can see.
OTHERS: Umm.
G.W.: The main reason bein' we was all sliced up on the east side like little chocolate pies by the Great White Fathers 'twixt and 'tween a bunch of lovely super-duper highways.
JOE: And therefore ...
ABE: The colorin' could not be lightened up none ...
ROCK: Because of ...
G.W.: Pollution, brothers and sisters, pollution!
OTHERS: Ah!
JOE: It stand to reason.

ABE: If you can't get no light bright wash 'cause of them fumes ...
G.W.: You can't get no light bright skin neither.
OTHERS: Ah!
ROCK: Due to a priori conditions.
ABE: You hush, brother. Erudition and education is said to be our sure salvation.
JOE: Where was we in this race for equality?
ROCK: Nowheresville, just north of Calhounsville in a state of oblivion.
ABE: A-playin' with sharp objects amongst ourselves.
JOE: A-blowin' it in the wind.
ABE: Take one needle and one knife and stick it me, baby.
ROCK: Would you care to see my punctured arm or my punctured gut?
JOE: That sound like revenge tragedy, boy, and that don't play at this house.
G.W.: No it be comedy and that brother there is in stitches.
ABE: Might we have you name, suh, for our records?
ROCK: Franklin Roosevelt-Rockefeller with a hyphen.
ABE: Franklin Roosevelt-Rockefeller-with-a-Hyphen. Well now, Mr. Hyphen ...
ROCK: They call me Rock for short.
ABE: Well now, Mr. Short-Rock.
ROCK: Could you tell me, suh, where I am incarcerated at?
ABE: Since you is in need of stitchin', naturally, you is at the horse-spital.
ROCK: I beg your pardon, suh, but I usually checks in at the jail first as a kind of civic duty.
ABE: A kind of voluntary incarceration, you mean.
ROCK: That all depend on how much the hand on my neck is chokin', how far the night stick in my back is pushin', how tight the cuffs on my hands is squeezin'.
ABE: Surprise, surprise. What if I was to tell you you ain't in the horse-spital?
ROCK: I ain't?
ABE: That you ain't in no jail.
ROCK: Now that *is* a surprise.
ABE: That you is in the playhouse.
ROCK: Hunh?
ABE: I can see you ain't very appreciative of your public.
ROCK: To tell the truth, I ain't never had no playhouse. And no toys — except one which I ain't about to show you, buster-boy.
G.W.: He means a the-ate-ter.
ROCK: Where I come from a dark picture-show is the worst place for a boy and his toy.
G.W.: This ain't that kind of the-ate-ter.
JOE: This is the kind where you is alive and in color.
ROCK: Well, I have always been in color.
JOE: This is the kind where people come to see you.
ROCK: Alive or in color?
JOE: They out there now. (He points to the audience).

THE CEREMONY OF THE SOUPS

ROCK: Why, so they are.
ABE: They come to hear our saga, our epic.
JOE: Our trials and tribulations.
G.W.: Our wonders and our woes.
ROCK: Then they are incarcerated, too.
ABE: More or less.
ROCK: Perhaps they would like to join us.
G.W.: In the soup?
JOE: I'll see. Would anybody like to join us in the soup?
ABE: I guess they not a very social group.
ROCK: Well, they ain't formally met us. Now if we was to get out of the soup ...
ABE: I admires a man who thinks big. Erudition and ...
ROCK: Never mind that now. Let us depart from this dank and soupy place to other environs. We is in the the-ate-ter! (He pulls up his ladder and sets it outside against the bowl).

ALL but G.W. climb down to the stage.

ROCK: Wait a minute now. Just look at yourself.
ABE: Do I have to? I'm not sure it's the thing to do.
ROCK: Fix your tie.
ABE: Oh! I am so sorry.
ROCK: And spit on your shoes. Don't you know you in the the-ate-ter now?
ABE: Oh I say! Protestations, brother, I thought I was still in the soup. Hey, I ain't even wet or greasy.
JOE: Now that be miraculous.
ROCK: No, that be the the-ate-ter, brothers.
ABE: Ah! (To G.W.) Ain't you comin'?
G.W.: I am tryin' to unwind my historical-type epic saga which I would like to finish before the soup cools off. (He climbs down the ladder).
ABE: You go right ahead. We're off to take the grand tour. C'mon, Old Black Joseph.
JOE: Naw, I ain't comin'. (He flops down on the floor and yawns). I is too lazy and triflin' to get up. Yawl know how black folks is and I am playin' my role. Yawl just go ahead. (He yawns). Be non-violent now.
ROCK: Oh don't worry none about that. We outnumbered, as usual.

They go down into the audience and bow politely to all they stop and meet, "Good evenin', suh," "Good evenin', m'am." Black members of the audience are deliberately ignored.

JOE: (He yawns). Well, suh, I'd like you to know I done all I could for the world. Why, I got folks who done made the Role of Honor.
G.W.: (Awed). The Role of Honor.

JOE: Yes suh. The Great White Lady she come 'round every month to make sure nobody ain't rolled off the Role of Honor.
G.W.: Now ain't that nice. To have somebody to see to their welfare.
JOE: Yeah, and that Great White Lady do love it so. You know, givin' us directions. Tellin' us what we got to do. You know, givin' light to our darkness. (He stands).
G.W.: Oh we bless her and her good deeds, don't we? But where is my tale?
JOE: Why, it's right there attached to your spine.
G.W.: No, no, dear brother, I meant the direction of my thoughts.
JOE: Well while you findin' your direction, I'll entertain us with a song. (He climbs the ladder slowly, solemnly, singing). I hear the gentle voices calling—shoot the liquor to me, John, boy!
G.W.: Ah! I got it now! I got off there at the terminal place.
JOE: Ah! Was you dead?
G.W.: Frost-bit. My marbles was ...
ROCK: (Calling from the audience). Hoo-hoo-hold it! Man, you be careful. You can't say that in the the-ate-ter.
ABE: (From the audience). No, man. Now if they were wings, it'd be on the up and up, but from the waist down, it ain't permitted.
G.W.: Well I say with all them golf courses white folks got in big-little town, USA, there oughta be a place where I can play with my marbles.

ABE and ROCK stare at each other down front.

ROCK: You gonna argue with that, man?
ABE: Not me, brother. Say on.
G.W.: My marbles was froze inside my handbag.

JOE falls into the soup bowl.

ABE: uh-oh. Periscope up!
G.W.: Periscope up, sir!

A periscope comes up from the bowl of soup with vegetables stringing down from it.

ROCK: Um. He'll be back in a minute, folks. He's recuperatin' from the strain on the side of his noodle.
ABE: Noodle? Could have sworn it was cream of chicken.
G.W.: You got a short memory, brother.
ABE: Short memories burn long fuses.
JOE: (He rises from the bowl, singing). Thanks for the memories—
ROCK and ABE: (singing to the audience) Yeah, we thank you so much.
G.W.: (begins a chant). Well, I strolled on in that terminal—

OTHERS: Yes, brother.
G.W.: my handbag in my hand—
OTHERS: Yes, brother.
G.W.: took a dime from out my pocket—
OTHERS: Yes, brother.
G.W.: and gave it to the man—
ABE: (To audience). Things was cheap them days.
OTHERS: Well, brother?
G.W.: (No chant). I'd like my coffee black, man, with a spoon of sugar.
JOE: (On the ladder, calling back). Coffee black.
ABE: (Calling back). Spoon of sugar.
ROCK: (Calling back). To go.
G.W.: Hold it. Hold everything. Didn't say that.
JOE: You said coffee black.
ABE: You said spoon of sugar.
ROCK: Dig it, boy. Dig out of here now.
G.W.: It cold, man. Got that walk, man. Like six long blocks to the east side to the campus. C'mon, man. Who's to know?
ROCK: The crow will know, boy, and peck my little body with his beak. Besides, it ain't sanitary.
JOE: Your kind breed flies, they say.
ABE: And raunchy roaches, they say.
ROCK: See, it be all right to plate it if other folk ate it.
ABE: Education got to follow rules and regulations, you understand.
G.W.: I understand.
OTHERS: Ah!
JOE: He understand.
ABE: He understand.
ROCK: He a understanding man.
JOE: When you calls him "boy," he understand.
ABE: Be it law or custom, he understand.
ROCK: The honored traditions of this great little city is at stake, ladies and gentlemen.
JOE & ABE: He understand!
ROCK: And it be good for business.
JOE & ABE: Whew! He understand.
G.W.: (Resuming chant). So I strolled on out that terminal—
OTHERS: He understand.
G.W.: my handbag in my hand—
OTHERS: He understand.
G.W.: put my dime back in my pocket—
OTHERS: He understand.
G.W.: 'stead of giving it to the Man.
OTHERS: (Gleeful smiles). He understand.

G.W.: I WAS MADDER THAN SHIT!

The OTHERS stare at each other. JOE comes down from the ladder and the three of them go into a football huddle and mumble, mumble, mumble and point at the angry G.W. In a moment, they surround him.

JOE: Ahum.
ABE: Well now.
ROCK: What you trying to do, brother, blow this harmonious arrangement we done developed with the paid admissions?
ABE: Alienation could mean incarceration which ain't no way to sure salvation.
JOE: I figger he blew his coolie.
ABE: Oh I say!
ROCK: A little repentshun of your black sins is in order here, George Washingtonio Jones.
JOE: For the benefit of our little congregation which is gathered here. And remember to keep it clean.
ABE: Wholesome for conspicuous consumption.
ROCK: Amen. On your grubby knees, brother Jones, and confess your sins to the Almighty-Who. (He puts on a Great White Mask).
G.W.: (He goes to his knees). Almighty-Who forgive me for my sins.
ROCK: Be moved, brothers, a tear here and a tear there.

The OTHERS weep for a short two seconds.

ROCK: I forgive you, sonny. Now just what was those sins? (To the others). You boys get lost 'cause sometimes these sinners tells some right hot tales. Wouldn't want you lads to be corrupted.
ABE & JOE: Amen and yes suh. Yes suh and amen. (They move away but eavesdrop).
ROCK: Now then you go right ahead, brother, and dispose of the trash which is in your despicable mind. Item one.
G.W.: I mumbles to myself.
ROCK: (To the others). He mumble to hisself! Now you lissen to me, brother, you save your riddles for the You-Know-Who-in-Blue and not the Almighty-Who. Now let's have it. Relieve thyself.
G.W.: Imprecations in the night.

ALL whistle.

ROCK: The trash is in the barrel. Voulez-vous, parlez-vous, and what else? Pick a barrel for your trash.
G.W.: Don't know if I can. It so hard, Almighty-Who.

ROCK: Drop a dollah in the cup, Brother Jones. It make it easy. Easy for thee, easier for me.
G.W.: It my last dollah, Almighty-Who.
ROCK: That's all right, brother. St. Francis, he understand.
JOE & ABE: He understand.
ROCK: Hush back yonder or it's back in the soup with you. Now proceed with the unloadin' of your cerebral burden, that which has regurgitated into your mind.
G.W.: Don't know. Don't know if I can.
JOE: What's with him? Ain't he playin' no more?
ABE: Give him time, man. It's a long game.
ROCK: Hurry up, brother. Got me a luncheon date with the bishops and rabbis and others with testimonials to the right-side-upness of the world. Right now, brother, we is spinning on a predetermined axis toward an imperceptible glory which, if we ain't in step, may pass us by; which, being imperceptible, may have already done so, takin' with it the ever-elusive bluebird of happiness.
JOE & ABE: So they say.
ROCK: Right. But we doubts it, brother, because we would need no testimonials to the supreme right-side-upness of things if the world was, indeed, ipso facto, right-side-upwards, as so claimed. Does you follow me?
JOE & ABE: Amen, brother, in your fashion.
ROCK: Therefore, it is my determination that the predestined rotation of the axis has, in effect, left the brotherhood of man sitting in his place with his fork at the ready, waitin' to pitch into a good hot lunch. The lunch is being held at the Holiday Inn, by the by, with the Reverend Charlie Uptight White picking up the tab on a menu that begin with the shrimp cocktail. Umm! Which is why I am goin'. Now then, if you didn't gather all that under your black kinky wool, for another dollah in the collection plate, I should be glad to elucidate further on the subject. You wouldn't have a toothpick on you, wouldja?
G.W.: Nay, brother.
ROCK: Sinner livin' in sin, back to your cursin'. And in order of occurrence, please. There'll be no deviatin' from the text.
G.W.: Cursed me, brother.
ROCK: Well, he deserve it. If there ever was a scoundrel in this world it ... .You say you, that what you say?
G.W.: Me, brother.
ROCK: Oh. Well, you gotta start somewhere. And it do seem logical after all, considerin' the pigmentation of your skin which do appear somewhat darkly.
G.W.: I cursed me for having to bear the load!
ROCK: Um-hum, bearing the burden.
G.W.: Why me, I say. Why I got to do it?
ROCK: Why you, indeed, you cotton pecker.
G.W.: Why not some of these other muthers?

ROCK: Absolutely. Why not, indeed. Why not them paraplegics? Them muthers can go anywhere. They got a deal with a wheel.

G.W.: That so? What about them *black* paraplegics?

ROCK: Oh, they much better off than you, brother. The difference being evident. You see when you enters certain specified areas, you walks around to the back door and knocks, right?

G.W.: Say on.

ROCK: Whereas this here black paraplegic muther, he is *rolled* around to the back door and knocks. You clearly see from this example, brother, that the black paraplegic has got it all over you since he gets a free ride to the back door whereas you don't. Furthermore, since he ain't got nothin' to knock with, somebody got to knock for him which is a qualified advantage over you.

G.W.: He is lucky.

ROCK: Indeed he is. However, there is some triflin' small disadvantages in that he got no hooks, which in turn, keep him out of all the plush jobs that is available. For instance, without no hooks, he could not rise to the position of garbage collector. Nor is he available for ditch digging. Nor can he slop pigs. Can't grease no cars or run no elevators or carry no white folks bags. This place him in what we might call the double-zero negative position. In addition, since he got no stumps, he have difficulty runnin' from the You-Know-Who-in-Blue.

G.W.: That clinch it. I is the lucky one. I is red with shame.

ROCK: Anyone can see, brother, that you is blushing. Furthermore, black paraplegic muthers can't drink no coffee either at home or abroad, not having the means to do so.

G.W.: Well that put us more or less in the same tub.

ROCK: More or less since neither can get out in the usual manner. Therefore, you is correct, brother, in choosing to curse yourself first and foremost.

G.W.: There is a blackness within me.

ROCK: No, no, that ain't the problem. The problem is that you let it hang out in a somewhat exposed position. That is to say, where it can be seen.

G.W.: I curse my mama for that.

ABE: Fornication seems a doubtful course to sure salvation.

JOE: Nonetheless, it have some entertaining and satisfying aspects—which reminds of a story ...

ROCK: Lissen, brother, another interruption from you and it's back in the soup.

JOE: My mouth be lock-jawed, Almighty-Who.

ABE: I still say fornication ...

ROCK: Quiet, Goddamnit, during confession! Now then, to item three. Who else was the subject of these here black imprecations as you promenaded from the terminal place in the cold of a January night in the year of our Lord and Saviour, nineteen hundred and sixty?

G.W.: (He points to the audience). Them. Cursed them.

ROCK: (He points to the audience). Them?

G.W.: Them.
ROCK: Well now — that is somewhat all-inclusive, wouldn't you say, boy? Ain't you aware that some of them folks come from nice homes and families. And been here for generation after generation. And they always had indoor toilets and therefore built up a toleration for those folks that ain't.
JOE: That's so. I know people who really don't mind that some black folks have outdoor toilets. Why, they hardly notice them.
G.W.: Does he mean by that that some of those folks are what they call liberal thinkers?
ROCK: Why certainly, my boy. Why they been wishin' for you and yours to have indoor toilets for years and years. Generation after generation.
G.W.: That's so, I reckon.
ROCK: And right now ain't you set up in a nice dormitory room at that college with electricity and running water and a bed that got a mattress?
G.W.: That's true. Hey, man, you know where a fella like me can get a cup of coffee on a cold January night?
ROCK: Patience, brother. Why in another generation or two …
ABE: All right, hold it right there, brother. Your time's up. The repentshun scene is now over and out.
ROCK: Now just a minute here. I ain't absolved him from his sins yet.
ABE: (Significantly). It is lunch time, brother.
ROCK: (He takes off the Great White Mask. His expression is troubled). I suddenly ain't very hungry.
JOE: You hear that? The former Almighty-Who ain't hungry.
G.W.: Listen here, former Almighty-Who my soul is overloaded with my despicable black sins. I find myself starved for refreshment.
JOE: Who'll share our soup with us?
ROCK: Now lissen here, dinin' hall right 'crost the street, boys. Ain't no river and ain't no trees or other obstacles to impede progress to the belly. It be easy and without conflagrations and imprecations.
JOE: Who gonna share our soup with us?
ABE: Thought we'd take a little walk.
G.W.: Uptown to the Great White City.
ABE: Get us a little of the freshest air.
G.W.: And relieve my overloaded soul.
JOE: Who'll share our soup with us?
G.W.: There's a Great White Tower up there I want to touch. In the early morning light the sun shines on it from the east.
ABE: Ain't no man from the east side of town touched that tower.
JOE: Who's gonna share our soup with us?
G.W.: Say you can look down from ten floors and see the Street of Progress.
JOE: Where? Where?
ABE: Look down, boy, not east.

ROCK: Easy there, lads. You all excited about nothing. Why every morning some Supreme Almighty-Who blows up that orange balloon and sets it loose clear and free.
G.W.: Over the east side it come up tarnished with smoke and fumes and dust.
ABE: Then go west in clear and golden tones, shimmering acrost great manicured lawns my daddy dressed.
JOE: Who'll share our soup with us?
ROCK: Soul food is this way, brothers. There ain't no obstacles. No rivers, no trees, no strategies—just a short stroll. You think touchin' that Great White Tower gonna satisfy your soul?
ABE: Up that tower!
G.W.: Not the touch I want. It's the bein' able to I want.
ROCK: Ha! What you gonna do, brother? Push on it or push it over?
G.W.: It's goin' to be one way or the other, brother.
ROCK: Naw, man. Think about it. Think about sittin' down at the table real friendly and talkin' relaxed like with your own. It ain't no presidential dinner, but …
JOE: Who'll share our soup with us?
ABE: I'd like a counter. I'd like puttin' my hands across a counter.
G.W.: Yeah, man, and reachin' for a menu. I've seen it done, you know.
ABE: I seen it done. Was in there with a gal buying her some hair dye when I seen it done. She was gonna be a Afro-American-Hollywood blond. Needless to say …
JOE; Who's gonna share our soup with us?
ROCK: Ain't nobody gonna know your name, Abraham Lincoln-Turner.
JOE: My oh my. That is indeed strange fruit.
ROCK: You all confused up in your name and fame. Ain't no Bigelow goin' to be on your floor. Just blood and thunder.
G.W.: T.N.T. and sympathy. But they ain't on the menu today.
ABE: (Singing). A cup of coffee, a sandwich and me. A cozy corner, a counter that's free.
JOE: Soup, brother, soup. Who'll share our soup with us? Hey, how long I got to say that before we breaks bread, brother?
G.W.: Just say on until the time come when we share our little pleasures.
ROCK: Share? What you mean, share?
ABE: With them. (He points to the audience).
JOE: You know, the Great White Hope.
ROCK: That is comedy. That do indeed rip my stitches.
G.W.: Nonetheless, former Almighty-Who, that is the situation we are contrivin'.
ROCK: (He laughs). Brothers, you are bending the mind of History.
JOE: History has been known to repeat itself in the shoes of other feet. Or is that the feet of other shoes? Would somebody please untie my metaphor? In any case, the whole idea is non-contraceptive.
ROCK: It is dime store philosophy.

ABE: You guessed it, brother. And it means it's cheap enough for you to buy.
G.W.: Only the idea is expensive.
ROCK: Now you gone and upped the price.
G.W.: The demand is greater.
JOE: There you go, History and Economics packed in one meaty role.
ABE: Erudition and education is said to be our sure salvation, by cracky-boo.
ROCK: Got it all planned like the other time, eh, Mistuh Lincoln-Turner?
ABE: No suh. This time we gonna split hairs instead of heads, being educated in the subtleties of modern warfare.
JOE: Boom! Everybody fall down dead.

All fall down and lie flat on the stage.

JOE: (He sits up). There was Concord and Lexington and Harper's Ferry and Appomattox and reconstruction of the obstructions and foreign diversions and incursions—and then us.
ALL: (They all stand up). Us!
ABE: An accident in life, you might say.
JOE: Boom!

All but ABE fall down. ABE moves away from them and addresses the audience.

ABE: We got to jaw-bonin' and flappin' with brother G.W. here, you see, about his experiences at the hound terminal in big-little city.
JOE: (He stands and crosses to Abe). Just a little rap session, you might say, to cool that man.
ROCK: (He stands and crosses to the other). See, he come in from the cold that night—hot.
ABE: So we re-hash it all. We put more than a hundred years in a nutshell and couldn't figure how to crack it.
JOE: Just us and this nut thing bouncin' off the walls.
ABE: By then, it was all dark everywhere else. Everybody had used all the good running water they needed, generated all that good electricity they needed, and was snoozin' on them nice soft mattresses. Everybody except us.
ROCK: You know how it is. You've had those nights—when you couldn't put all the day together and rest it.
ABE: Tryin' to figure how you could crack that nut. Tryin' to figure how you could keep it from bouncin' back—how you could smash it. How you could crack it good and get the goodie out.
ROCK: Well it weren't my idea, I can tell you that.
JOE; Count me out, brother. Must have been you.
ABE: Me? Oh no, man. I was thinkin' more in terms of splittin' that nut with the atom.
JOE: Boom.

ABE: (Points at G.W.). And not him either. He was cracking a foot locker with his toes.
ROCK: He come in from the cold—hot.
G.W.: (Up now and pacing angrily). Oh man, was there ever such a night. The futility of the night!
ABE: A collection of nights. A scrapbook of nights. Volumes of nights. An encyclopedia of nights!

ALL whistle.

ABE: And therefore, ergo, and all that stuff, a selection of incidents and anecdotes in our lives and in the dark time of our History evolved into ...
JOE: An erection of ideas!

They laugh and whistle together.

ABE: The super symbol! Fertilization and education might well be our sure salvation. Turn a page in your scrapbook, boy.
G.W.: This page is blank. This page is for us. What evolved is a simple fact.
JOE: You mean a simple act.
G.W.: This page says—make it happen.
JOE: Who'll share our soup with us?
ABE: And how did you say you like your coffee, suh?
G.W.: Make it black. No, make it white. Creamy white. Just bring it here. No, hell, I'll get it myself. Any flavor, man. I'll take tootie-fruitee. Any size, man, a mug or a jug or a thimble. Hot or cold or anything in-between. My dime is good, mister. Here, put it between your teeth and bite it.
ABE: Yeah, crack a molar on it.
ROCK: What kind of a thing is this, Charlie Uptight? What kind of a thing to have me dining in the kitchen of your mind? Who give you permission to divide and sub-divide three-fourths of the whole world?
G.W.: Don't preach, former Almighty-Who.
ROCK: Hell, I ain't preachin'. Talkin' about madness. Talkin' about the ultimate upside-down-ness of the mind. I'm talkin' about a real nut, the essence of nuttiness, the quintessence of craziness. I'm talkin' about asylums and head-shrinkers and witch brooms and white robes and batheadedness!
JOE: Who'll share our soup with us?
ABE: And thus brothers and sisters and ladies and gentlemen of the conservative and liberal majorities, that is how we collectively collected our collection of thoughts on that cold black night when Mistuh G.W. Jones walked frost-bitten from the hound terminal. I think we are now ready for the ceremony.
ROCK: Being father confessor and former Almighty-Who, self-appointed, and self-afflicted, don't you think I should preside over the ceremony?
G.W.: By all means, brother, if you wish.

ROCK: After all, it is I who has made myself most harmonious by stretching out my hand and assuming the somewhat bent-down and twisted posture of Uncle Tom. It is I who has chided those who would imprecate blackly, who would plot the repetition of black deeds on their counterparts, those who would promote blood tragedy and black revenge, all of which is out of fashion in these glorious contemporary and hip times. Besides, brothers, I do so love bein' in charge of things.

JOE: He do go on, don't he?

ABE: All right, Almighty-Who, alias Franklin Roosevelt-Rockefeller with a hyphen, and fourth nigger in order of appearance on the program, I hereby appoint you Exalted Director and Chief Chef of the Amalgamated Ceremony of the Soups which is about to begin.

ROCK: I is honored. (He puts on the Great White Mask).

JOE: (He has dipped a bowl of soup from the big bowl). Raise your right hand and put your left in this here bowl of soup.

ROCK: Hum. This here is certainly wet—greasy stuff. (He licks his finger). But it's right tasty.

JOE: Put your paw back in that pot, boy.

ROCK: Yes suh.

ABE: Repeat after me. I, Almighty-Who—

ROCK: I, Almighty-Who—

ABE: Do solemnly swear—

ROCK: Do solemnly swear—

ABE: To conduct the Ceremony of the Soups and all its liquid contents—

ROCK: To conduct the Ceremony of the Soups and all its liquid contents—

ABE: So that the proper persons—

ROCK: So that the proper persons—

ABE: Receive its succulent flavor, its rights and privileges, and all the vegetables and broths that come with it—

ROCK: Receive its succulent flavors, its rights and privileges, and all the tasty vegetables and broths that come with it—

ABE: So help you Who—

ROCK: So help me Who.

ABE: Congratulations, you is it.

ROCK: (He takes a sip from the bowl and takes out his hanky to wipe his hands). Now come my inauguration address, right?

JOE; Short-Rock have a long mouth.

G.W.: Well, dip your lip in the ladle and let's get on with it.

ROCK: (He hands bowl to Abe, clears his throat and addresses both them and the audience). Dear brothers, ask not what the soup can do for you, but what you can do with the soup. And so my fellow brothers of tarnished descent, victims of whiplash, backlash and bullshit, let us come together again in the kitchens of the world and lower our voices to a roar. There you are, gentlemen, we ready for history to be made, short and greasy. Let the commencement of the Ceremony

ROCK: (continued) of the Soups begin. (He looks offstage right). Let us redeem our redundancy once again ...as before and after ... forthwith and again ... Would one of you wake up the nigger sound man?
JOE: Hey! Uncle Remus! Wake up back yonder, it's your cue!
ROCK: Told you about puttin' your relatives in the show. (To audience). Ain't these niggers a lazy, triflin' lot?

The SOUND of a fanfare—elephants trumpeting—followed by ceremonial music in the form of African drums. JOE goes round back of the big soup bowl and brings out three more soup bowls and hands them to the others and keeps one. With great ceremony, each climbs to the big soup bowl and dips in, then climbs down. They line up center stage.

The large soup bowl is pulled offstage left and a dime store lunch counter is moved on simultaneously to right center stage. TWO GREAT WHITE WAITRESSES in white uniforms stand behind the counter chewing gum vigorously, mechanically, in rhythm. TWO GREAT WHITE FATHERS and the GREAT WHITE WITCH sit at the counter eating lunch, mechanically and in rhythm. When the counter is in place, G.W. and ABE cross downstage right to the side of the stage and JOE and ROCK (mask off now) cross downstage left with great ceremony. They turn and face each other, soup bowls in hand, then look to the counter and watch solemnly.

Enter FOUR BLACK YOUTHS in coats and ties looking very similar to G.W., Abe, Joe and Rock. They move to the counter and sit down. The others continue eating, then slowly in rhythm, wind down mechanically, look up simultaneously, first curiously, then appalled. The FOUR BLACK YOUTHS sit like statues throughout.

The SOUND of the drums stop abruptly.

1ST WAITRESS: Oh! I would if I could but you see that I can't. (She giggles).
2ND WAITRESS: (She picks up a scroll and lets it roll down. It reads):
"By jiggers, it's niggers that's come in our place.
By jiggers, these niggers is taking up space." (She rolls up the scroll).
1ST WAITRESS: (She crosses her legs tightly as she stands and wiggles). I would if I could but you see that I can't. (She giggles).
2ND WAITRESS: (She rolls down a second scroll. It reads):
"By jiggers, you niggers can come in for shopping,
but you know there's a law that keeps you from stopping." (She rolls up the scroll).
1ST WAITRESS: You see that I can't, but I sure would if I could. (She giggles).
THE GREAT WHITE WITCH: (She is an elderly lady with a pointed nose and lacking essential teeth). Awk! Awk! Awk! I knew I should have brought my

broom. (She looks downward toward Hell). So this is the black curse you gave me on your death bed, Horatio. By damned, if I had known this I would have poisoned you sooner, you lecher. If it weren't for the trouble of it, I'd conjure up my own death and come down to Hell after you for this. Awk! (Piteously). Come the time when even a sweet old lady like myself can't take a morsel of bread and do a little shopping for herbs without some cursed black cloud stirred up in Hades descending on her like a plague. Awk! Awk! I'll take my business elsewhere!

Enter the distressed GREAT WHITE STORE MANAGER, but the GREAT WHITE WITCH pushes him aside.

GREAT WHITE WITCH: Awk! Awk! Awk! (She flies off).
STORE MANAGER: Madame, wait! (He regains his composure and addresses the audience). Ahum. Hello everybody. I'm the Great White Store Manager. Notice the flower in my lapel. Isn't it lovely? Notice my neatly folded hankie in my coat. Isn't it neat? Do you like my tie? It's all silk. And here we all are at our nice big counter having a good little lunch in big-little city, USA. So typical, so joyous, so friendly , so lucrative, so ...

The 1ST GREAT WHITE FATHER grabs him by his lapel and begins pushing him, whispering in his ear and pointing at the counter.

MANAGER: Easy there—how do you do—watch my flower. Now what can I do—watch my flower! .... What was that? Would you let me go? What did you say? ... Oh my Lord. Oh my Lord!
1ST WAITRESS: I would if I could but you see that I can't. (She giggles).
MANAGER: (He crosses to the four blacks). Now see here—how do you do—what do you think—don't you know—didn't you notice—oh Lord! How do you like my tie? Isn't it—you wouldn't do this deliberately, would you? No, I won't believe that. I just couldn't, I just wouldn't. (He laughs). Is it a joke? An apparition, that's what it is. It's certainly a dark one. No, no, you're there all right, yes you are. There's one, two, three—four of you right there!
2ND WAITRESS: (She throws down her wipe cloth). By jiggers, they're niggers.
MANAGER: I'll handle this, Miss Jablonski.
2ND WAITRESS The name is Schmidt! Schmidt!
MANAGER: Well what happened to Miss Jablon—never mind that now. Now gentle—boys—if you'd be so good as to—that is, I'd appreciate it if—you know what I mean and I mean what I say!

No response.

MANAGER: (He ducks down behind the counter and jumps up). BOO!

No response.

MANAGER: Dear me, what to do? They can't—you didn't expect—oh Lord what does this mean? Can't people sit at our nice big counter and enjoy a good little lunch in big-little city, USA without—I mean, after all, this is a public place—I mean to say a private place, I mean to say the public has a right to—to—without being disturbed. I mean *our* public—*our* regulars—*our* people.

The MANAGER puts his arm around each WAITRESS and turns to the audience and all smile in tableau.

1ST WAITRESS: I would if I could, but I'm sure that I can't.
MANAGER: Hush! My Lord, they're just going to—sit there.
2ND WAITRESS: Call the You-Know-Who-in-Blue. They'll fix 'em. (With appropriate gestures). They'll pick 'em up and stuff 'em in their great white wagon and take off their heads with a club if'n they give 'em any crap.
MANAGER: Oh my, I'm not so sure—Yes, that's just what I'll do! Yes, we'll just see about all this. Don't anybody let them leave until I get back. (He starts to go, then stops). On second thought, let them leave if they want to—only make them promise never to come back. (He pulls out his hankie and wipes his brow). My Lord, how awkward! Oh look here, I've ruined my hankie! (He throws it down and goes off).

Two to four GREAT WHITE YOUNG MEN have entered and stand around gawking.

1ST GREAT WHITE FATHER: (He walks around looking at the four black men, responsibly). Hello there. Let me introduce myself. I am Mister Great White City Father, a composite and symbolic embodiment of the responsible thinking people of this community.

The GREAT WHITE YOUNG MEN whistle and cheer.

1ST WHITE FATHER: I would shake your hands except that I just washed them for lunch. Germs, you know. It's nothing personal. Where was I? Oh yes, as Mister Great White City Father I should like to take this opportunity to tell you that you are welcome in our fine city at any time.
WHITE YOUNG MEN: BOOOOO!
1ST WHITE FATHER: However—
WHITE YOUNG MEN: YAAAAAH!
1ST WHITE FATHER: Though it is a pleasure to have you here to purchase the necessities of life from our fine merchants—
WHITE YOUNG MEN: BOOOOO!
1ST WHITE FATHER: It is also necessary for us to progress and grow in an

orderly manner, respecting the laws and traditions handed down to us by our forefathers.
WHITE YOUNG MEN: YAAAAAH!
1ST WHITE FATHER: After all, we have a heritage here. Many of our ancestors came to these shores on the Sunflower.
1ST WHITE YOUNG MAN: Excuse me, sir, don't you mean the Mayflower?
1ST WHITE FATHER: Shut up, you smart ass, before I kick your teeth in.
2ND WHITE YOUNG MAN: My great-great-great-granddaddy was a pirate!
1ST WHITE YOUNG MAN: So what?
2ND WHITE YOUNG MAN: He'd steal guns from the British and sell 'em to the Americans.
1ST WHITE YOUNG MAN: So what?
2ND WHITE YOUNG MAN: Then he'd steal 'em *back* from the Americans and sell 'em to the British. Pretty cool, eh?
1ST WHITE YOUNG MAN: A damned Indian-giver.
2ND WHITE YOUNG MAN: He weren't no Indian. He was part-wop, part-spic, and Polack on his mother's side. They say he was really a bastard.
1ST WHITE FATHER: You useless pot-smoking pimps, shut up back there! What do you know about anything! (To the four blacks, responsibly). Now then, fellows, I hope I've made myself clear. I hope I have expressed what I believe is the community's position on this grave matter. I hope that it is clear that no ill-feelings are intended. That just as soon as you return to your rightful place in our big-little city community, then all — this will be forgotten. We'll just pretend that this disruption, this flagrant violation of the rights of the majority, this revolting display of abstinence — did not happen.

The WHITE YOUNG MEN cheer and clap. The FOUR BLACK MEN do not move.

2ND WHITE WAITRESS: (She throws down her wipe cloth). They ain't moved a smidgen. Not one smidgen.
1ST WHITE FATHER: Yes, I see that, Miss — eh —
2ND WHITE WAITRESS: (She smiles). You can call me Pearl. I mean ever body calls me Pearl. (She looks at the four blacks) Well most ever body. (She throws down her wipe cloth).
1ST WAITRESS: (to 1st White Father). Here's your soup-pee. (She sets bowl on counter and giggles).
2ND WHITE FATHER: Why come they ain't movin', Mister Great White City Father? Why come?
1ST WHITE FATHER: Well, they're going to. I'm just certain of that. I'm just certain they're peaceful responsible citizens just like the rest of their kind — most of 'em. I'm just certain they wouldn't want to arouse the anger of those useless smart asses back there. I'm just certain they'd rather keep matters peaceful and in the hands of the responsible citizenry of our fair city.

1ST WHITE WAITRESS: (To 2nd White Father). Here's your soup-pee. Split pea, weren't it? (She giggles).
2ND WHITE FATHER: Jus' set it down and shut up. Can't you see I'm involved here with concern for my civic duties? (Confidentially). Now see here, City Father, what bother me is that it appear them bucks is plain stuck to them stools and I plain don't like it. And speakin' as a plain citizen ...
1ST WHITE FATHER: As you know, I stated in my last public appearance my admiration for plain talk from plain citizens in this plain — this fine community.
2ND WHITE FATHER: No, I didn't know that. And I ain't got time or the notion to listen to a bunch of bullshit. All I know is them bucks is stuck to them counter stools and it look bad for the community.
1ST WHITE FATHER: Now you just give them a chance. You just give them a minute to think about the — consequences of defying authority. They've worked out some sort of deal, but now they're seeing how wrong that was, how irresponsible and dangerous — especially with all these young thugs around, this despicable generation of SOB's we've grown and nurtured.

The WHITE YOUNG MEN cheer and whistle and begin to move in on the four black men.

2ND WHITE FATHER: Those smart asses makin' a fool of you, that's plain to see.

The WHITE YOUNG MEN laugh and jostle the 1st Great White Father.

2ND WAITRESS: (She unrolls another scroll and shows it all around):
"I could've told you before you can't trust no nigger.
They just like a mule only their backsides are bigger." (She rolls up the scroll).

The WHITE YOUNG MEN whoop and holler.

1ST WHITE YOUNG MAN: That a girlie, Pearlie.
2ND WHITE YOUNG MAN: Our pimpled peach.
1ST WAITRESS: I would if I could, but you see that I can't. (She giggles).
1ST WHITE FATHER: (To four blacks). All right now, you've seen how I've been trying to keep the peace. Trying to make you see a little reason.
2ND WHITE FATHER: Got a crowbar in the trunk of my car. Be glad to help you out.

The WHITE YOUNG MEN pretend to "bong" the four blacks with the crowbar and snicker among themselves.

1ST WHITE FATHER: (To four blacks). What you doing down here this time of day anyway?

1ST WHITE YOUNG MAN: Ask us, daddy-o. Why don't you ask us? (He laughs).
2ND WHITE YOUNG MAN: Yeah, he ain't payin' us no attention. Feel lonely and neglected, don't you? (He laughs).
1ST WHITE FATHER: Oughta be in classes, that's what. Showing a little responsibility.
2ND WAITRESS; Lissen to him, lowerin' hisself. (She throws down the wipe cloth).
2ND WHITE FATHER: Jawin' and jewin' with four dumb niggers. Why doncha just eat your soup and let 'em sit there 'til they starve?
1ST WHITE FATHER: I suppose you're going to eat with them?
2ND WHITE FATHER: Hell, they ain't eatin'. They sittin'. Glued to the stool.

The WHITE YOUNG MEN jeer at the 1st White Father.

1ST WHITE FATHER: Then by God I'm going to give them something to eat for their trouble. (He picks up his bowl of soup and pours it on the head of the 1st Black Man).

The stage LIGHTS flare up.

G.W., ABE, JOE & ROCK: (Chanting). Who'll share our soup with us? Who's gonna share our soup with us? (They move down into the audience repeating the chant, carrying their soup bowls with them "inviting" the audience to "share" their soup. They move close to the audience members as though they just might be tempted to pour their soup in their laps or on their heads).
GREAT WHITE CHEF: (He enters banging his ladle against the kettle). Soup's on, yawl come and get it. (He smiles his great white smile and exits).

The 2ND WHITE FATHER dumps his soup on one of the blacks at the counter. The WHITE YOUNG MEN crowd the counter.

ALL: Bowl of soup, please ... .Bowl of soup, please ... . May I please have a bowl of soup?

The GREAT WHITE WAITRESSES begin dishing out bowls of soup as though it were an assembly line and the WHITE YOUNG MEN take the bowls of soup and pour it on the FOUR BLACKS. The FOUR BLACKS do not move. The action becomes mechanical as it is repeated. Enter a GREAT WHITE REPORTER and a GREAT WHITE PHOTOGRAPHER taking notes and pictures, respectively, followed by the GREAT WHITE STORE MANAGER who runs behind them.

MANAGER: Shoo! Shoo! You never come around when things are nice. Shoo, I say! Oh Lord! My suit's all rumpled! Good heavens, look at my flower! (He finally shoos them offstage and follows them).

The action freezes on stage into a tableau.

G.W., JOE, ABE & ROCK: Who'll share our soup with us? Who's gonna share our soup with us? (They have set down their bowls at the back of the theatre. G.W. grabs a designated GREAT WHITE AUDIENCE MEMBER).
G.W.: He'll share our soup with us.
ABE: (He grabs the audience member). He's gonna share our soup with us.
JOE & ROCK: (They join the others). He'll share our soup with us.

All grab the GREAT WHITE AUDIENCE MEMBER and drag him down the aisle. The FOUR BLACKS at the counter cross to stage left and bring on the huge soup bowl. Simultaneously, the counter and all the GREAT WHITE PEOPLE move off stage right.

GREAT WHITE AUDIENCE MEMBER: Wait! Help! What are you doing? Let go of me! I'm not in this! Help!
G.W.: We all in this show, brother.
GREAT WHITE AUDIENCE MEMBER: (He struggles in vain). I'm not going up there! You can't make me! Help! Somebody help!
JOE: Up he go!
ABE: Easy does it.

The FOUR BLACKS move now to help the others move the GREAT WHITE AUDIENCE MEMBER up the ladder and into the soup bowl.

ROCK: Baptize him, brothers—like these four brothers was baptized. In the name of those who went before him or us on February the first, in the year of our Lord, nineteen hundred and sixty in big-little city, USA.

They lift him up and throw him in the soup. The GREAT WHITE AUDIENCE MEMBER screams. The SOUND of a great splash. Enter the GREAT WHITE YOU-KNOW-WHO-IN-BLUE, night stick at the ready. He is followed by all the other GREAT WHITE PEOPLE. He blows his whistle.

ROCK: Hold it! Hold everything right there!

All the GREAT WHITE PEOPLE freeze.

ROCK: Don't you worry your head none, Mister Captain of the You-Know-Who-in-Blue.
G.W.: He's not dead. He's not even wet. It's all fantasy, a ceremony of make-believe. You're in the playhouse.
JOE: Didn't happen quite this way, Cap'n.
ABE: Well not exactly.

ROCK: After all, brothers, if we were to really behave like the other side, we would *be* the other side.
G.W.: (to the audience). A reflection of you.
JOE: (to the audience). Would you want us to be a reflection of you — in black?
G.W.: Who wants to be a reflection of you in any color.
ABE: So take our little play with a grain of sugar.
ROCK: While we dissolve in light and shadow.
G.W.: We'll go marching back to our end of big-little city.
JOE: Maybe we'll sing a little song for you along the way to remember us.
ABE: Do a little dance.
ROCK: Do a little jig in the middle of the city square. Then we might just sit down right there and rest a little while.
G.W.: You always react to our performance — but never to the script.
JOE: So there's another production coming up, brothers.
ABE: Another little fantasy.
ROCK: Another dream.
ALL: I have a dream.
G.W.: Reality is my dream. To see this façade of make-believe gone at last! To see all the mirrors and illusions smashed! Nothing is decided on a stage. In the pits is where it's at. Where *they* are. (He points out into the audience). All right, men, let's move into the shadows. Let's move east to our side of town.
ROCK: Yeah, brother, the mysterious east where they can't tell one of us from the other.
ABE: Yeah, man, a little shadowy game we play.
G.W.: If they're not able to see reality, perhaps one day we'll see it for them.
ROCK: Amen, brother. I believe that ends the ceremony.
JOE: What about Charlie there in the soup?
ABE: There's no soup in there, you know that.
JOE: Man, I forgot. Just goes to show how things are in this the-ate-ter business. (He climbs up the ladder beside the bowl). I'll just see if he's all right. (He waves). Hi there, how you doing?
GREAT WHITE AUDIENCE MEMBER: Great. Say, when do we get paid?
JOE: Yeah, he's all right. He's his same self again.
G.W.: C'mon, let's walk.
ROCK: Uh — you forgot something.
G.W.: What's that?
ROCK: The You-Know-Who-in-Blue, with friends.
G.W.: Don't worry about him. He's our escort. You know, he always escorts us back to our end of town after a performance.
ABE: (He laughs). Don't you love being protected by the You-Know-Who-in-Blue?
ROCK: Well, sometimes his benevolence blows my mind. (He touches the top of his head tenderly).
ABE: No, brother. He helps you keep your mind on what you are doing. (He smiles). Shall we go?

G.W.: If you will lead.
ABE: My pleasure, brothers. (Singing). "Oh woke up this morning—"
ALL: "with my eyes on freedom."
ABE: "Woke up this morning—"
ALL: "my eyes on freedom."
ABE: "Woke up this morning—"
ALL: "my eyes on freedom, allelui, allelui, allelui—ui—ui—a."
ROCK: C'mon, brothers, make it big. This here is the big scene.

    They repeat the song and are joined by the FOUR BLACKS as they begin to move off stage left. The YOU-KNOW-WHO-IN-BLUE puts away his night stick and follows them as escort. He looks back watching the GREAT WHITE PEOPLE as he follows them off. The GREAT WHITE PEOPLE look from one to the other shocked, not knowing what to do.

    BLACKOUT. The Ceremony is over.

MISS DORIS ANDERSON

A One-Act Play in Three Scenes

(Based on a commentary by Nicholas von Hoffman which appeared in *The Washington Post*)

First published in *Southern Theatre* XVII (Winter 1974)
Produced by Converse College to tour the South Carolina public schools, 1975
Produced in workshop at the University of Mississippi, 1976
Produced in workshop by the Back Alley Theatre, Washington, D.C., 1976
Produced by Longwood College Theatre, 1984

Revised, 1999

CHARACTERS

(5 to 7 males, 3 females, plus 3 to 4 non-speaking roles. All characters should be white except for Miss Doris Anderson who is Afro-American. Most non-speaking roles should be Afro-Americans).

MISS DORIS ANDERSON — 35-year-old Afro-American
1ST MAN — also The Police Sergeant
2ND MAN — also a Police Officer, a Doctor
RECEPTIONIST — also the Nurse, in her 20's
1ST GUARD — also the 1st Attendant
2ND GUARD — also the 2nd Attendant
JUDGE — very elderly, silver-haired
DR. BARNES*
DR. STEIN*
MISS LUCILLE ANDERSON — disheveled, in her 50's or 60's

(*These roles could also be played by the 1st and 2nd Man)

THE SETTING

The play is in three scenes with minimal set requirements and flexible staging appropriate for thrust, black box or proscenium stage.

Miss Doris Anderson

Scene 1

The LIGHTS come up on a plain hard-backed chair exactly center stage. Stage right and left below the chair in the shadows are desks and desk chairs. MISS DORIS ANDERSON is sitting in the plain hard-backed chair. She is 35-years-old, black, prim, neat, shy. She wears a tailored suit that is old. She is nervous. It is the light that makes her nervous. She does not wish to be in the light. She does not wish to be before us, before anyone. She casts her eyes furtively toward the light, then looks about uneasily. She waits.

Enter the 1ST MAN stage left. He takes a seat in the chair at the desk stage left. Like the chair and the desk he remains in the shadows. His face eludes us. MISS DORIS ANDERSON strains to catch a glimpse of his face, but his face eludes her.

1ST MAN: Your name?
MISS A.: Doris Anderson.
1ST MAN: Miss or Mrs.?
MISS A.: It's miss.
1ST MAN: Your address?
MISS A.: One-oh-oh-four B Orleans.
1ST MAN: One-oh-oh-four D Orleans.
MISS A.: One-oh-oh-four *B* Orleans.
1ST MAN: One-oh — was that C or B?
MISS A.: B. It's B.
1ST MAN: B. Of course, B. Are you a native of the city?
MISS A.: I — what was that?
1ST MAN: Were you born here?
MISS A.: I — don't think so.
1ST MAN: Oh I see. Then ...
MISS A.: I've lived here since I can remember. I mean, that's all I can remember.
1ST MAN: Oh I see. Number of children?
MISS A.: What?
1ST MAN: How many children?
MISS A.: Oh. Well, there was eight in the family, only Leroy and Hazel — and little Beth, they passed on.
1ST MAN: Oh I see. Then there are five children at home.
MISS A.: What? No, I don't know where they are now — except Gracie. Gracie, she went off to New York. She read this ad in the paper where they needed somebody and she went on up there and — she writes to me now and then. (A beat). Well, Christmas time, any way.
1ST MAN: (Pause). Then you have four children at home.

MISS A.: I don't have no children.
1ST MAN: We have to have the proper information for this application, you understand ...
MISS A.: Well, you asked me how many children ...
1ST MAN: The proper information, it's necessary that we have that, you see. First you tell me eight children, then you tell me five, then it's four and now you say ...
MISS A: I told you it was Miss. You asked me ...
1ST MAN: Who is the father? Do you know the father? Where is the father?
MISS A.: My daddy's passed on. Mama, too. My daddy was hurt at his work. They say the truck backed up and him behind it.
1ST MAN: How old were you when this happened?
MISS A.: (Pause). I can't remember. I think I was thirteen, maybe older. Nobody knew what happened.
1ST MAN: I don't quite follow that. Nobody knew what happened to him or what happened to you? Could you make that clearer, please?
MISS A.: Didn't—anything happen to me. I said nobody knew what happened to him. Didn't nobody tell us. Finally, Mama went down to the place of business—and they told her and ...
1ST MAN: This is very confusing. If you'd just kindly answer the questions on the application for assistance, perhaps there's something we can do. Otherwise, there's just going to be nothing we can do. I mean, you saw all those people out there waiting. It's making it terribly difficult. Now if you'll kindly just answer the questions. Will you do that?
MISS A.: Yes sir.
1ST MAN: Good. Now then, where were we? You stated that you were not married. Now is that correct?
MISS A.: Yes sir.
1ST MAN: And that there are four children in the home.
MISS A.: No sir, I never said ...
1ST MAN: Please! Let's not confuse things again, Miss Andrews.
MISS A.: It's Ander ... (She stands).
1ST MAN: I think the situation is quite clear now. Yes, you see, we have a number of cases similar to yours. It's not really an unusual circumstance among you people. We understand that. It does appear, however, that the receptionist has sent you to see the wrong person. She's rather new and—in any case, I'm going to pass your case on to our ADC man. Now if you'll take this application for assistance out to the receptionist and tell her you want to see the ADC man, I'm sure he'll be able to help you, Miss—er- Williams. Now if you'll excuse me. (He goes).
MISS A.: (She stands). It's Anderson. Miss Doris Anderson.

The 2ND MAN has entered and seats himself at the desk stage right. He, too, is in the shadows and MISS DORIS ANDERSON cannot see his face.

2ND MAN: Your name?
MISS A.: Doris Anderson.
2ND MAN: (A command). Please sit down. Miss or Mrs.?
MISS A.: (She sits down, almost stumbling over the chair nervously). It's — Miss.
2ND MAN: Your address?
MISS A.: It's — one-oh-oh-four B Orleans.
2ND MAN: One-oh-oh-four — was that D or B?
MISS A.: B. It's B.
2ND MAN: B as in Boy?
MISS A.: Wh-what?
2ND MAN: B as in the first letter of Boy.
MISS A.: Yes, yes sir.
2ND MAN: One-oh-oh-four B — did you say Orleans?
MISS A.: Yes sir, Orleans.
2ND MAN: Are you a native of the city?
MISS A.: No sir, I wasn't born here.
2ND MAN: Just Yes or No will be sufficient. How many years have you lived in the city?
MISS A.: I — since I can remember anything.
2ND MAN: (A beat). I didn't ask you that. I asked you specifically how many years. How old are you?
MISS A.: Thirty-five.
2ND MAN: Did you live in this city ten years ago?
MISS A.: Yes sir.
2ND MAN: Fifteen years ago?
MISS A.: I — yes sir.
2ND MAN: Twenty years ago?
MISS A.: Yes.
2ND MAN: Twenty-five years ago?
MISS A.: (A whisper). Yes.
2ND MAN: Thirty years ago?

MISS DORIS ANDERSON nods her answer.

2ND MAN: There — you see? Now that's more than we need to know. That wasn't so difficult, now was it? Own your own home?
MISS A.: I — no.
2ND MAN: Rent?
MISS A.: Rent, yes I rent it.
2ND MAN: Monthly? Bi-weekly? Weekly? What?
MISS A.: (A beat). You want to know what I pay?
2ND MAN: I haven't asked for that yet. Please wait until I'm ready to ask that. Monthly? Bi-weekly? Weekly?
MISS A.: I — it's by the week. Yes, the week.

2ND MAN: More than eight families in the building? Less than four families? Two-family dwelling? Single family? Which?

MISS A.: What—do you want to know?

2ND MAN: I want to know how many families live in the building—or the house, as the case may be.

MISS A.: (She looks into the shadows and fumbles with her pocket book). The project. It's in the project. Not a house—a apartment. It's first floor ... It's first floor. I live on the first floor. (No response). I—I'm sorry. I—didn't answer the question.

2ND MAN: No. But you're getting there.

MISS A.: (She looks up at the light, confused). It's just that—that ... . (Her eyes dart about, trying to find the man in the shadows).

2ND MAN: You seem upset. You people are in here so often you should be used to the procedures, or at least have heard about them.

MISS A.: No sir, I never been here before.

2ND MAN: It's not so difficult really. It simply requires complete co-operation. I wish we could have that understood. We need to open the lines of communication and that requires some clear and concise procedural documentation. But we're always getting this kind of antagonism and confusion rather than the needed co-operation to get our programs implemented. We find this attitude discouraging, I can tell you. Perhaps you're ill. You keep looking about. Do you often get upset like this?

MISS A.: No, I'm sorry. It's just—what was it you said?

2ND MAN: (A beat). I didn't say anything. I just cleared my throat. You didn't think I said anything, did you? I mean there's no need to say anything if no one is going to listen. Well, where were we? Oh yes, I asked how many families live in the apartment?

MISS A.: I—don't know that.

2ND MAN: Right. More than eight?

MISS A.: Yes sir.

2ND MAN: Good enough. Number of children? Wait—let me re-word the question. I don't want to know how many children live in *all* the apartments, is that clear?

MISS A.: It's Miss Anderson and I don't have no children.

2ND MAN: What I'd like to know is the number of children in *your* apartment. In other words, how many children have *you* had and how many children are at present living with you? (No response). Well? Dear God, isn't that clear?

MISS A.: I told you.

2ND MAN: Told me what? Are you going to answer the question or not?

MISS A.: It's Miss Anderson and I don't have no children. I told you.

2ND MAN: (He stands). Is this some sort of clever game we're playing here? Look, this is a social service agency where people come for help. Don't you want help? If you do, then you ought to at least try to answer the question.

MISS A.: I'm telling you everything! What can I do?
2ND MAN: You're not telling me everything. I ask you how many children you have and you're telling me you don't have any. Look, if you're ashamed of it, I can understand that. A lot of people like you come in here and don't care one way or the other, it seems to me. Well, I can tell you this, if this agency is to help people and to function properly, we must have correct procedural information or else ...
MISS A.: I don't have no children. (She stands trying to find him in the shadows). I don't have no children!
2ND MAN: (He slumps into his chair). Why are you here? Why did you come to my office?
MISS A.: It was the other man. He said ...
2ND MAN: What other man?
MISS A.: The other man.
2ND MAN: I asked you *what* other man?
MISS A.: The one down the hall.
2ND MAN: This building is full of offices down the hall. Don't you have a name?
MISS A.: He never said his name. Nobody told me his name.
2ND MAN: Well, he has an office number. They gave you his office number, didn't they? You couldn't get there without an office number, right?
MISS A.: Yes sir.
2ND MAN: Well—what was the number?
MISS A.: (She tries frantically to remember the number, fumbling with her purse as though it might somehow be there. Finally, her whole body just sags). I don't remember it... . I'm sorry. (She looks for his face in the shadows). I'm sorry.
2ND MAN: (Pause). Why did you come to this agency?
MISS A.: I—always paid my rent before. I never missed in nine years—but I wanted to take this course, you see. If I could take this course and study a little I could get this good job with this company—so I spent the money for that. Only then I found out the school don't have the right machines I had to learn to get the job. But they never told me that and they wasn't about to give me my money back, so I took this other course which ... It was to get a better job, it was to ... The people that rent me the place, the project people, they sent me this. (She fumbles in her purse and pulls out the notice). It says unless I pay up in five days, they going to take my place from me. Nine years I live there. Always pay on time. It's not right for them to do this. They shouldn't do this. (She looks for him in the shadows). I can't see you. Are you there?
2ND MAN: I'm right here.
MISS A.: I—that's why I come here.
2ND MAN: To the office of Aid to Dependent Children?
MISS A.: (She stares into the shadows, then withdraws the paper and puts it back in her purse). He sent me here. He said to come here.

2ND MAN: To the ADC? Really now. Do you know what I think, Miss Allison? I think you're ill. But don't you worry, I'm going to see if we can help you. Now then, I want you to take this application back to the receptionist and tell her to make you an appointment with our psychiatric clinic. Is that clear? You just tell her that you've not been feeling well lately and that you think you need some psychiatric help. Here, I'll just write a little note on this assistance application and you give this to the girl at the reception desk. Now do you understand what you are to do, Miss Arnold?

MISS A.: Miss Doris Anderson. My name is ...

2ND MAN: You better hurry now. We'll be closing for the day soon and I don't think this should be put off. I think we should definitely take care of the procedural matters today and get you an appointment as soon as possible. (He hands her the paper). Now if you'll excuse me. (He goes).

MISS DORIS ANDERSON takes the paper and stares at it blankly. The area LIGHTS come up revealing the reception room, shadowy and nondescript like the people who wait and wait on a long bench upstage. The reception desk is down left and behind it several doors exactly alike with numbers on them. MISS DORIS ANDERSON crosses down left to the reception desk. The drab blond RECEPTIONIST is busy shifting piles of paper on her desk.

RECEPTIONIST: (She does not look up). Yes, what is it?

MISS A.: I was here a while ago.

RECEPTIONIST: So was I. Now what do you want? We're closing in a moment. If you'll have a seat.

MISS A.: I want to see that man again.

RECEPTIONIST: What man?

MISS A.: You—didn't tell me his name. In one of those rooms back there.

RECEPTIONIST: What number is that?

MISS A.: I—can't remember.

RECEPTIONIST: You're a big help. (The papers drop from her hand). Your name?

MISS A.: Anderson. Miss Doris Anderson.

RECEPTIONIST: (She finds a paper). You were sent to ADC.

MISS A.: That was the wrong place.

RECEPTIONIST: (She looks up for the first time). I guess you know the right place, eh? You come in here off the street and you know all about it.

MISS A.: I don't have no children.

RECEPTIONIST: Congratulations. We need more around here like you.

MISS A.: That man, he made me go to the ADC—the Aid to Dependent Children man.

RECEPTIONIST: Why would he do a ridiculous thing like that?

MISS A.: I—don't know.

RECEPTIONIST: Well, I bet I can guess. Sit down over there and wait. I'll tell him you're back.

The RECEPTIONIST continues to move papers around her desk. MISS DORIS ANDERSON remains at the desk, waiting.

RECEPTIONIST: I thought I told you to sit down.
MISS A.: You didn't tell him.
RECEPTIONIST: We're closing in a few minutes, I said.
MISS A.: You didn't tell him.
RECEPTIONIST: (She slams down the papers). Oh damn! (She turns and goes off).

MISS DORIS ANDERSON waits, becomes apprehensive, plunges her hands in her purse, finds the papers, looks at them, unsure. She holds them in her hand and closes her purse and waits uneasily. Enter the uniformed 1ST GUARD from one of the doors stage left.

1ST GUARD: All right, folks, our office is closing now. If you wasn't seen by nobody come up and sign the appointment sheet for tomorrow morning. You'll be first on the list for tomorrow morning. (He moves along the bench). Folks, the office is closing now. If you can't sign your name, you just tell me what it is and I'll fix you up for tomorrow morning. Let's hurry along now, it's closing time.

MISS DORIS ANDERSON moves behind the receptionist's desk.

1ST GUARD: Hey, you! You can't go back there. What do you think you're doing?
MISS A.: I got to see the man.
1ST GUARD: What man?
MISS A.: The one I talked to.
1ST GUARD: I'm sorry, lady. If you'll just sign this appointment sheet—
MISS A.: She's gone to get him—to tell him.
1ST GUARD: Who? What are you talking about?
MISS A.: The girl who was at the desk—she went to get him.
1ST GUARD: Oh c'mon now, she's already gone for the day. Leaves right at five. You just sign on this here appointment sheet.
MISS A.: I got to see the worker. I got the notice right here. I got to see him.
1ST GUARD: What notice? I don't know anything about that. That's something you'll have to discuss with a case worker. Now if you'll just sign this appointment sheet.
MISS A.: He sent me to the wrong place.
1ST GUARD: We all make mistakes, lady. Now you just sign here.
MISS A.: He won't know nothing tomorrow. It'll be somebody different tomorrow.
2ND GUARD: (He enters from another door). What's the trouble, Harry? Somebody giving you a hard time? C'mon let's get it done and go home.
1ST GUARD: This lady here claims she's got to see her worker now.

2ND GUARD: We're closed. She can't see nobody now.
MISS A.: I got to see my worker now, Mister. I been living that place nine years and they going to put me in the streets.
1ST GUARD: (To 2nd Guard). Maybe we should find out something?
2ND GUARD: What's to find out? The office is closed. It's past five o'clock.
MISS A.: He's in there. I know he's in there.
2ND GUARD: Is that so? Well, you know more than I do. Some of you people come in here and think you know it all.

MISS DORIS ANDERSON tries to move past him. He grabs her.

2ND GUARD: Now just a minute, lady, if you can't follow the rules and regulations—listen, you can't come around here acting like this.
1ST GUARD: Man, she's getting all uptight, ain't she?
2ND GUARD: Yeah. Go call 'em, Harry.
1ST GUARD: Yeah, I'm going. I mean if she can't be reasonable about things. (He goes off).
MISS A.: My arm. You hurting my arm. Let go of me.
2ND GUARD: (He restrains her). Listen, lady, I've about had it with you.

The 1ST MAN with a briefcase has entered from one of the doors. His face cannot be seen. He moves like a shadow across stage and off right.

MISS A.: Hey, Mister! Hey, man. That's the one. He looks like the one. Can't see his face. Let me go! I can't—he looks like the one.
2ND GUARD: You're nuts. Did you call 'em, Harry?
1ST GUARD: (He has entered). They're on the way.
MISS A.: (She breaks away from the Guard and starts to cross stage right). Mister, you sent me to the wrong place! I told you I ain't got no children. I told you that!

The GUARDS grab her.

MISS A.: Let me go! What did I do?
2ND GUARD: Jesus, she sure can wiggle! (He bends her arm behind her back). Gotcha!
1ST GUARD: She's pretty uptight, ain't she?
2ND GUARD: Well, I got her now. Boy, this is some friggin' job we got.
MISS A.: (She stops struggling). All right, I'll sign it. Let me sign it.
1ST GUARD: If people would just do as they're told.
MISS A.: Let go of me and let me sign that paper!
2ND GUARD: Don't you yell at me, damn it!
MISS A.: You sign that paper and you get in first thing in the morning, ain't that what you said?

2ND GUARD: You ain't signing any paper now except maybe the one for your personal possessions.
MISS A.: Help me, please. You said if I sign that paper ...
1ST GUARD: I don't have no paper for you to sign.
MISS A.: But you said ...
1ST GUARD: You'll have to talk to them about it now.
MISS A.: Who? Who do I talk to?

The center area LIGHTS come up on the two desks, a POLICE SERGEANT sits at one, another police officer called GILLY is at the other. At center between the two desks, a Judge's bench has been added. The Judge's bench is vacant at the moment.

SGT.: Bring her over here.
2ND GUARD: Right, Sergeant.

MISS DORIS ANDERSON turns around and sees the policemen. She recoils and the GUARDS grab her again, but she manages to squirm away from them. The SERGEANT and GILLY get a kick out of this and laugh.

2ND GUARD: Bitch! This is some friggin' job.
SGT.: Yeah, yeah, we all got problems. Lady, you just come over here. Don't you worry about nothin'. We ain't hard to get along with, are we, Gilly?

GILLY nods, smiles excessively, picks at his face and stares at her. MISS DORIS ANDERSON moves apprehensively between the desks, facing out, again in the blinding LIGHT.

SGT.: Your name?
MISS A.: (Softly). Miss — Doris Anderson.
SGT.: Pardon, I didn't get that. Could you speak a little louder, please? It's just a routine question. Procedural stuff, you understand. Nothing to worry about.
MISS A.: Miss Doris Anderson.
SGT.: Miss or — sorry, you answered that. Your address?
MISS A.: One-oh-oh-four B Orleans.
SGT.: One-oh-four B Orleans.
MISS A.: One-oh-*oh*-four Orleans.
SGT.: I thought you said One-oh-oh-four *B* Orleans.
MISS A.: (A beat). Yes. I said that.
SGT.: Okay, let's just try and get it right. Ever been arrested?
MISS A.: Arrested?
SGT.: Yeah. You know, to the police station. You got any previous record?
MISS A.: Am I arrested? What am I arrested for?
SGT.: Lady, I am asking the questions now. You'll get your chance later if you behave.

MISS A.: I never had nothing to do with the police. Only trouble I had with the police is once when I got lost and went to a police station. They wasn't no help. They thought it was funny and laughed at me.
SGT.: Lady, I just asked if you ever been arrested. You wanna tell the story of your life, you write a book, eh?

GILLY laughs excessively at this, but makes no sound. He shakes his head. The SERGEANT smiles at him, appreciating his response.

MISS A.: I never been in any trouble with anybody.
SGT.: Sure. Nobody that comes in here ever has, ain't that right, Gilly?

GILLY gives him the same response as before.

SGT.: How long you lived in the city?
MISS A.: Thirty years.
SGT.: Born here?
MISS A.: No sir.
SGT.: Uh-huh. Some personal description now. Color of eyes?
MISS A.: (Pause). Brown.
SGT.: Color of your hair?
MISS A.: (Pause). Black.
SGT.: Any outstanding skin discolorations, birth marks, scars, that sort of thing?
MISS A.: (Pause). No sir.
SGT.: Your race? .... I asked you your race. (He stands). I want you to tell me your race—now. (No response. He sits down). Listen, lady, I got these questions all written out for people to answer. It ain't nothing personal, but the procedure is that the arrestee is to answer all these questions, even the obvious ones. How am I to know you ain't one of them dark I-talians? Huh? How am I supposed to know that?
MISS A.: I'm black and I'm afro-American.
SGT.: Afro ... American. Um. Yeah. All right, Gilly, do your thing.

GILLY pulls a big camera from under the table and quickly flashes a picture. The flash is sudden and very bright and unexpected. MISS DORIS ANDERSON flinches in terror.

SGT.: Awright, turn that way toward the other officer there. Turn! Turn a little more. Get your chin up. Get it up higher. Awright, Gilly?

GILLY nods and the camera flashes again.

SGT.: Awright, now you can face the front so's we can get your profile. Didn't you hear me? I said face the front. Good. That awright, Gilly? … One step forward, please … No, no that's too far. Half step backward, please. Good. Stand still. Don't move. Hold it!

The flash of the camera is like an electric shock to MISS DORIS ANDERSON. She is trembling.

SGT.: Face the other way, please. No, no the *other* way.

MISS DORIS ANDERSON is turning about in a circle of confusion.

SGT.: Damnation! Woo there, mule.

They all laugh. MISS DORIS ANDERSON, as it happens, stops in the correct position.

SGT.: Do your thing, Gilly.

The flash. MISS DORIS ANDERSON is immobile.

SGT.: Awright, now put your hands on the officer's desk… . Put your hands on the officer's desk, I said… . Goddamn, what tribe is she from anyway?

They all chuckle.

SGT.: Put her hands on your desk, Gilly. Reckon we need a breathilizer?

GILLY touches MISS DORIS ANDERSON's hands and she pulls them away, close to her body. GILLY stares at her, smiling, but the effect is ominous.

SGT.: No, no. Down, boy, down. (He moves around the desk). Why the hell you have to be so ugly, boy?

The GUARDS chuckle.

SGT.: Now look, lady, the rules and regulations say I got to take your fingerprints for the record. It ain't no big deal. Once I get your fingerprints, that'll be it—at least for the time being. Now if you'll just put your hands on the officer's desk there.

MISS DORIS ANDERSON does not move. The SERGEANT takes her hands and guides her to the desk, not forcefully, but as though they were a pair of brown gloves.

SGT.: Ready, Gilly? Awright now, just roll your thumb—all the way over. (He guides her thumb). Roll it now. That's it. Now roll it in that there square. That's the way it's done. Now you do it. The forefinger. Now just r-o-l-l it over. Good. That's the way. There, it's all done. No pain. Now wipe your hands on this cloth. That's the ticket. Now we all done, right, Gilly? (Calling). Ready, Judge.

The LIGHTS come up on the Judge's bench which is higher than the desks. The JUDGE enters. He is very elderly, silver-haired, face wrinkled with age, voice cracked and crusty. He takes his seat on the bench. He looks at no one, at nothing, seemingly curled inside himself as he sits. They wait. He does not look up.

JUDGE: Tell the court your name.

Silence. The GUARDS and POLICEMEN fidget nervously. They wait. The JUDGE waits, not moving, with great patience.

MISS A.: (Mumbling). Doris Anderson.
SGT.: Louder, please.
JUDGE: I heard her! ... Miss or Mrs.?
MISS A.: Miss.
JUDGE: Tell the court your address.
MISS A.: Four-oh-oh-one—no, I mean—one-oh-oh-four—B Orleans.
JUDGE: Tell the court how long you've lived in the city.
MISS A.: (Pause). Thirty years.
JUDGE: Tell the court if you're a native of the city.
MISS A.: No.
SGT.: The procedure is that you address the Judge as "Your Honor" or "Sir" at all times.
JUDGE: What was that?
SGT.: I was explaining to the defendant the procedure of the court, your honor.
JUDGE: Oh yes! Yes, of course. Would the defendant tell the court how—he? (He looks up and out carefully). She—pleads. (No response). Would the defendant please tell the court how—she pleads to the charge? (He waits patiently, but gets no answer. He begins searching about on his desk. He knows where it should be exactly, but it is not there). I—don't seem to have—to have the thing here. No, I don't seem to—have, to have it.
SGT.: What? Well, I—you see, your honor ...
JUDGE: Is someone not following procedure here? You know I have to have here on this desk some—some indication of—how's the court to do its work without some indication—correct procedure being—being followed in these—this case? How's that to happen? Whose—how to explain this?
SGT.: (To Gilly). Didn't you—I thought you—

GILLY shakes his head.

SGT.: The clerk. They must've—(He looks to the Guards. They look positively blank. His arms drop to his sides). You mean we didn't ... Jesus.
2ND GUARD: Eh—your honor, please the court, could I say something?
JUDGE: Say something? What's there to be said? What?
2ND GUARD: Please the court, it's in regard to information regarding this here woman.
JUDGE: Information! You have information? Please, the court would be most interested in having such—who are you?—never mind that! The Sergeant will deal with that later when—when we've got ourselves—straightened out.
SGT.: Yes sir, your honor.
JUDGE: Go on, quickly, quickly.
2ND GUARD: Your honor, I was one of the guards in the social agency where this here woman come and caused the trouble.
JUDGE: Trouble? What trouble? Be specific!
2ND GUARD: Sir, she did forcibly try to break my hold on her to enter a unauthorized area in the social service building after she was specifically told not to do so.
JUDGE: Ah! Now then—ah!
MISS A.: Please, sir, I had to see my worker. He sent me to the wrong person. They going to put me out of my place in five days. They going to put me in the street. Your honor, you never been to those places ...
JUDGE: Wait! Madam, in God's name, what are you talking about? What places haven't I been? How do you know that? What is this?
MISS A.: The social agencies, the welfare—they got all those files and things, yet they can't remember nothing. They told me not to go there, they told me it wouldn't do any good. I never went there before. They said it'd bring trouble to me, but I didn't know what else to do.
JUDGE: Stop! .... Wh-what are you doing? What—just what is all this?
MISS A.: Your honor, don't you see ...
JUDGE: I see nothing, madam. Except that this court cannot function in all this—this confusion. Such a—such an emotional outburst cannot be tolerated. You succeed only in prejudicing the—this case. The court wants—must remain fair. I hope that is understood. Yes! Yes I do. (He mops his brow). Where's that guard?
2ND GUARD: Right here, your honor.
JUDGE: Please—continue.
2ND GUARD: This here black lady caused quite a ruckus, your honor.
JUDGE: What's black? I don't see—caused what? What was that again?
SGT.: He means, your honor, this woman entered the said unauthorized area without the permission of the authorities.
JUDGE: (A thoughtful pause). Proceed.

2ND GUARD: It caused quite a—it was necessary for us to call the police, sir, to gain control of the situation.
JUDGE: Us? Us? What's that about?
2ND GUARD: Me and Harry. Harry's the other guard.
JUDGE: There are two guards? Did someone mention two guards, Sergeant? I don't recall anyone mentioning two guards.
SGT.: I—don't know, sir.
JUDGE: Are there two guards, Sergeant?
SGT.: Yes sir, two guards.
JUDGE: Then someone should have mentioned that. Where's the other guard?
1ST GUARD: Here, sir. Here, your honor.
JUDGE: Ah! Now we're getting things in their proper order, yes we are. You, sir, you have heard the incident described. Were you a witness?
1ST GUARD: Yes, your honor. You see, I was approached by this woman first and I told her it was time for the agency to close.
JUDGE: What time was that?
1ST GUARD: 'Bout two minutes to five o'clock, sir.
MISS A.: Your honor, sir ...
JUDGE: What time does this agency office close?
1ST GUARD: Right at five, sir. Every day at two minutes to five on the button—
JUDGE: Button? What button?
1ST GUARD: At exactly two minutes to five is what I was saying, sir. I come out see, with this paper and pencil and I take a list of people who couldn't be seen by the workers that day. I get their names and make appointments for them for first thing the next morning.
JUDGE: Just a moment! (Pause). Yes, that's quite clear. I understand that perfectly. You may proceed.
1ST GUARD: Well, this here woman wouldn't sign the list. She insisted on seeing the case worker right then and there and she starts trying to push her way by me.
MISS A.: I told you the receptionist went to get my case worker. I told you that.
JUDGE: By God, madam, you are out of order! And just when the court was beginning to grasp—understand the situation. You people have no respect for the court with these—outbursts. Time and time again, you disrupt procedure. There is no legal sense, no understanding of the proprieties of—of justice. You act like savages, that's what. Savages!
MISS A.: (She looks around wildly and seems close to fainting. Finally, to the Sergeant). Could I—sit down some place?
SGT.: Your honor ...
JUDGE: Stop! (He sighs and mops his brow with a handkerchief). The court—would like to apologize for that last statement. The court—its level of judicial tolerance was—taxed, one might say. I trust, Miss Andros, you will accept the court's apology, but would you please keep in mind in the future the court's procedures. I hope that's—clear.

MISS A.: It's Miss … . I don't have nothing to say, your honor. I'm just tired and I'd like to go home, sir.
JUDGE: Yes well, I can assure you that the court is in complete agreement with you on that. However, our obligations and duties must be fulfilled first, as you must know. With—with that in mind, what further evidence can the plaintiffs present to the court now? (He again rifles through his papers).
1ST GUARD: Give him the paper.
2ND GUARD: What?
1ST GUARD: The paper you took off her.
2ND GUARD: Oh. Oh yeah. Your honor, I have this paper signed by one of the agency workers which I think should be presented to you—to the court.
JUDGE: Paper? What sort of paper?
2ND GUARD: It tells how this here black woman is psycho. You know, upset. I mean in the head.
SGT.: Your honor, I think he's trying to say that he has evidence that shows this woman is probably a mental case.
MISS A.: (To 2nd Guard). What did I do to you? Lord, tell me what I did to you and I'll say I'm sorry. Anything you want and I'll say I'm sorry. I must have done something really bad to you, Mister.
JUDGE: What is it? What's happening out there? Where's that paper?
SGT.: (He grabs the paper from the Guard and places it on the Judge's bench). Here's the paper, your honor.
JUDGE: Ah! Let me see that. (He reads it over).
2ND GUARD: Your honor, you can see by that paper there that a mental doctor is recommended. The agency is pretty sure this woman's crazy.
MISS A.: Crazy! Lord God, what's happening now? Where's the doctor that ever said that? Where's somebody to prove that?
JUDGE: Madam, please! I am trying to read this paper. No, as a matter of fact I have done reading this paper. Now then, I can tell you that this document recommends that you have a psychiatric examination. What have you to say to that?
MISS A.: He made a mistake, your honor. He didn't understand what I was trying to say to him. He wasn't no doctor. None of you is doctors.
2ND GUARD: You're nuts, lady! If you'd just done what you was told, none of this would've happened.
JUDGE: You're out of order! I ought to put you in contempt of court for that. I—you're obstructing justice, that's what. Not another word from you in these proceedings, is that understood?
2ND GUARD: Yes sir.
JUDGE: Now then—now then, Miss—Mrs.—Madam, your point is well-taken regarding this matter. We—the court cannot possibly accept this paper as evidence until we have a proper evaluation of your mental condition from an authorized physician. Yes, that's quite clear. Therefore, it is this court's ruling that any judgment against you be suspended until such time as you have been

JUDGE: (continued) properly evaluated and that you remain in the custody of this court until such time as that evaluation is complete. Sergeant, I trust the decision of the court is clear?
SGT.: Yes, your honor.
JUDGE: And I trust that before this woman comes before me again, you will have something more explicit concerning the nature of the offense. Do I make myself clear?
SGT.: Yes, your honor.
JUDGE: Preferably in the form of a warrant for her arrest. Do I make myself clear?
SGT.: Yes sir, your honor.
MISS A.: Your honor, sir, could you tell me — can I go home now?
JUDGE: This case is continued until such time as — inform her, Sergeant — now if you'll excuse me. (He hurries off).
MISS A.: Your honor — (To Sergeant). What did he say? What does it mean? Can I please go home now?
SGT.: Oh no, you've got to be evaluated.
MISS A.: Evaluated? Does he think I'm crazy? You know I'm not crazy. You know that!
SGT.: Lady, I don't know nothing about it. I just do as I'm told.
MISS A.: You're going to take me to jail, aren't you.
SGT.: Let's go, Gilly.

They each take an arm of MISS DORIS ANDERSON.

MISS A.: Oh my God, was what I done so bad? Was it so bad?
SGT.: You just take it easy, lady, so there'll be no trouble. (To Guards). You guys go up to the clerk's office and wait there. I gotta talk to you.

The GUARDS go one way, the SERGEANT and GILLY the other, holding on to a frightened MISS DORIS ANDERSON.

BLACKOUT.

Scene 2

The LIGHTS come up in the stage left area. MISS DORIS ANDERSON sits behind bars on a stool in a jail cell. Enter DR. BARNES and DR. STEIN, two elderly doctors. They are neatly dressed, but their suits border on the shabby. They look about for a moment unsure of the proper direction.

DR. BARNES: This the one?
DR. STEIN: How should I know. Check the card. You should always check the card.

DR. BARNES: Yes, well — I haven't got the card. You've got the card.
DR, STEIN: I've got the card? So when did I get the card?
DR. BARNES: You took the card from the Sergeant and stuck it in your pocket.
DR. STEIN: You're hallucinating. It was you took the card and — so what did you do with it?
DR. BARNES: I'll just look in my — (He begins searching through his pockets). My toothpicks ... Driver's license ... Some notes. Wonder what they're about? Some change. A Canadian penny. Somebody gave me a Canadian penny for change the other day. I didn't realize it until ...
DR. STEIN: You lost the card?
DR. BARNES: Well — it appears that I don't have it.
DR. STEIN: Must you be so careless, Doctor? Every time I work with you, you lose something.
DR. BARNES: We'll just go back to the desk —
DR. STEIN: No, no! No need to do that. You know how they are.
DR. BARNES: Right. We'll get another card and fill it out when we get back.
DR. STEIN: Good idea. You question, I'll write. I got paper. You got a pencil?
DR. BARNES: (He checks his pockets). Um. More toothpicks. Ah, here's one. It's a little short.
DR. STEIN: Never mind, it'll do.
DR. BARNES: (He looks in the cell). Anybody in there?
DR. STEIN: She's right there.
DR. BARNES: I know, I was making conversation.
DR. STEIN: You're wasting time. You there, girlie. The doctor here is evaluating. Just answer the questions, all right?
DR. BARNES: Yes, you just answer all the questions and there won't be any trouble, isn't that right, Doctor?
DR. STEIN: One hundred per cent, Doctor.
DR. BARNES: Now then, your name? (No response). Your name?
MISS A.: Nobody can remember nothing.
DR. BARNES: Did you get that down, Doctor?
DR. STEIN: A curious response.
DR. BARNES: Yes, I thought so, too.
MISS A.: (She stands wearily). Doris Anderson. Miss Doris Anderson. I live at one-oh-oh-four B Orleans — at least I did. I've lived in the city for thirty years but I wasn't born here. I'm not married and I got no children.
DR. STEIN: Stop already! I'm writing!
DR. BARNES: I thought I noted a slight hysteria in the tone of voice.
DR. STEIN: Hers or mine?
DR. BARNES: Hers. We're not evaluating you.
DR. STEIN: Exactly. I noticed it, too.
DR. BARNES: Now then, Miss — er — do you find yourself often getting excited about things?
MISS A.: No, not anymore.

DR. BARNES: Um. Might be showing some signs of depression, don't you think?
DR. STEIN: Don't evaluate so quickly.
DR. BARNES: Do you have bad dreams?
MISS A.: Doesn't everybody?
DR. BARNES: True. I can recall some of my own. What are your bad dreams about?
MISS A.: About being evicted by the landlord in five days. Three days now.
DR. STEIN: She dreams in sequence.
DR. BARNES: It's not the norm, would you say?
DR. STEIN: Ask her if she day dreams.
DR. BARNES: Day dreams?
DR. STEIN: Sees things that aren't there.
DR. BARNES: Well, how would she know ...
DR. STEIN: I'll ask the question. Ever day dream? You know, see things that really aren't there?
MISS A.: (A beat). If you see things, they're really there.
DR. STEIN: True. It's a difficult question. She handled that one nicely—with some qualifications, of course.
DR. BARNES: Philosophical implications, maybe?
DR. STEIN: That's much too sophisticated for her. Go on to the next question.
DR. BARNES: Tell me this, Miss—er—did your mother ever beat you?
MISS A.: Yes.
DR. BARNES: How about your father?
MISS A.: Yes.
DR. BARNES: I see.
MISS A.: When they thought I did something wrong, they beat me.
DR. BARNES: Doctor?
DR. STEIN: I'm getting it down. These people are such primitives.
MISS A.: I don't suppose your father ever beat you.
DR. BARNES: Me? Well, as a matter of fact, he really tanned my rear when I borrowed his new car and—you have a point there. I think I'm finished, Doctor. You have anything you'd like to add?
DR. STEIN: You never asked her did she ever want to murder her mother or her father.
DR. BARNES: You never wanted to murder your father or your mother, did you?
MISS A.: I wanted them to live and I wanted them to be happy. But all they did was work and die at it.
DR. BARNES: Did you follow that?
DR. STEIN: I got it all down.
DR. BARNES: I'm not sure she answered the question properly. My goodness, look at the time! Come, Doctor, we've others to see. You'll be all right, Miss—er—you've nothing to worry about.
DR. STEIN: You didn't ask her. Never mind, I'll ask. Ever been in a mental institution?
MISS A.: No.

DR. STEIN: Ever seen a psychiatrist?
MISS A.: I did once—at that clinic.
DR. BARNES: Let's go, Doctor.
DR. STEIN: Wait! She said, yes. Didn't you hear her?
DR. BARNES: What did you say that for, you stupid bitch! Look at the time.
DR. STEIN: When did you go to this clinic?
MISS A.: I was sixteen. My daddy died and nobody told us. Just took him away without nobody telling us. Like he was part of the garbage he collected for the day. Like when the truck backed over him, they could've just tossed him in with the other stuff and wouldn't have made no difference. There was no clinic and no doctor nowhere that could explain that. All they could do was to give me a shot to cool me down 'til I worked it out for myself. Ever since, I've worked out my answers and known how it was and where I stood and what might happen. (Her hands clutch the bars). And I been careful. I move quietly and I hide myself away when I have to. I always stay clear of things. Since I got that shot to cool me down, I've managed. Then the day before yesterday when I got that notice from the renter I just clean forgot everything. I panicked and like some dumb mouse I walked right into the trap. You'll have to understand how that was. I mean some people I never seen or heard from before was telling me I had to get out of my hole, leave my place I'd made for myself for nine years and go out into the streets. The streets is no place for no mouse, anybody knows that. A mouse that show herself on the street is dumb, 'less she know exactly what she doing. But if she don't know, if she ain't sure, then she'll lose her coolness and get lost and run right into the trap. (She grabs Stein by his coat lapels through the bars). You see how that is, don't you, Doctor? I'm too dumb to be crazy! That ain't hard to see, is it?
DR. STEIN: (He pulls away from her). Sure, sure. I think we see your problem now. (His hand slides into his pocket. He discovers the missing card). Come on, Doctor.
DR. BARNES: Give me that card. (He grabs it). We'll see you later, Miss—er. Where's that pencil? What a case. Our first bona fide loony in quite a while. A psychiatrist will see that right away.
DR. STEIN: Hallucinating. It's a clear case.

They hurry off. MISS DORIS ANDERSON looks after them a moment, then slowly her hands and body slide down the bars to the floor. She remains there for a long moment. Enter the two GUARDS, dressed now as two ATTENDANTS.

1ST ATTEND.: Get up, please.

MISS DORIS ANDERSON gets up mechanically. The 1ST ATTENDANT opens the cell door.

2ND ATTEND.: Your name?

MISS A.: Miss Doris Anderson, one-oh-oh-four ...
2ND ATTEND.: This is the one.
1ST ATTEND.: Just relax, Miss Andrews, while I put these on.
MISS A.: (In a monotone). What is it now? What's happening now?
2ND ATTEND.: Nothing to worry about. We're going on a short trip is all.
MISS A.: (Mechanically). There's nothing the matter with me. Don't put those things on me.
1ST ATTEND.: (He puts on the handcuffs). Sorry. Those are the regulations.
MISS A.: The nut house, that's it, isn't it? That's where I'm going.
2ND ATTEND.: An institution, Miss Anniston, not a nut house. Don't worry, you'll be given good care.
MISS A.: Please take these things off me.
1ST ATTEND.: No trouble now, Miss Andy. Just come along now.
MISS A.: Is somebody talking to me? You really talking to me? (She laughs, close to hysteria).
2ND ATTEND.: Now listen, we're not going to take any crap from you.
1ST ATTEND.: Take it easy. You can see she's really sick. (To Miss Anderson). Look, there's nothing you can do. It's nicer out there. A lot nicer than this hole.
MISS A.: A hole is safe.
1ST ATTEND.: They got doctors out there. It's a lot nicer.
2ND ATTEND.: C'mon, let's go.
1ST ATTEND.: There's nothing you can do.
MISS A.: No.
1ST ATTEND.: You ready then?
MISS A.: Yes.
2ND ATTEND.: Then move.

The ATTENDANTS escort MISS DORIS ANDERSON to center stage, then release her from the handcuffs and exit.

The area LIGHTS stage left have dimmed as the area LIGHTS stage right come up. The area is much the same as the reception area seen earlier except that now this is a nurse's station and the doors at the stage left wall are now barred and screened. The long bench is as it was, but now has shadowy figures of troubled individuals in various body positions. The NURSE, who was the RECEPTIONIST, shifts papers as before. Finally she looks up and sees MISS DORIS ANDERSON standing immobile. She crosses to her.

NURSE: You're the new one, aren't you?
MISS A.: What?
NURSE: Let's see if we can remember our name. (No response). I asked you a question, dear. Did you not hear me? Your name.

MISS A.: Can you tell me how long I have to stay here?
NURSE: Your name?
MISS A.: Miss Doris Anderson, one-oh-oh-four B Orleans.
NURSE: That's good, dear. Let's see, I believe we've had our physical examination.
MISS A.: Please, can you tell me how long I have to stay here?
NURSE: My, it appears we have a very healthy girl. We like to keep ourselves in good condition here at the hospital. Time now for our physical therapy to see if we have good muscle coordination. (She points upstage by the bench). Take that mop and bucket and scrub the floor and hall. We've done that before, haven't we, dear? I don't think we need instructions, do we? ... Miss Allison, we are speaking to you, dear. We must keep busy, you know. If we expect to be discharged we all have to do our therapy jobs.
MISS A.: I'm tired. I want to go home.
NURSE: The exercise will do us good, won't it? I'm just certain we've done this kind of therapy before, haven't we? .... I told you to mop that floor. Are you trying to give me a hard time, dear?
MISS A.: I'm not the maid.
NURSE: You want to get out of here, don't you?

MISS DORIS ANDERSON turns away and does not answer.

NURSE: Then you'd better show a little co-operation and a little respect for the procedures of the hospital. You make trouble and you might find yourself here permanently.

MISS DORIS ANDERSON turns back to her, but says nothing.

NURSE: (Sweetly). There now, I'm certain we understand each other, don't we, dear? I'm certain we'll get along nicely when we understand each other. (She smiles and crosses to the nurse's station).

MISS DORIS ANDERSON looks after her, then moves upstage, takes the mop and bucket and begins scrubbing the floor. MISS LUCILLE ANDERSON, a middle-aged white woman, clothes in disarray and looking wrinkled and disheveled, approaches her. She does it cautiously, glancing toward the nurse's station as she does so. She carries a dust rag in her hand which she had been using on the bench.

LUCILLE: (Confidentially). I heard all that, honey. I'm witness to it. They done the same to me almost three years ago it is now. Dear me, it seems like thirty .... That's it, you keep mopping like you ain't heard me. That's the best thing to do and she'll be none the wiser. Ha! You learn things quick, I can tell.

MISS DORIS ANDERSON stops her mopping.

LUCILLE: Well not me, I can tell you. Oh I kicked and screamed, I did. I told 'em, piss on you, I pay taxes to get this here work done and I'll not do it for you.... 'Course in the end I done it. But they ain't forgotten how I skipped my therapy and no tellin' how much extra time I'm gettin' for it. Damned if I was goin' to let them treat me like the colored.

MISS DORIS ANDERSON begins mopping again.

LUCILLE: There wasn't nothin' personal in that, honey. You needn't worry, they treat everybody the same here. The same, same, same. Nurse says I'm adjustin' myself. I'm hopin' she'll let me see a doctor soon and he'll sign me out. But they say I'm old and got nobody to go out to—and that I need my therapy.

LUCILLE wanders a little stage right. MISS DORIS ANDERSON mops slowly and listens.

LUCILLE: But I have friends to help me, you know. If I could just settle down and write some letters. (She turns to Miss Doris Anderson). I'm certain they read your mail, honey, so you be careful. (She speaks more to herself now). Yes, so many good friends in my young days, so many happy times. Why I'm just certain some one of my friends would be glad to help me—except that it's been so long ago—and I'm not sure of the addresses and—I can't for the life of me think what to say to 'em, what to tell 'em .... Dearest Agnes, Surprise! Surprise! To be hearin' from me after all these years. Remember all the wonderful times we used to have when—when .... I hope you're doin' well. As for me, as for me .... (She trembles). Dear God, if they leave me here much longer I will be crazy. Dear God, it's bein' in here that makes you crazy, don't you understand that?

MISS A.: You're not crazy. None of us is crazy.

LUCILLE: (Defensively). What do you know about it!? Everybody here is crazy as bats. And the doctors worst of all. Like molds of jello, they are, and tryin' to make you the same. All starched-collared flops, that's what. And them nurses, all of 'em been lobotomized by the pricks of them doctors. All of them doctors got huge enormous pricks that rip you out and destroy all your feelins.

MISS DORIS ANDERSON draws back from her.

NURSE: Lucille, we're not making much progress with our mopping, are we?
LUCILLE: Ah God, you don't suppose she heard?
MISS A.: Is that going to matter?
LUCILLE: Don't you get smart with me.
NURSE: Doris, we must finish our dusting therapy early today. The doctor will be coming soon.
LUCILLE: Hear that? She got us mixed up. She's always doin' that. Ha! She's a bitch!

MISS A.: We know who we are. We know we got names.
LUCILLE: (Frightened). What are you talkin' about?
MISS A.: We—I said we got names. We know who we are. What's my name? (No response). My name is Doris ... . It's Doris, do you hear me? Lucille?
LUCILLE: (With distaste). You're colored, that's all I know.
MISS A.: What do you want from me? Why'd you come talking to me?
LUCILLE: I don't know who you are! ... Doesn't make no difference to me anyway. I've had a terrible accident. Yes'm, a terrible accident. Only—I don't know exactly what it was. Something happened to me.
MISS A.: Maybe somebody slapped a wet mop across your face.
LUCILLE: Don't be ugly. Look at you, I suppose you ain't no accident. I suppose you come in here on your own. Well, you wait'll you're here three years. That nice hair of yours'll turn the color of that filthy mop and your skin'll wrinkle up like an old brown wharf rat.
NURSE: All right, Doris, if we can't do our therapy on that floor, perhaps we'd like to do something a little more elementary in our bathroom.

MISS DORIS ANDERSON begins mopping the floor vigorously, angrily.

NURSE: Lucille, we *don't* talk during therapy. I think we *know* that.
LUCILLE: Thank the Lord, we're unmixed again—but that won't last long. One of them doctors'll prick her again and she'll not know chocolate from vanilla.

LUCILLE wanders back to her bench chuckling wildly. Enter a DOCTOR, the same person who played the 2ND MAN. MISS DORIS ANDERSON sees him, drops the mop, and crosses quickly to him.

MISS A.: Are you the doctor?
DOCTOR: That's right. Now if you'll excuse me—
MISS A.: Doctor, they promised you'd see me.
DOCTOR: I don't recall—if you'll excuse me, I have quite a bit to do today.
MISS A.: The man said I didn't belong here.
DOCTOR: What man? I've quite a lot to do today.
MISS A.: That other doctor—the one out front, that one. He said I didn't belong here, that someone would see me.
DOCTOR: That must be Dr. Bristol. I'm sure that Dr. Bristol only meant—you'll have to be patient. Now if you'll excuse me.
MISS A.: It's been three days!
DOCTOR: There's no need to get upset. Now if you'll excuse me.
MISS A.: (She grabs the lapel of his white jacket). But he said I didn't belong here!
DOCTOR: Your name?

MISS DORIS ANDERSON releases her hold and backs away.

DOCTOR: I asked you a question.
MISS A.: (Reluctantly). Anderson. Miss Doris Anderson.
DOCTOR: Why did you do that?
MISS A.: What?
DOCTOR: You grabbed my coat. Why did you do that?
MISS A.: Please, you got to listen to me!
DOCTOR: You reached out and grabbed my coat. Why did you do that? Did you want to hurt me?
MISS A.: If it'll make you listen, yes!
DOCTOR: Oh I see. Have you always felt that to get someone to listen to you, you must first hurt them?
MISS A.: No — you — I mean, listen ...
DOCTOR: How did you feel toward your parents? Was it necessary to make physical contact with them to get them to listen to you?
MISS A.: He said I'd get help. He said they'd get me out of here.
DOCTOR: You seem a little confused, Miss Adams. Do you have any idea what might have confused you? (No response). I'm trying to help you. Tell me, did you ever want to — hurt your father and mother?
MISS A.: Yes.
DOCTOR: And when was that?
MISS A.: Now.
DOCTOR: Oh I see. You mean today?
MISS A.: I mean now.
DOCTOR: Oh I see. And why today, Miss — er ...
MISS A.: For giving me a name nobody can remember. For giving me a life I'd like to forget!
DOCTOR: Now, now, something has confused you. You're getting upset. We'll talk later. Now if you'll excuse me.
MISS A.: How many years will that be?
DOCTOR: Really, Miss — er —
MISS A.: Lucille. It's Lucille. Lucille Anderson. Miss Lucille Anderson.
DOCTOR: Oh of course. I recall everything now. Dr. Bristol did mention you. We'll see to things right away. Now if you will excuse me. (He crosses to the nurse's station).
NURSE: Good morning, Doctor.
DOCTOR: Good morning. Nurse, we've got to make a number of procedural adjustments in the hospital today.
NURSE: Yes, Doctor.
DOCTOR: The state has called for another round of budgetary cuts. We're affected, of course.
NURSE: Yes, Doctor.
DOCTOR: It's going to be necessary to discharge some of the older indigent

patients, the ambulatory ones, of course, and transfer them to community facilities or to other state agencies or to relatives, if we can get them to take them.

NURSE: Yes, Doctor. I have the files right here. (She picks up folders and puts them on top of the desk).

DOCTOR: Good. Please be sure the distribution of them is systematic according to the formula adopted by the state. I believe you have a copy of that.

NURSE: Yes, Doctor.

DOCTOR: Good. We mustn't allow one community or agency to bear too great a burden. In other words, not too many parcels at one doorstep, if you get my meaning.

NURSE: Yes, Doctor.

DOCTOR: I'll just have a peek at these files.

NURSE: Yes, Doctor.

DOCTOR: Hm. Miss Lucile Anderson, yes.

NURSE: She's the one over there pretending to dust.

DOCTOR: You mean the one who's doing the mopping.

NURSE: No, Doctor, I believe she's the one ...

DOCTOR: Never mind, I'll take care of it. (He picks up the file). You can prepare the others for distribution.

NURSE: Yes, Doctor.

DOCTOR: (He crosses to Miss Doris Anderson). Come with me, Lucille. We'll take care of you right away. You see? I told you not to get upset. You've been here three years, is that right?

MISS A.: That's right, Doctor.

DOCTOR: I see. Come with me, please.

MISS DORIS ANDERSON follows the DOCTOR off.

NURSE: Doris, we must finish our therapy as quickly as possible. We've transfers to make and you need to finish your mopping.

LUCILLE: All right, honey. (She picks up the mop and begins working). Hee, hee, hee! Tell me, honey, what ever happened to that nice black lady who used to mop the floors?

NURSE: Please, Doris, we haven't time for chatting this morning. Please continue our therapy.

MISS LUCILLE ANDERSON continues to mop the floor.

BLACKOUT.

Scene 3

>Several beats. The LIGHTS on MISS DORIS ANDERSON center stage as in the beginning. She is sitting in the chair. She is not nervous. She does not fumble with her purse. The lights do not bother her. She makes no effort to see the shadowy figure of the 1ST MAN who is sitting at the desk.

1ST MAN: Your name?
MISS A.: Mrs. Lucille Anderson.
1ST MAN: Your address?
MISS A.: Thirteen-oh-two Bristol Street.
1ST MAN: Bristol, Bristol — I don't seem to be familiar with that. What section of the city is that?
MISS A.: Oh, it's way out, sir. A long ways out. To the west, sir.
1ST MAN: Oh I see. But in the city, right?
MISS A.: Oh yes sir.
1ST MAN: Your age?
MISS A.: Thirty-five.
1ST MAN: How long have you lived in the city?
MISS A.: Forty years.
1ST MAN: Native of the city?
MISS A.: Yes sir.
1ST MAN: Married?
MISS A.: Yes sir.
1ST MAN: Husband living with you?
MISS A.: Yes sir.
1ST MAN: Employed?
MISS A.: Yes sir.
1ST MAN: Occupation?
MISS A.: Sanitation Department.
1ST MAN: Number of children, if any?
MISS A.: Four.
1ST MAN: How many living at home?
MISS A.: None. All got good jobs. None on the welfare.
1ST MAN: Good. Then you'll only need one of our smaller units.
MISS A.: That's right, something small.
1ST MAN: That completes our preliminary form. Now if you'll just sign here, we'll put you on our waiting list.
MISS A.: You got a vacancy in the Orleans project.
1ST MAN: I'm sorry we have no vacancies at this time. If you'll just sign here.
MISS A.: I knew the woman who lived there. She lived there nine years and she missed her rent one time and you sent her notice.

1ST MAN: Now Mrs. Anderson, I realize you have followed all the proper regulations on this application, but you must understand that there is always a waiting period. That is simply normal procedure.
MISS A.: She went crazy and was sent to an asylum for life. So I know there's a vacancy in the Orleans project.
1ST MAN: You people are always getting things confused. I can assure you—what was the number of that apartment again?
MISS A.: One-oh-oh-four B Orleans.
1ST MAN: (He pulls out a file). One-oh-oh-four—did you say D or B?
MISS A.: B as in the first letter of Boy.
1ST MAN: B as in the first letter—I'm awfully sorry. Apparently you are mistaken. I have a Miss Doris Anderson residing there.
MISS A.: You mean—you didn't send any notice? You—didn't evict her?
1ST MAN: Notice? How would I know about that? This office doesn't handle that. That's another department. We find matters are kept more orderly that way. Now please, we're taking up a great deal of time. Until we get formal notice from that department, I'll just have to put you on our waiting list. Now if you'll just sign here.
MISS A.: And she wasn't arrested?
1ST MAN: Please! Others are waiting. If you'll just sign—wait a minute, what did you just say?
MISS A.: Nothing. I didn't say nothing. Just forget it.
1ST MAN: Oh I see. Now just sign here. You're holding up the line.

MISS DORIS ANDERSON has left the chair and moved away from it, the LIGHT following her.

1ST MAN: Mrs. Anniston, you forgot to sign the waiting list. You're holding up the line .... Next!
MISS A.: (She stands alone in the light). All that trouble for nothing. Miss Doris Anderson was all safe in her little hole all the time—and not even knowing it. Like she never came out at all. Nobody saw her or heard her. Like waking up tired after a bad dream, knowing if it all happened it wouldn't have mattered anyway. An accident, just the way it was with my daddy. Something to get rid of as though it never happened. (She pulls a letter from her purse). It wasn't no dream, though. Somebody knew who I was. (She holds up the letter and looks at it). There's the proof of it—right on the envelope. (She reads). "Occupant, one-oh-oh-four B Orleans." So—somebody knew.

The LIGHTS fade out on MISS DORIS ANDERSON.

ON THE MORNING OF THE FIRST DAY

A One-Act Play

CHARACTERS

RUFUS WALLER—an ugly beanpole of a man, but very strong; in his middle 20's
MURDOCK BROWN—tight-fisted store-keeper, dirty and unkempt, in his 60's
ORVILLE JONES—master checker player, lazy, paunchy and middle-aged

THE SETTING

The interior of a rural country store/café in eastern North Carolina, located across the highway from a county school in the mid-1960's.

On the Morning of the First Day

A small general store and café in a rural area in eastern North Carolina in the late 1960's. An old wooden counter is upstage center with several stools in front of it and sparsely stocked shelves in the back wall. The door to the outside is stage right and an old potbelly stove is up right from the door. Downstage toward the audience is an imaginary window where outside events will be observed by those in the store. The store is cluttered and dirty.

It is early morning. MURDOCK BROWN, in his late 60's and the proprietor, stands in front of the counter chewing on the stub of an unlit cigar. He is as unkempt and dirty as his store. He is watching a game of checkers at a center table, one of several wooden tables, most of them placed in the stage left area.

One of the men at the center table is ORVILLE JONES, middle-aged and graying, who is slumped in his chair gazing at the checker board indifferently. He is a chain-smoker and has a racking cough. The man seated across from him is RUFUS WALLER, an emaciated-looking beanpole in his mid-20's, who sits with a baseball bat in his lap. His looks are deceiving, for when he swings the bat, it is clear that his wrists are powerful and his movements quick.

There is a moment of absolute silence as RUFUS hunkers over the board. MURDOCK BROWN almost falls on to the table as he watches intensely. Finally, RUFUS makes his move. ORVILLE suddenly breaks into a spasm of coughing.

RUFUS: Aha-aha. Reckon you thought you had me there, din't you, Orville? Yes suh, I reckon you thought you had me good. Aha. I 'spect you did. I 'spect so.
MURDOCK: Ha, hunh, thas sumthin'.
RUFUS: (To Orville). What'd he say? (No response). What it was Murdock is that I had my red man right cheer mist all his black 'uns and sailed right out of it slick as a wet cunt hair.
MURDOCK: Um. Hunh. Sumthin'.
RUFUS: (To Orville). What'd he say?
ORVILLE: He didn't say nothin'.
RUFUS: Aha. Orville din't see I had this here red man over here floppin' free as the breeze neither. Din't see that, didja, Orville? Eh?
ORVILLE: I seen it.
RUFUS: Shit you did. Sh-it.
ORVILLE: Whatcha think? Think I was to tell you 'bout it? You wanna play like a charity game? We can play a charity game if you want, boy.
RUFUS: You gonna wisht it were a cheerity game when I captures all your black nigger men and puts them in my dungeon. (He puts his hand on his crotch). Aha.

ORVILLE: Hear that, Murdock? You gonna hafta boil these here checkers in hot water to get the crud off.
MURDOCK: (Mumbling). Hunh. Ain't his goddamned checkers. (He moves behind the counter).
RUFUS: What'd he ...
ORVILLE: Said they ain't your checkers.
RUFUS: Wisht they was. It's what I need. (He stands and grips the bat like a pro). Jus' what I need. If I was to have my own checker board—(He takes a terrific swing of the bat). I could practice all night long.
ORVILLE: (He ducks his head). Watch what the hell you doin' with that bat.
RUFUS: Be just like I done with this slugger. Built my wrist good and got my eyes trained so's I could pick out a fly on a heap of garbage thirty feet away. That's no lie neither.
ORVILLE: Don't know why you bring along a baseball bat to play checkers early of a mornin'.
RUFUS: Yes suh, it's good wrists and—(The bat slips to his side). Aha. You don't, eh?
ORVILLE; Think I'll make my move.
RUFUS: Murdock, Orville here don't know why I brung my baseball bat to play checkers this mornin'.
MURDOCK: Hunh. (He takes the cigar stub out of his mouth). Got a nice set of checkers away back in the back somewhere. Sell it to you for three-fifty. A mite dusty but I'll sell it to ya.
ORVILLE: He'll sell anything to ya that ain't attached.
MURDOCK: Discount price, what it 'tis. It's a mite dusty. Got the checkers in a paper sack, though.
RUFUS: (He strokes the bat). What I done was to figger out all the moves so's none of them smart pitchers could trick me up, I did. Do the same with you, if'n I had my own checker board. Even work nights at it—when I wasn't busy with somethin' else. Aha.
ORVILLE: I made my move.
MURDOCK: Might even go as low as three dollah.
RUFUS: Maybe I could find me a piece of cardboard and draw me a checker board. I betcha if I was to practice, I could whip ya.
ORVILLE: Well, you win a few, you lose a few, as I calculate it.
RUFUS: (He sits down again). Aha. You don't fool me none, Orville. You like nothin' better'n beatin' my ass with your nigger black checker men.
ORVILLE: You the one who picks the colors, Rufus. Makes no difference to me. Your move.
RUFUS: Jus' kill your ass if I was to beat you oncet.
ORVILLE: Checkers is checkers.
RUFUS: Jus' kill your ass, that's what.
ORVILLE: Startin' to play checkers of a mornin' with a damned baseball bat.
MURDOCK: Why doncha jus' shut your mouth about that.

ORVILLE: (Amused). What'd he say?
RUFUS: (Not amused). Ain't it your move? You takin' your own sweet time about it.
ORVILLE: I done told you, I moved. (He leans back). Makes no difference to me.

MURDOCK crosses to the imaginary window down left and looks out.

RUFUS: Aha. Orville I din't see you make no move.
ORVILLE: Made one.
RUFUS: (A beat). Shouldn't do that. I mean, I wasn't expectin' no move. I mean, while we was havin' that little dis-cuss-shun there.
ORVILLE: Not me. It was you doin' all the talkin'.
RUFUS: Aha. You sly, Orville. You like a—fox, you are. Lawd me, ain't no tellin' what you was up to while I was jawin'. No tellin'. I know you ain't one to trick me up, now I know that. But all the same.
ORVILLE: Hell, I told you I was movin'. Christ's sake, all I did was move a checker. (Not looking up). Seein' anything, Murdock?
RUFUS: Shouldn't do that while I wasn't lookin', Orville. Shouldn't do that.
ORVILLE: Thought you was lookin'.
RUFUS: Shit you say. Sh-it.
ORVILLE: (Not looking up). Yes sir, Murdock, I love to see a man enjoy the beauties of nature.
RUFUS: Seems to me that there space was empty. Seems to me that black nigger checker was over yonder.
ORVILLE: Suit yourself. (He gets up and stretches). Never found no reason to cheat you. I could shove 'em around with my nose and beat you. Makes no difference to me.
RUFUS: Well—aha. It's jus' that you have to watch out for trickery, Orville. Like them smart pitchers that go to finger lickin' 'fore they throw. It ain't cheatin', unnerstand.
ORVILLE: (Observing Murdock). Checkers is checkers. Don't need no baseball bat to play checkers.
RUFUS: Aha. Ain't he sly, Murdock? Lawd me, he like a—fox.
ORVILLE: Oh, the beauties of nature, eh, Murdock? The sun, all them trees, right pretty sky, too, this mornin'. Cold, though. By God, it's a bit nippy. No day for a sandlot game with no baseball bat.
RUFUS; Aha.
MURDOCK: I ain't lookin' at no goddamned sun or the friggin' trees. I'm lookin' at the goddamned school house over yonder and well you know it!
ORVILLE: That a fact? Well, I'll be boiled in oil.
RUFUS: You funny, Orville.
ORVILLE: Thank you, son. God bless you, son.
RUFUS: Funny. Like you din't care nothin' for it. Like you come to play checkers at seven-thirty of a mornin' ever mornin'.

ORVILLE: Makes no difference to me. (He rubs his neck). By God, believe this cold weather done give me a crick in my neck.

MURDOCK: (Peering out). Nigger janitor come today. Out sweepin' the porch, like always.

ORVILLE: That's that dumb damned Grady. He don't never get the word about nothin'.

MURDOCK: Hunh. Well, he's sweepin' like his goddamned broom is on fire.

RUFUS: He know, all right. That's what I hate about them niggers. Knowin' and pretendin' the way they don't. It smell of trickery, the way they smell. Ask 'em somethin' and they knowin' and you know they knowin', but they not sayin'.

ORVILLE: Maybe it's the way of askin'.

RUFUS: (He stands, smiling). Yeah. Aha. You know, I'd jus' never in this world thunk of it that way. Jus' never in this world. Wouldja, Murdock?

ORVILLE: Thinkin' ain't one of your strong subjecks, Rufus, boy.

RUFUS: I'm thinkin' I know why Orville come down here to play checkers at seven-thirty of a mornin'.

ORVILLE You listenin' to what the Louieville slugger here is sayin', Murdock?

MURDOCK: (Peering out). Grady done gone back in now.

ORVILLE: Talkin' to you, Murdock.

MURDOCK: I ain't deaf. Both of ya don't do nothin' but talk through your ass and bicker.

ORVILLE: Well you might tell him all the same.

MURDOCK: Tell him what?

ORVILLE: Nothin'. Jus forget it.

MURDOCK: Hunh. What's to tell? Ain't laid your hand to work in must be fifteen years far as I know. That plot of land your daddy left you look like a weed patch, and I reckon God hisself put a coin in your hand now and then. Wasn't for checkers and Rufus here, you'd likely starve, I know that. What's to tell?

ORVILLE: You talk like St. Peter on Judgment Day, you peckerhead. You ... (He has a terrible coughing spell).

RUFUS: (He waits for the coughing to subside). Aha. Aha. That was a good one, Orville. Aha. St. Peter. That was sure a good one.

ORVILLE: You want to finish this game or not? Or you gonna play sandlot with a snowball?

MURDOCK: Still nobody showed up. Most eight o'clock. Strikes me as funny.

RUFUS: (To Orville). Teasin' again, ain'tcha? Jus' teasin' away. Ain't no snow.

ORVILLE: Well, pardon that. Thought there might be. If Murdock wasn't too cheap to add another lump of cold in that potbelly, I'd likely forget all about it.

MURDOCK: (Turns from the window). You think I'm gonna waste coal so's you can come in and sit on your fat ass all day and not buyin' nothin', you gotta 'nother think comin', I can tell you. 'Sides, most folks come in and out so quick, they never notice. Trouble with you, Orville, is you never learned the value of a dollah. Yes sir, that's your trouble.

RUFUS: You ever notice how Orville's favorite color is black, Murdock? Ever notice that?
ORVILLE: Well sir, when you ask me to leave, I'll accommodate ya. Makes no difference to me.
RUFUS: Yes suh, he sure got a fondness for it.
MURDOCK: I figger on a miracle. I figger one day you'll buy somethin' besides smokes. And maybe him somethin' besides them little cellophane bags of pecans.
ORVILLE: Pee-cans, Murdock. He calls 'em pee-cans. Never spoil another man's dirty joke.
MURDOCK: Pee-cans, pee-cans, you can't pay your bills with nicotine and nuts, I call tell ya.
RUFUS: You got any of them black nuts? Orville prob'ly like them black nuts.
ORVILLE: Yeah, somethin' buzzin' in here all right. Thought it was a crick in my neck, but sound now like somethin' buzzin' around.
MURDOCK: (At the window again). There went a highway patrol car. Jus' passed right on by.
RUFUS: Ain't seen nothin' dark with fat lips and shiny eyes, has you? Aha. Now Orville jus' might be in-ter-rested in somethin' like that.
MURDOCK: Orville ain't in-ter-rested in nothin' but sittin' on his fat butt in my store from mornin' 'til night playin' checkers and smokin' them cancer sticks.
ORVILLE: What's that? What you talkin' about?
MURDOCK: I got TV at home. It's what they sayin' about them things you puff.
ORVILLE: That's guv'ment stuff.
MURDOCK: It's TV. TV ain't guv'ment.
ORVILLE: Don't you know guv'ment own ever thing you see, breathe, eat and shit?
MURDOCK: No sir, not TV. TV don't cost a nickel.
RUFUS: He's right, Murdock. They mixed up in it, like ever thing else. They tryin' to mix up the colors even. Mixin' up the colors so you'll not know the diff'rence. So's you'll not know red from green or black from white.
MURDOCK: That's color TV. I don't have no color TV.
ORVILLE: He don't quite get ya, Rufus.
RUFUS: (He sits down, absorbed in his own thoughts). Usta watch them baseball games when they first come on TV ever Satiddy and Sunday. Usta get me some corn to pop and sit by that TV hour by the hour and watch them games and cheer and yell 'cause I knowed I was goin' to be up yonder with them major leaguers one day. Would have, too, if I hadn't throwed my arm away. But I'm glad I done that now 'cause if I hadn't I might've been tempted to go up yonder and get myself all mixed up with them colors and not knowin' no more who I was. Playin' with those black bush league niggers that was put there by them black-robed nigger-Jew judges in Wash'ton. Don't nobody keer to watch them games no more. Don't nobody keer to watch them bush niggers or cheer for 'em

RUFUS: (continued) or see 'em touch them nice white balls or put their nigger hands on a nice clean Louieville slugger. (He stands and the bat drops to the floor). It's nigger teams with niggers cheerin' for 'em. Even startin' to get nigger ump-pires and niggers sellin' the popped corn and a-touchin' it with their black paws and all that. And wantin' to come down here now and do the same to my school and wantin' me to go sit with niggers in the stands to watch my school play. (Pacing furiously). Those black-robed nigger-Jews in Wash'ton wantin' to make my school one of their nigger heavens with a nigger devil in charge makin' a whole rotten nigger town of the place where I took my schoolin'! Nigger apes with their nigger black flies and nigger sores and nigger-Jew judges and nigger sin and sickness. You can't go nowhere no more that there ain't nigger this and nigger that and nigger, nigger, nigger!

ORVILLE and MURDOCK stare at RUFUS in disbelief. RUFUS's whole body is trembling and his mouth is covered in saliva. Finally, he sinks down in his chair.

RUFUS: (Long pause). Aha … . Aha. Lawd me. Aha. Lawd me. Lawd me. (He looks down at the checker board). My move, ain't it? Ain't it my move?
ORVILLE: (Pause). You scared to death, boy, that's what I think. What if you was to go over yonder this mornin' with your slugger there and see a bunch of them big black bucks and turn tail and run? What if you was to do that? Wouldn't be able to live with yourself. Some nigger buck pull a switchblade on ya and you turn tail and run. Wouldn't be able to live with yourself, now ain't that true? Ain't it?
RUFUS: (He gets up and picks up his bat and grips it tightly and leans over the table). You sly, Orville. You slick, you are. Yes suh. Foolin' around, that's what. I know ya.
ORVILLE: Fine, boy. Hope you know yourself as well.
RUFUS: Aha. Know poison, Orville. Poison sure scare hell out of me. Know how to treat poison. Know I'm not to take a dose of no poison.
MURDOCK: There go the sheriff's car.
RUFUS: This here is like poison. Like givin' little children a dose of black poison. That sure scare me, Orville, them children takin' black poison.
ORVILLE: Bullshit. You 'fraid of them bucks. You 'fraid you'll get over yonder with them black bucks and turn tail and run.
RUFUS: You a fox, Orville. Like all niggers and nigger-lovers. Murdock, you know Orville here's got a fondness for black?
ORVILLE: Lissen here to hot pants. I 'spect you done your share of prowlin' in the hollow.
RUFUS: Aha. Lissen here, Orville, you can bet your ass when this old boy pulls the curtain to fill his needs, what's underneath me is goin' to be pearly white.
ORVILLE: Ha! Well I'll be boiled in oil. You think I believe that?
RUFUS: (In his face). Lawd God help me if I was to lie about that! Lawd God strike me dead if I was to trade my race like others I know!

ORVILLE: Get outa my face, boy. (He pulls out a handkerchief and wipes his face). You got a screw loose, Rufus. Let's just play checkers.
RUFUS: Aha. You funny, Orville. You always so private and secret-like. I'd say you was up to some kind of trickery, I would. You wouldn't keep no secrets, would you, Orville?
ORVILLE: Murdock, this boy talks like a wildcat that done got himself caught in a corner.
RUFUS: I 'spect not. Aha. But I do like to fill my needs. Why there's times when I rise big as my slugger here. Aha. I ain't as sly as you, Orville, but when the time come to fill my needs, I'm like an old fox with them ladies if I'm to be attended to. Got the proof of it case you wants to know.
MURDOCK: (An obscene laugh). God Jesus, you beat all, Rufus. Ugly as sin itself and women comin' after you like alley cats. You'd think they enjoyed punishin' theirselves. I hear the talk. Beat all I ever seen.
RUFUS: Aha. Jus' tendin' our needs is all, Murdock. (He grips the bat tightly). They know what I got for 'em. You watchin' out yonder?
MURDOCK: Huh? Oh. Ain't nothin' yet. Not one bus yet. You beat all, I tell ya, boy.
ORVILLE: Yeah, it kinda make you wanna — (A coughing spell) pin a medal — (Coughing). On his stump. (Coughing).
RUFUS: (He is fascinated by the cough). Aha. Aha. Aha. (He waits). You know, Orville, I heard tell of people who ain't able. And that's a fact. I've heard tell of people right chere in this county who ain't able. You know that? People right chere not able to even git a rise out of their stump. Didja know that?
MURDOCK: (An obscene laugh). You beat all, boy. Always jokin' 'round like that. Ha! That's sick for sure.
RUFUS: What make it sick, Murdock, is one who can't get no rise out of his stump 'cept for some hot black ape out in the woods like a animal.
MURDOCK: Ha! What a thing. You beat all, boy. Got the devil in ya.
RUFUS: Ain't me that's got a devil. Whatcha think, Orville? Wouldn't you say it was a sickly fella who was to have to do a thing like that?

ORVILLE just stares at the checker board.

RUFUS: Orville of a sudden ain't talkin' no more, Murdock. Aha. Funny. Sure funny when Orville here don't have nothin' to say. Sure is. I'll just make my move now.
ORVILLE; Think maybe you done made your move while I wasn't lookin'.
RUFUS: But that'd be trickery, Orville, ha. Aha.
MURDOCK: What in hell is goin' on over yonder?
RUFUS: (He stands, his bat in hand). They come yet? They out there?
MURDOCK: Hell, I ain't talkin' about out there. I'm talkin' 'bout you and him. I ain't followin' what's goin' on. By damn it, if'n there's somethin' goin' on in my own store, I'm damned well goin' to know about it else I'm likely to get robbed

MURDOCK: (continued) blind. You can't trust nobody or nothin' these days else they'll take ever dime you got. By God, I've never seen the likes of it, the way folks is after ever dime you got.

RUFUS: Ain't nothin' to worry over, Murdock. It's jus' a little dis-cuss-shun Orville and me is havin'. Ain' that so, Orville? (No response). Aha. Like a I said, Orville got him a little secret he ain't gonna tell — but it ain't nothin' for you to be worryin' over. (He flops down in the chair and stares across at Orville, a triumphant smile on his face).

MURDOCK: (Upset and on a tirade). Oh, you think I got nothin' to worry about, eh? That what you sayin'? Well, a helluva lot you know about it. If'n them black bastards get their black asses in that school over yonder, you know what's to happen? Ever body is goin' to commence to pullin' their young'uns out and puttin' 'em some other place in the town or the county. So, by God, where they gonna eat lunch? Well, I tell ya, it ain't gonna be here! Years and years those little pimple-faced shits been comin' here for lunch what with the school bein' right 'crost the road. They can't smoke and fuck around in the cafeteria so they come over here. Years and years, I say! By God, you come to depend on trade like that even if you have to run the little shits out of the store half the time so's your eardrums won't bust. Least their daddies and mommies knows they got a good hot sammich when they lunch here, I seen to that. And only one thin dime extra charged to heat it. Hunh. That school likely to close down and you tellin' me not to worry. Why the hell ain't you over there with that slugger standin' in the doorway? Why the hell ain't you over there makin' sure those black nigger communists don't get in that place? You want to see me run out of business? I reckon twenty-thirty-forty dollahs a day from those pig-young'uns and you tellin' me not to worry! Why the hell ain't you out there rollin' a few heads, you big, ugly fuck-face?

RUFUS: (Subdued). 'Cause ain't nobody there yet.

MURDOCK: Ain't nobody there! How you know ain't nobody there? You been over there? No. You been sittin' on your skinny butt playin' checkers and makin' riddles with that cancer machine.

RUFUS: I'm waitin'.

MURDOCK; Waitin'! What the goddamned hell are you waitin' for!?

RUFUS: You supposed to be watchin'. You supposed to tell me when them busses come. I mean, I'm waitin' for you to tell me, Murdock.

MURDOCK: What? (A beat). Yeah. That is right. Forgot that.

ORVILLE has a coughing spell.

MURDOCK: Well how the hell you 'spect me to do that with all this mumbo-jumbo goin' on 'tween you and him? I've a mind to go over there jus' to get away from you two. Yes sir, if it wasn't for mindin' the store, I'd get over there myself.

ORVILLE: You go ahead, Murdock. I'll mind the store. Got nothin' else to do.

RUFUS: Now ain't that somethin'? Orville here gonna mind the store so's you can go over yonder and bust a few niggers. Aha. Sounds mighty sly to me, Orville, like maybe you was hopin' to get somethin' outa it. Or keep some secret you got from Murdock Brown here?
ORVILLE: (disgusted): I'm gonna make my move. Maybe that'll shut you up for awhile.
RUFUS: Aha. Secrets is the hardest things to keep, Orville. 'Specially nigger secrets.
ORVILLE: Can't you quit yakkin' for a minute and play checkers!? No wonder you never win.
RUFUS: Orville—oncet a woman spreads her legs out there ain't no secrets. You finds out all kinds of things.
ORVILLE (He looks up at him sharply and gets halfway up in his chair): What you sayin'?
RUFUS: Aha. Your move, Orville.
ORVILLE: (A beat). I know what you're sayin'. You been out there, ain't ya? To the trailer. I'll be son of a bitch.
MURDOCK: If I was to leave Orville here he'd make off with ever pack of smokes in the store. I'd be run into bankruptcy. Who spread her legs? Who's puttin' out?
ORVILLE (He sinks down in his chair): You done it to her? Even to her? No lie, is it? You ain't makin' it up, are you?
RUFUS: I can't abide lies and trickery, Orville. Way I see things we all got to tend to our needs no matter what. Our needs is big and don't seem to be no way to set 'em aside. They got to be fixed one way or 'nother. Now that's so.
ORVILLE: Well I'll be boiled in ... That stupid bitch! Oh God, poor thing. Poor Millie.
MURDOCK: Thing of it is, I'm too old to go over there. Ain't scared to fight. Just too old. Be glad to crown one of them black bucks, but you can see I'm too old. Man oughta tend to his own business anyway. What's wrong with the country today, people turnin' all their business over to guv'ment and big companies so's nobody knows what the hell is goin' on.
ORVILLE (He stands): Goddamn, anybody but you! (Another coughing spell).
MURDOCK: What? What'd he say? What the hell's goin' on over there?
RUFUS: Aha. Orville jus' got to laughin' is all. You watchin' the window?
MURDOCK: What? Oh. They ain't doin' nothin' but ridin' by. Orville ain't laughin'. It's them cancer sticks. What the hell you talkin' about, boy?
RUFUS: Like I say, Orville, there's needs that need attendin' to and if you ain't able ...
ORVILLE: Jus' forget it. Jus' shut up about it. Makes no difference anyhow.
RUFUS: Sure. Sure wisht I could. I could too—if'n it weren't for the rest of it. You got the poison, Orville. (Intensely). Makes me so sick I could jus' throw up.
MURDOCK: By God, that's a fact. I seen it all on TV. He got the cancer. Ought not to hang around here like he does. Might be contagest. (Looking out). There go the highway patrol. Whose side they on anyway?

RUFUS: Aha. Well, I was jus' a-walkin' down the road of a late summer day past that trailer where she moved to from your place. Well, of a sudden I got this awful need. You jus' never believe how awful it was, Orville, it bein' so hot and all. So I says to myself, it's so awful hot believe I'll drop by to see that old sweet Millie, bein' as how I knowed you and old sweet Millie done split like you had.

ORVILLE gets up and crosses downstage right stifling a cough.

RUFUS: Get her to treat me to a glass of tea, I will. Aha. Loves tea in the hot summer time. It sorta fills my needs long as it's got some spoons of sugar in it. Figgered since you and old sweet Millie been split for a while, she jus' might be willin' to share a bit of tea with spoons of sugar on a summer day to satisfy a little thirst. Aha. She's still a right pretty little woman, now ain't she, Orville? Aha. Oh, yes she is.
MURDOCK: Well I'll be Jesus H. Christ! Rufus, you mean you been fuckin' Orville's wife!? Holy mother! (He starts to laugh, but stops abruptly). Lissen, you son of a bitch, I catch you within two hunder'd yards of my place I'll shoot your ass off and that's a fact.
RUFUS: Aha. Now you know your woman's way too old and wrinkled for me, Murdock. Anyway, ever body knows how you able to fill your old lady's needs. Wouldn't do me no need to come 'round your place. Aha.
MURDOCK (He laughs. Proudly.): I ain't had no complaints, I'll say that.
RUFUS: That's because you ain't got the weakness that some has.
MURDOCK: That don't sound like no cancer that I ever heard of. That's the damndest thing I ever heard. That beats all.
RUFUS: It ain't all. Ain't no sin to have a little weakness—if'n that was all.
MURDOCK (He laughs): Well, I guess not, but I'm glad I ain't got it. Whatcha mean if that was all?
RUFUS: Aha. You watchin' the window? What if them school busses was to come while you ain't watchin' at the window?
ORVILLE: Well, go on, boy, you dyin' to tell him, ain'tcha? Go on and tell him how I screwed a nigger. That's the big deal, ain't it? Go on, makes no difference to me. (He has another coughing spell).
MURDOCK: Son-son of a bitch! You lost your mind, Orville? (He slams his fist on the counter). You wanna get hung from a tree? Get a switchblade in your back? Holy mother!
ORVILLE: That's right, lost my mind. Be much obliged if you'd tell me how that happened—or how it din't happen no more with one, and did with another. (He leans against the counter, stifling another cough). Ain't blamin' Millie. The woman had hopes, wanted things. Like Murdock says I've not put my hand to work for more'n fifteen years. Ha. I'm what they call a butterfly chaser, a cockeyed howler at the moon. What the hell, one goddamned life and I'm supposed to spend it bent over a goddamned machine or shufflin' papers at that there

lumber office. Might as well have, I guess. Makes no difference anyway.
RUFUS: Good, weren't it, Orville? All that hot black poison old Laurie Mae Hawkins give was good, weren't it?
ORVILLE: That's right. Kind of poison you can't get enough of. Like smokes which you know is goin' to one day burn out your insides. But the comfort of it all. To sit and draw on a fag to steady your shaky bones when you're tired of it all. Makes you sick at your stummick to think about it all. Well, what's done is done. Makes no difference.
MURDOCK: How come, Orville? How come you to do a thing like that?
ORVILLE; Jus' went fishin' one day down by that sandy cut at the river.
RUFUS: Aha. Fishin' for what, Orville?
ORVILLE: Fishin' for nothin', or peace, or—fish! Yes, by God, fish.
MURDOCK: Niggers is the only ones that fish down yonder by the cut anymore, you know that.
ORVILLE: Niggers and Orville.
MURDOCK: She was down there?
ORVILLE: Yep.
MURDOCK: Hot damn! Then what?
ORVILLE: Fishin'.
RUFUS: Shit. Sh-it.
ORVILLE: Pretty day. Oh, a pretty day. But the fishin' wasn't no good. Laughed about that. Maybe she knowed right off what was to happen. I did. Sure funny how that works.
RUFUS: See there? Can't change no nigger. That black bitch of a school teacher a-whorin' around like the rest of 'em. That's niggers for you.
ORVILLE: Can't say why she did it. Got no idea. Jus' that kinda day. Seems to me that them that's schooled in books got needs like them that ain't.
RUFUS: I was schooled, Orville. But wasn't schooled to no race-mixin'. I was taught not to fool with no lazy black poison, and there's not been a day I ain't turned my hand to work, that I ain't done my job. I takes time to drink a little likker and play a bit of checkers and tend my needs, but, by God I've not missed a day at sawin' lumber—and that's bein' because I've not been poisoned by no nigger blood mixin'.
ORVILLE: That the reason? Boy, you jus' on your high horse today, aint'cha, boy?
RUFUS (He grasps the bat in his hand, angrily, threatening Orville): Like nothin' better'n see you hangin' on a tree limb by your balls for what you done! You nothin' but part black nigger ape now. Nothin' but a nigger-wop-nigger-Jew-nigger!

RUFUS appears about to swing the bat at ORVILLE. ORVILLE does not move.

MURDOCK: Hey, you knucklehead! You gonna bash heads you do it on the outside not on my property!

MURDOCK tries to grab the bat, but RUFUS is too strong and will not let go.

MURDOCK: What the hell, you tryin' to do run me outa business? Mess up the floor with the stuff in his head and I'll never get a woman in here shoppin' again. Be a damned scandal for sure. Hell fire, Rufus.

RUFUS (He lets the bat fall at his side): Aha. Wasn't goin' to, Murdock. Wasn't. Look yonder at Orville. He know that. He ain't moved a hair. Aha. Not moved a inch like it din't matter one way or another. Jus' go to show you wasn't nothin' to it. Jus' a dis-cuss-shun, ain't that so, Orville? (He pulls a coin from his pocket). Gimme a bag of them pee-cans.

MURDOCK: By Jesus, what a mornin'. Highway cops ridin' around wastin' taxpayer money and you raisin' a baseball bat to a white man.

RUFUS (He rips open the bag): Orville got the poison. Ain't no tellin' what he is.

ORVILLE: Orville's English on both sides. Pure as King George the Third.

RUFUS: Don't you see it, Orville? Your lovin' of niggers done made you sick. Done made you sick and lazy and shiftless like them. Made them as good as you. That's what the poison done. That's what come of race-mixin'.

ORVILLE: I ain't sayin' nothin'. All I know is I thought I done turned to stone and here was this woman who for a couple of minutes, for reasons I'll never know, got me thinkin' I was a man again. (He has a coughing spell that forces him into his chair). I'm tired talkin'. Even tired of this here game. What's done is done. Don't figger I'm any worse off than Millie is if she was took by you, boy.

MURDOCK: By God, this is raunchy. Good and raunchy! Make me sick to my stummick, I can tell you. Don't know if I can stand the sight of you no more. No sir, don't know if I can.

ORVILLE: Well turn 'round and go over to the shelf and bring me three packs of Camel cigarettes to relieve yourself of the strain.

MURDOCK (He gets the cigarettes and brings them to him): Well, I'll jus' tell ya, if I wasn't in need of trade — a man has to put up with a lot to make hisself a livin'. Wouldn't put up with it if I wasn't strapped with that dumb lazy-ass young-un of mine and my old woman.

RUFUS: Shit. Sh-it! Ain't no men anymore. They all sick. They all been got by trickery and race-mixin'. Ain't no sport to nothin' no more. Ever body pushin' theirselfs on others and mixin' and leanin', and it not makin' no diff'rence one way or the other.

ORVILLE: That why you come here this mornin' with your slugger?

RUFUS: Them was my good days over yonder at that school. I give all I had to 'em on the diamond. Then went to that there baseball spring trainin' camp and was out-pointed by a black nigger 'cause my arm was throwed away. Well, din't mind that so much 'cause I din't want to play in no nigger league anyway. But when it come down to my school, that be somethin' else. The day gonna come when I get enough of my needs filled and I'll be wantin' to settle in and maybe have a young-un or two. You think I'm gonna let 'em make a nigger team and a nigger league out of my school where my young-uns to go? Where I give my

best? Man got to have somethin' of his own that's best—that he best at. Ain't that right? Ain't that so?
ORVILLE: Yep.
MURDOCK: Goddamned right you are, boy.
RUFUS: Ain't just skin neither.
ORVILLE: Nope, not skin.
RUFUS: It's your feelin' about it, that's what. It's a-likin' it and knowin' there ain't no poison in it.
ORVILLE: Yep.
RUFUS: Oncet you mix, oncet it don't matter, oncet it don't make no diff'rence, then you gone. Ain't no privilege to bein' what you been. Anybody saw lumber as good as you. Anybody take them women good as you and fill the needs. Then you ain't nothin'. That's what them black-robed nigger-Jew judges been tryin' to do. Tryin' to trim us all down 'til we're all worth nothin' more than dust. Tryin' to make us—like Orville.

ORVILLE says nothing. He lights up a cigarette and moves up right by the potbelly stove.

The SOUND of the faint noise of a crowd which none of them hear as yet.

RUFUS: Aha. Aha. Ain't no trickery meant there, Orville. Ain't one for trickery, you know that. You unnerstand, Murdock?
MURDOCK: Hell no, not a bit of it. All I know is I ain't wantin' niggers in the schools or niggers no where near me—less'n of course they gonna buy somethin'. But when they buys, they leaves quick, see there? That's the thing, they can buy but they gotta get out of sight and in their place down to the hollow. Well, what I've heard this day is sure raunchy, I'll tell you. That's as far as I'll say about it. She come in here sometimes, you know, but I jus' dare that black bitch to put her long nigger legs on my doorstep again or she'll get a foot in her black ass. If she want to buy somethin' she'll have to send somebody in to get it, and that's all I've got to say on the matter. (He hears the sound of the crowd). What's that?
RUFUS: I don't hear nothin'. You watchin'?
MURDOCK: Watchin'? Watchin' what?
RUFUS: The school house!
MURDOCK: Oh damn! Plum forgot that in all this mess (He hurries over to the window). Holy mother! Get goin', Rufus. They here, the niggers is here.
RUFUS (He hurries to the window): Will you look at that. Nothin' but a swarm of black comin' off them busses!
MURDOCK: It's a plague! A toranada! A-a-a hurry-cane!
RUFUS: Where'a my slugger?
MURDOCK: There's too many of 'em, Rufus. Ain't no use.

RUFUS: Don't matter. Won't even have to take aim. Jus' swing blind and I got me a dead nigger fly. You watch and see if that ain't so. (He grabs his bat and starts for the door. Feverishly). Aha! It's like bein' out yonder in the games again, Murdock! A ache and a thrill.
MURDOCK: You be careful, boy.
RUFUS: Aha. Aha. (He sets and takes a vicious swing and dashes out the door).
MURDOCK (He chuckles). Now don't that boy beat all. Yes sir, there go a boy with fire in his balls. He'd go far at the saw mill if and when he learns the value of a dollah. Yes sir, quite a boy that.
ORVILLE: Murdock.
MURDOCK: Yes sir, that boy—what's that?
ORVILLE: Say it was offered to you—say there was nobody about to know. Say you could do it right slick like and nobody there to know. (He crosses toward him and stops). Would ya?
MURDOCK (Nervously). Would I—oh hell now—I mean, what the hell ... .
ORVILLE: C'mon, Murdock, would ya? Good and clean, Murdock. The day bright, the sand good and warm and you feelin' young again. And her brown and naked before you, and nobody to know nothin' or share nothin' but you and her.
MURDOCK: Nobody to know nothin'? Jus'—me and her, you say?
ORVILLE: That's right. Wouldja?
MURDOCK (He smiles and licks his lips, but the smile fades to a frown): What'cha—what'cha tryin' to do, Orville?
ORVILLE: Jus' 'tween us, Murdock. Jus' want to know 'tween us. Well, never mind. Can't make no difference. Jus' forget about it.
MURDOCK: What? Goddamn right I'll forget about it. I say a thing like that and you spread it 'round and I might as well close down and declare bankruptcy.
ORVILLE: Told you it was 'tween us.
MURDOCK: Lissen here, I'll swap stories, but you gotta watch what you say. Now what you done was a crime—a—a sin just like Rufus said. (A beat). Naked, was she?
ORVILLE: Yep.
MURDOCK: How come? I mean—you mean she jus' come over and lay it all out for you?
ORVILLE: God, no. Told you how it was. Beautiful day. I was feelin' good and prancin' 'round in the water like twenty years ago. Skippin' ripples and drunk on the sun. Foolish cavortin'. Then I hears this laughin' behind me. Felt foolish as hell, I can tell ya. Figgered the only way to face it was to laugh myself. So I did—then I turns and sees who it was and what it was. Had on shorts and it seemed I saw a mile of fine brown legs up on the bank of the river and plum forgot to whistle "Dixie."
MURDOCK: Goddamn! What happened next?
ORVILLE: Talkin' and laughin'. Plum forgot fishin'—and who we was.
MURDOCK; Then what happened?

ORVILLE: I done told ya, we ended up screwin' before we knew what we was doin'.

The SOUNDS from the distance have become louder.

MURDOCK: Well I know that. Ain't'cha gonna tell me how you—hell, the dee-tails, man. The dee-tails, goddamn it!
ORVILLE: What's goin' on over yonder?
MURDOCK: What's that? What are you talkin' about?
ORVILLE (He goes to the window): Over yonder at the school.
MURDOCK (He follows him to the window): I'm damned, Orville, you get a man all hepped up on a story, then change the subjeck.
ORVILLE: You got no right to know the rest. You'd a knowed none of it if that bitch of a woman I married hadn't fixed her mind on a little self-torture with that ugly boy and his iron prick. (A beat). God knows who told her or how she knew about it, but she knew right off. (Disdainfully). Glass of cold tea. If that don't top all.
MURDOCK (Looking out the window): Holy mother, look at that! There's bunches of white people out there now and they turnin' over the busses!
ORVILLE (He looks out): What the hell?
MURDOCK: The dumb bastards done turned over the busses! They think my taxes gonna pay for that, they got another think comin'!
ORVILLE: Yep, they done it all right. And look at that. You talk about mixin' the races. Now that there is really mixin' it up.
MURDOCK: Oh my, they sure is swingin', ain't they? There come the sheriff's deputies.
ORVILLE (He turns away and moves to the counter): Don't believe I can look at a thing like that before breakfast. (He has a coughing spell).
MURDOCK: There come the highway patrol. Done took off them wide-brimmed hats and put on helmets. Wonder what they cost?
ORVILLE (He refuses to look): They can buy theirselfs gas masks, if they want. Makes no difference to me.
MURDOCK: They got them, too. Next thing you know they'll be tradin' in all their cars for helly-copters. Oh, there's Rufus! I can tell by the swing. Bopped down two niggers in one turn. Gonna break his damned bat if he ain't careful. There go a window out in the school! There go Grady out the back way! ... Hunh. Smack dab into the arms of a trooper. Dumb nigger. Troopers startin' to break through out front yonder. Damn if this ain't better'n listenin' to Don Dunphy do the Louis-Conn fight on the radio. Never will forget that. Jus' a boy then countin' out the day's take for my daddy. Come out ten dollahs short that night. Couldn't sleep the whole blasted night worryin'. Come to find out I made a mistake 'cause I was listenin' to Don Dunphy call the Louis—Hey, ain't that her? Ain't that Laurie Mae Hawkins yonder?
ORVILLE: She ain't there. She teaches down the hollow at the nigger school, you know that.

MURDOCK: Sure do look like her with them long nigger legs and all.
ORVILLE (He goes to the window): Where? Where's that?
MURDOCK: See yonder. Now she done pulled out of the crowd. See? Leadin' them two nigger young-uns up the walk toward the school.
ORVILLE: Yep, that's her all right. What in the name of hell is she doin'? She lost her mind?
MURDOCK: Look! They after her! Look at them white boys go after her. There's Rufus! He's got that bat up. He's ... .

ORVILLE turns away and moves very slowly to the counter and leans on it.

MURDOCK (He has turned away, but now looks out again): They got her. Kids, too ... Now the troopers is scatterin' 'em. Hm. Hunh. Look like they got 'em a pretty big mess over there, Orville. (He rubs his hands along his trousers, thoughtfully. Suddenly he snaps his finger). Damn my ass! Let that sammich man talk me into buyin' my regular order today. Somethin' told me I wouldn't need all them sammiches today. Damn sammich man kept sayin' the niggers was too scared to show their black faces. That lyin' bastard talked me into it. What the hell am I goin' to do with all them stale sammiches? Whose gonna buy a damned day-old permentoe cheese sammich?

The SOUND of sirens in the distance.

MURDOCK: Here come the am-bu-lances. There's a bunch of 'em. Who you suppose is gonna pay for that?

ORVILLE has moved to his chair. He sits and stares blankly at the checker board.

MURDOCK: There go the gas! Look at them niggers run! The white folks is running, too, of course, but not as fast ... . Troopers is tryin' to catch 'em now. Dumb bastards shouldda caught 'em first, then turned on the gas. Wonder how much that gas cost? Here come Rufus! He done outflanked the whole lot of 'em. That boy beats all I ever seen. Comin' right over here now, slick as a whistle. Them others oughta have as much sense. Come right over here and buy theirselfs a sammich, like they been here all the while. Buy 'em a sammich and a fried pie, a drink and maybe a pack of smokes. Jesus! Could've been a bonanza. Could've sold ever one of them sammiches that dumb sammich man talked me into ... .

RUFUS enters, panting and out of breath. He falls hard against the counter, his shirt torn, a little blood on his cheek and shirt. He does not have his baseball bat.

MURDOCK: Well, by God, boy, if you don't beat all! I never seen such a thing in my life. Better'n than Don Dunphy and the Louis-Conn fight on the radio some years ago.
RUFUS (Panting): You seen—you seen it?
MURDOCK: Sure, I seen it. Like a reg'lar fan in the stands, a-sittin' in a box seat. And din't cost me a red cent.
RUFUS: You seen—you seen how—you seen how no black niggers went to my school today. You seen that, din't you, Murdock?
MURDOCK: Oh yeah, I seen. Seen it all from right here. Troopers and niggers and am-bu-lances. Holy mother! That was somethin'.
RUFUS: Showed them black-robed nigger-Jew judges what we was. Showed 'em we was somebody to reckon with. Showed we men! We men, not ants they can come steppin' on with their black nigger feet and their black nigger paws. Bunch of apes with their black nigger skin and their niggerness and .... (He is trembling and his mouth is drooling. He holds on to the counter for support). Aha. Aha. Aha.
MURDOCK: Wanna soft drink?
RUFUS: Yeah, gimme one. Gimme pack of them pee-cans, too.
MURDOCK: One quarter. How 'bout a sammich?
RUFUS: Some of them nice pee-cans yonder.
MURDOCK: Sure. I'll never get rid of them stale sammiches. Hey, where's your slugger?
RUFUS: Must've dropped it. Saw they was gonna shoot that gas off, so I run like hell. Guess I dropped it. Don't matter, though. That the best day I'll ever have with that slugger—and din't have to put up with no trickery from any of them pitchers neither.
MURDOCK: That's fact. Sure as hell, though, boy, they gonna catch your ass.
RUFUS: Don't matter. Catch the whole town and it don't matter. Gonna put the whole town in the jailhouse? We done what we went for and done won the day. Done won the old ball game, Murdock! Aha.
MURDOCK: Well I'll say that for you. Yes sir, I seen that for myself. Not one black nigger got to the door of that school house today.
RUFUS: Ain't none goin' to get there neither. No sir. Aha. Remind me of the day we won the state championship. Lawd me, sure does.
MURDOCK: I seen that Laurie Mae Hawkins walkin' up toward the school door in her short skirt with them two little pickaninnies holdin' on. I seen that clear as day.
RUFUS: Aha. And you seen how they din't get there?
MURDOCK (He laughs): Oh yeah, me and Orville watched that from right here, like sittin' in a box seat and not payin' a red cent.
RUFUS: Aha. You say Orville seen that?
MURDOCK: Yeah, he seen it.
RUFUS (He crosses to Orville): Orville, you seen that, didja? Didja, Orville?
ORVILLE (Not looking up): Makes no difference to me.

RUFUS (Tauting): Aha. Laurie Mae Hawkins, she able to get Orville's race-mixin' stump up and goin'—but don't make no diff'rence to him. You hear that, Murdock? You hear what Orville here say? (He takes a big drink from the cola bottle and slams it on the counter with resolution). Know what, Orville? I feelin' so good 'bout right now I reckon I could beat your ass at this here checker game. Believe I could put all your black nigger men in my nigger dungeon here, that's what.
MURDOCK: You beat all, boy. Never happen.
RUFUS (He pulls out his wallet): Got ten dollah of workin' money says it will. Yes suh, ten dollah says I can. What you say to that, Orville? You ain't afraid, are ya?
ORVILLE: 'Fraid of what?
RUFUS: I mean to say, if you ain't too upset?
ORVILLE: Upset about what?
RUFUS: Aha. Aha. You funny, Orville.
MURDOCK: Never happen. He'll get the cancer and die 'fore you'll ever take him at checkers.
RUFUS: Shit. Sh-it!
MURDOCK: Well, there's the board, boy. Look like you're near even-steven in that game right now, don't it?
RUFUS (He checks out the board counting with his finger): It seem so. Seem so. Do it suit you, Orville?
ORVILLE: Told ya, makes no difference ...
RUFUS: Would swear you was part nigger blood if'n I din't know ya!
MURDOCK: Now wait there, boy. I knew Orville's daddy. Got crippled up on a tractor in his young days. So I knows he wasn't able to make no trips down to the hollow.
ORVILLE: We gonna play this game or not?
MURDOCK: As for his mama, those that knowed her claim she was so cold she musta had a virgin birth. Course that couldn't be right, could it? That'd mean that Orville here would be—(He bursts out laughing). That sure is funny. Took me a while to catch on to that, but sure is funny.
ORVILLE: Why the hell don't you check out the window yonder and count dead niggers? Might charge the tax-payers for the funerals, you know. (He moves a checker).
MURDOCK: Hell you say! I ain't payin' for no—You jokin', eh? Well, it ain't a very funny one, I can tell you. Mighty sick, I'd say. That's what I'd say.
ORVILLE: Can't you jus' shut your mouth for damned minute!?
RUFUS: Aha. Look like Orville done got hisself all upset, Murdock.
ORVILLE: I moved, boy! I moved my black nigger checker! Now jus' get on with it. I need the money.
RUFUS: Aha. I seen, Orville. I seen you move, sure did. I was watchin, sure was. That mean it my turn, don't it? Ain't that right?
ORVILLE: Pest. Dumb-ass pest, get on with it.

RUFUS: I seen it. I sure seen that move, Orville. Aha. Sure did. (He leans over the table like a vulture. Then he slowly and methodically jumps every black checker on the board except one. He picks up each one and slowly puts them in his pocket, looking at Orville with a gaping grin on his face).
MURDOCK: Son of a bitch, Orville! What the hell is the matter with you?
RUFUS: Aha. Aha. One black nigger checker 'gainst five of my red 'uns.

ORVILLE makes no response. He just stares at the board.

RUFUS: Look like maybe you done made a dumb move, Orville. Real careless. Aha. Reason it took me a time to move was I jus' couldn't figger how you could make such a dumb move without some kind of trickery in it. But couldn't find no trickery in it. Ain't like you to make no dumb move, ain't that so, Murdock? Orville he like a—fox. Aha. A fox! But now he done made a dumb …
ORVILLE (Quietly): Jus' shut up.
RUFUS (To Murdock): What'd he say?
ORVILLE: I said I wisht you'd close that flycatcher you got for a mouth.
RUFUS: Aha. Aha. Reckon you got to pay up, Orville. (He empties his pockets of the black checkers and lets them fall on the board, his eyes on Orville). All of them black dead niggers there belongs to you, Orville. I done took them and put them in their place. Tucked them in my dungeon so's they can't play no more of their tricks and jokes on nobody again. They all dead niggers 'cept that one that's left yonder and I was to get him. He'd step in front of my big reds and I'd hop his ass, too. So pay up, Orville. Pay up for all your nigger tricks and sins.

ORVILLE, his eyes on Rufus, reaches slowly in his back pocket for his wallet, then drops the ten on the board.

RUFUS: Aha. Made an awful dumb move, din't you, Orville! Sure did.
ORVILLE (Softly): Checkers is checkers. Makes no difference to me.
RUFUS: Shit. Sh-it! (He grabs the money and pockets it).
MURDOCK: Well, I done seem ever thing. You beat all, boy.
RUFUS: Aha. I 'spect I'll saw me some lumber today. I 'spect I will. Aha. Aha.
MURDOCK: Oh you havin' yourself quite a day, boy. I'll say that, I sure will.
RUFUS: And there wasn't no trickery to it neither.
MURDOCK: Hell no. Ever thing you done was straight. There's nobody can say otherwise. Here, you take one of these here permentoe cheese sammiches with you for ya lunch. (He tosses it to him).
RUFUS: You ain't gonna give it, are ya?
MURDOCK: Sure. Sure, I'm givin' it. It's a big day for you, boy. Eh—Well maybe I'll jus' slip it on your account where you can take care of it later. Say you gonna saw some lumber today, eh?
RUFUS: 'Spect I will, sure do. Aha. Be seein' you, Orville. Aha. Don't look like Orville there is too happy.

MURDOCK: You beat his ass, boy. What'd you expect?
RUFUS: Orville he shouldda kept his mind set on the game, that's what. Sure thing, if'n you lose track of the game, if your mind ain't set on it, you makes a dumb move. Aha. Sure do. Any time you let your mind go fishin', as they say, you makes a dumb move, ain't that so, Orville?
ORVILLE (Not looking up): Checkers is checkers. Makes no difference to me.
RUFUS: You funny, Orville. Lawd me, you funny. (He goes out the door).
MURDOCK: See ya, boy. By God, if that boy don't beat all. Well now, ain't it been a day and barely nine o'clock in the mornin'. Orville, bet you ain't even et breakfast yet. How 'bout lettin' me sell you one of these fresh permentoe sammiches?
ORVILLE: Open me a beer, Murdock.
MURDOCK: A beer? You goin' to drink a beer and it barely nine o'clock in the mornin'? No sir, some of them ladies might come in to do some shoppin' and seein' you settin' drinkin' in my place at this hour, they likely to set the preacher on me. No sir.
ORVILLE (He takes out the money and sets it on the table): Wisht you'd learn the value of a dollah, Murdock.
MURDOCK (He eyes the money for a moment and looks all around): Well — tell ya what — I'll jus' put it in this here brown coffee mug and nobody be the wiser. See, I wouldn't want to hurt nobody's feelins, unnerstand? That be all right, won't it? Put it in a brown coffee mug?
ORVILLE (He slumps in the chair): Makes no difference. Makes no difference.
MURDOCK: Well — you know there's nothin' like a coffee mug to keep beer good and cold, I can tell ya. 'Specially early of a mornin'. (He pours the beer in the mug and hides the bottle under the counter and brings the mug to the table). Yes suh, it beat all. Quite a day. Ain't ever day you crown a new champ. (He crosses to the window). No suh, not ever day you do that. 'Course there is those damned sammiches — but I reckon it'll all settle back tomorrow and be jus' the same. There come a wrecker truck. Gonna put them busses up right, I guess. Yes suh, quite a day. Remind me of the Louis-Conn fight on the radio. Always was one to root for the underdog, you know. Jus' a thing about me, I guess. Yes suh, Billy Conn, he sure give that big nigger a run for his money, I can tell ya. That Rufus he remind me of that. Out yonder a-fightin' the guv'ment, the state and all the niggers in the hollow all at onct — and comin' out on top like he done. And not one nigger teacher and not one nigger kid darkened the door of his school, jus' like he said. He sure beat all, that boy. Yes, he does.

ORVILLE picks up a handful of black checkers and lets them slide through his fingers to the board.

MURDOCK: Good big bright sun out this mornin', Orville. Little frosty out, it look like, but a big bright sun up there. There go another am-bu-lance. Look like school ain't to open today. Nice day like this, too. Would've sold ever one of them sammiches. Guess now it'll settle back, though. Ha! Now that Rufus, he beat all. Yeah, it'll all settle back, like I say. Damned chilly, though. Maybe I'll add jus' a lump or two of coal to the stove. Almanac call for an early spring. (He crosses to the stove). I damn well hope so 'cause this is the last load of coal I'm buyin' 'til next winter. It's enough to drive a man to bankruptcy, I can tell ya. (He dumps two lumps of coal in the potbelly and slams the door).

The LIGHTS fade quickly to BLACKOUT.

ON THE WARPATH
A Comedy about War in One Act

CHARACTERS

1ST MAN — a big burly soldier in his late 20s

2ND MAN — a small, thin soldier, late teens or early 20s

THE SETTING

Two brick barricades, one stage left and one stage right. A thinly trunked shade tree and a knoll up center left.

On the Warpath

Two brick barriers, one stage left and one stage right. They are fortifications with a hole in each one wide enough to fit the barrel of a rifle, but not large enough for the person firing to see what he is shooting at. The 1ST MAN is behind the barrier stage right and the 2ND MAN is behind the barrier stage left. There is a shade tree on a knoll up center left.

When the LIGHTS come up both men in full military gear are firing a barrage from their automatic rifles. The 1ST MAN is a big strong burly fellow in his late 20's; the 2ND MAN is small in stature and thin and very youthful, in his late teens or early 20s. The firing continues for a few beats, then the 2ND MAN stops firing.

The SOUNDS of explosions, machine gun fire, etc. in the distance.

2ND MAN (Calling): Hold it! Hold it! Stop shooting!
1ST MAN (He looks up over the brick barrier): Are you ready to surrender?
2ND MAN (He stands and looks over the barrier): Certainly not. I'm just re-loading my rifle.
1ST MAN: You want me to stop firing so you can re-load your rifle!? Are you crazy?
2ND MAN: Well, you want to be fair, don't you?
1ST MAN: Fair! Man, this is war. Whoever heard of anybody being fair in a war!?
2ND MAN: Well, if you ran out, I'd let you re-load.
1ST MAN: Why!? What is this? Don't you want to win?
2ND MAN: Of course I want to win. You think I want to die? That's why I have to re-load.
1ST MAN: Is that what you're doing now?
2ND MAN: Yes.
1ST MAN: And I'm supposed to quit shooting at you until you re-load? That's the most ridiculous thing I ever heard of.
2ND MAN: That may be, but it's fair.
1ST MAN: Fair! Why the hell would I want to be fair? Tell me that?
2ND MAN: I don't know, but you are.
1ST MAN: Are what!?
2ND MAN: Being fair, damn it!
1ST MAN: I'm being fair? How the hell do you figure that?
2ND MAN: Well, you stopped shooting when I asked you to.
1ST MAN: Damnation! You think I stopped shooting because of you?
2ND MAN: Well, I asked and you stopped.
1ST MAN: You asshole, that wasn't because of you.
2ND MAN: It wasn't?
1ST MAN: Hell, no!

2ND MAN: Oh. I thought that was the reason.
1ST MAN: Well, it wasn't.
2ND MAN: So what was the reason?
1ST MAN (A beat): I don't know.
2ND MAN: You don't know? That's odd.
1ST MAN: Odd, my ass! What you did — what you said was so goddamned stupid, so goddamned weird, so — so far out I couldn't believe my ears.
2ND MAN: What do you mean far out? It was just a simple request.
1ST MAN (Frustrated): But this is war, man! You don't ask the enemy to stop firing so you can re-load your goddamned rifle. Nobody does that in war. It's clear you have no sense of history.
2ND MAN (He comes out from behind the barrier): History? I don't know anything about history. What's history got to do with it?
1ST MAN: Look at you standing in the open like that. As soon as I fire this weapon, you'll be history and food for the buzzards.
2ND MAN: Listen, all I was trying to do was re-load my rifle so I could save my life and I don't need any history lesson from you to do that.
1ST MAN (He throws down his rifle and comes from behind his barrier): Damnation! How bloody ignorant can you be!? I just said that there's no place in the history of war where one enemy says to the other, "Stop shooting, I've got to re-load my rifle; stop shooting I've got to feed my horse; hey, hold it, my armor's come loose; you guys hold up over there, my artillery piece is jammed." (He steps toward center stage). Christ's sake! That's not history, that's just common sense.
2ND MAN: Well, I've got common sense, but I'm not much on history.
1ST MAN: Oh yeah. Then what are you doing standing out in the open like that? You call that common sense?
2ND MAN: You're the one standing in the open. You don't even have your weapon. You might as well be naked.
1ST MAN: Listen, kid, I'm losing patience with you. All I'm saying is you don't ask the enemy to stop firing while you re-load your weapon. Just take my word for it.
2ND MAN: Why should I take your word for it?
1ST MAN: Because I *know*, damn it!
2ND MAN (He moves to him center stage): And I'm supposed to just trust you, right? My mortal enemy.
1ST MAN: Well, I let you re-load your rifle, didn't I?
2ND MAN: Yeah, but you didn't mean to. I just surprised you.
1ST MAN: That's not the point. I violated all the rules of war by letting you re-load your goddamned rifle.
2ND MAN: Well, I told you I appreciated it. Don't think I'm going to suck up to you just because of that.
1ST MAN: That's not the point!
2ND MAN: Just what is the point?

1ST MAN: (Exasperated, he turns to go back to his barrier): Forget it.

An artillery shell EXPLODES near them just offstage left. BOTH hit the ground for several beats, then slowly get up.

2ND MAN: I've really upset you, haven't I?
1ST MAN: I'm not upset! You runt, you think somebody like you could upset me!? I'm bigger, older and a helluva lot tougher than you are. That's obvious. And I'm smarter.
2ND MAN: Well, you may know more history than I do, I'll say that.
1ST MAN: And there's one other thing.
2ND MAN: What other thing?
1ST MAN: I want to kill you a helluva lot more than you want to kill me.
2ND MAN: Oh, I don't know about that. The people in my country have been hating and killing the people from your country for generations.
1ST MAN: And we've been hating and killing the people from your country for generations. And now it's going to be your turn.
2ND MAN: Oh, now you're going to make this a personal thing, are you? Like I'm some inferior person to you. I'll have you know that back home, I was voted "Most Likely to Succeed" in my high school class.
1ST MAN (He laughs): What kind of horse shit is that? You're on the battlefield, runt, not back home and you're sure as hell not succeeding with me.
2ND MAN: I wasn't trying to impress you. I was simply making a point.
1ST MAN: A point? What's the point?
2ND MAN: That — that you are probably the most thoroughly unlikable person I've ever met and you would certainly never be welcomed in my country.
1ST MAN: You little shit, I wouldn't be caught dead in your country. Seems to me you're the one who's getting personal.
2ND MAN: Don't be ridiculous. You're utterly inconsequential as far as I'm concerned. Unless you kill me, of course.
1ST MAN: Well, that's what I'm going to do.
2ND MAN: Not if I kill you first.
1ST MAN: You won't.
2ND MAN: I was the top marksman in my battalion, I'll have you know.
1ST MAN: Your weapon is inferior. You have to keep re-loading it. Our side has superior weaponry.
2ND MAN: You know as well as I that rockets and missiles and all that stuff don't matter. It all comes down to us guys in the trenches.
1ST MAN: I thought you didn't know anything about the history of war.
2ND MAN: Hells bells, who needs history to know that?
1ST MAN: Yeah, and you don't need history to know that our weapons are superior to yours.
2ND MAN: Well, we'll just see about that. (He moves stage left).
1ST MAN: Where are you going?

2ND MAN: To shoot at you.
1ST MAN: Well, wait a damned minute, will you!? (He runs stage right behind the barrier).
2ND MAN (Calling): Are you ready?
1ST MAN (Calling): Yes! What kind of dumb question is that?

They open fire on each other. It is of course impossible for either to hit the other while they are behind the barrier. This firing continues for several beats. Then the 1ST MAN stops firing. He is having trouble with his rifle.

1ST MAN (Calling): Okay, hold it a minute! Hey, I said, hold it a minute!
2ND MAN (He stops firing): What for?
1ST MAN: I got a problem here.
2ND MAN (His head above the barrier): Re-loading?
1ST MAN: Hell no! I told you our weapons are superior to your weapons.
2ND MAN: So what's the problem?
1ST MAN (His head above the barrier): I think it's jammed.
2ND MAN: Ha! I thought your weapons were superior to our weapons.
1ST MAN: It's not the weapon.
2ND MAN: I thought you said it was jammed.
1ST MAN: It is—but it's not the weapon.
2ND MAN: If it's not the weapon what is it?
1ST MAN: It's me, damn it! It jammed. I've fucked it up some way. I'm—I'm not into these new-fangled gadgets they've put on this rifle.
2ND MAN: Just history, right?
1ST MAN: This weapon is so fucking complicated it takes a fucking wizard to figure the fucking thing out.
2ND MAN: My, what language. That's just another example of your country's decadence.
1ST MAN: Shut the fuck up! You don't know anything about my country.
2ND MAN: Are dictionaries obsolete in your country?
1ST MAN: Shut up, smart ass! I'm trying to figure this thing out.
2ND MAN: I might be able to help.
1ST MAN: This is sophisticated stuff. What the hell would you know about it?
2ND MAN: You're right. All I have to do is load and pull the trigger.
1ST MAN: You have to re-load more often than we do. You've got an inferior weapon.
2ND MAN (A beat): I could take a look at it. I'm kind of interested in how things work. After high school, my mom made me enroll in this technology class where we worked on cars and electrical stuff until our countries decided to fight another war and I had to go. See, my dad died when I was twelve and he kind of left us penniless. Mom worked in a garment factory which didn't pay much, so I had to go into this technology class so I could learn stuff and get a job. I was really good at it so …

1ST MAN: Hey! I'm not interested in you or your goddamned family history. I got problems of my own.
2ND MAN: Right. I was just explaining my background. You know, how I got interested in stuff.
1ST MAN: Well, I'm not interested, see! (A beat). What happened to your father? How come your father died when you were so young?
2ND MAN: He was on furlough from the last war we had. So we decided we'd go hiking up a mountain and he had a heart attack.
1ST MAN: Why?
2ND MAN: Why did he have a heart attack?
1ST MAN: No, dummy. Why was he taking you hiking up a mountain?
2ND MAN: So we could get to the top.
1ST MAN: What? Why? What's up there?
2ND MAN: Well, nothing really. Just the top of the mountain.
1ST MAN: And there's nothing there?
2ND MAN: Well, you hike, see, and get a really terrific view up there.
1ST MAN: That's the silliest goddamn thing I ever heard. To climb to the top of a mountain just to get a nice view.
2ND MAN: Well, we liked doing that.
1ST MAN: Ha! Leaves his wife and son penniless while he romps up and down mountains. Some father.
2ND MAN: Well, he really wanted me to see how things were at the top.
1ST MAN: That's too bad. Instead he has this heart attack.
2ND MAN: Oh we got to the top. That's where he had his heart attack.
1ST MAN: Well, so what? He had this heart attack and left you and your mom penniless.
2ND MAN: Well, it was quite a challenge for dad and me getting up there all the way to the top. It was a lot of fun and it was really beautiful. We saw the greatest sunsets.
1ST MAN: You don't need to climb a mountain to see the goddamned sun set! You can see that anywhere, for Christ's sake! Why are you telling me all this stuff? I told you I got a problem here. (Struggling with his rifle).
2ND MAN: Well, you asked me ...
1ST MAN: Press this, push that—I can't figure this frigging thing out!
2ND MAN: I could take a look at it. I mean you might show it to me.
1ST MAN: You'd never understand it. (A beat. He struggles with the rifle, then stops). I might show it to you. I could meet you halfway. But I warn you, runt, there better not be any funny stuff, understand?
2ND MAN: Right. I'll just leave my weapon behind the barrier here.
1ST MAN: Don't be a fool. You'd be defenseless.
2ND MAN: All right. I'll just bring it with me.

They each come from behind the barrier and meet center stage. The 1ST MAN shows him his weapon.

2ND MAN: Gosh, that's some weapon. Really neat. Could I handle it?
1ST MAN (He hands it to him): Just be careful. There's a bullet jammed in the chamber.
2ND MAN: Yeah, I see that. It won't lock in.
1ST MAN: Right. There's some sort of gizmo on there that's supposed to throw it out. Something that turns one way and then another way then you're supposed to push something or other and turn it. I don't know, it's complicated as hell.
2ND MAN: On ours you just load and pull the trigger. If it jams it just comes right out.
1ST MAN: Yeah? Let me see yours.
2ND MAN (He takes his rifle off his shoulder and gives it to him): Here. You'll see how easy it is. Be careful, there's a round in the chamber.
1ST MAN (He examines it and ejects a bullet from the chamber): Yeah, that is really simple. It's obsolete, of course.
2ND MAN: Well, it really works.
1ST MAN: You mean it really works after you re-load it all those times. Hey, I really like it, though. It's light—you know—it's a lot lighter than mine.
2ND MAN: Yeah, this is a heavy muther you've got here. I'll just fool around with some of these gadgets a minute.
1ST MAN: Be careful. That bloody cartilage is stuck in there.
2ND MAN: What you've got here is a bent cartilage.
1ST MAN: Well, I know that, idiot. The problem is I can't get it out.
2ND MAN: It's too complicated for you, right?
1ST MAN: That's not the problem. It's all them gadgets on the thing. That's the problem. Something that turns this way and something else that turns another way, then you push something or other. Then—I don't know what comes next.
2ND MAN: Yeah, yeah ... . It's this thing ... . No, goes the other way ... . Ah, now this thing ... . And push and turn. (The cartilage pops out).
1ST MAN: Isn't that something? Popped right out.
2ND MAN: Yeah, popped right out.
1ST MAN: Yeah, that's what I said.
2ND MAN: What?
1ST MAN: I said it popped right out!
2ND MAN: Oh right. Right there on the ground.
1ST MAN (He picks up the cartilage): It's bent. Some sucker in the factory back home let this one get by inspection.
2ND MAN: Probably thinking about something else.
1ST MAN: What?
2ND MAN: Whoever inspected it was probably thinking about something else.
1ST MAN: Yeah. He was probably thinking about what he was going to have for lunch, or something like that. Not keeping his mind on what he was doing. Probably thinking about what he was going to stuff his face with for lunch. Let that damned bent cartilage get by him while he was ...
2ND MAN: He might have carried his own lunch.

1ST MAN: What?
2ND MAN: I said he might have carried his own lunch.
1ST MAN: Oh. Well, that's possible. Maybe had one of those metal lunch boxes you see.
2ND MAN: Maybe wondering if it was a ham and cheese sandwich or a peanut butter and jelly sandwich.
1ST MAN: Could've been both.
2ND MAN: That's true. Maybe trying to figure out which one to eat first.
1ST MAN: Yeah and meanwhile the goddamned bent cartilage slips by him.
2ND MAN: Could've been a woman.
1ST MAN: What?
2ND MAN: The guy inspecting—could've been a woman.
1ST MAN: How could the guy inspecting be a woman?
2ND MAN: In my country, it could've been a woman. We have equality of opportunity.
1ST MAN: Well, in my country we have equality of opportunity, but I don't think the guy inspecting could've been a woman. I think it was a man.
2ND MAN: You think maybe men aren't as conscientious as women?
1ST MAN: I didn't say that. Don't put words in my mouth, damn it!
2ND MAN (A beat): You're right, though. He or she was probably thinking about lunch.
1ST MAN: What's lunch got to do with it?
2ND MAN: Well, you said that the inspector was probably ...
1ST MAN: Whoever inspected this thing was a careless son of a bitch! That's all I'm saying. Why, I could've been killed. I'd like to see her come out on the battlefield and live in the trenches for a while.
2ND MAN: I thought you said it was a man.
1ST MAN: What difference does it make!? I could've been killed because of some lame-brained careless production worker! They should have put me on one of them production lines instead of out here.
2ND MAN: Well, I got the cartilage out for you.
1ST MAN: No kidding. I'm holding it in my fucking hand, ain't I? Oh—uh—I appreciate the help.
2ND MAN: No problem.
1ST MAN: What do you mean, no problem? You had a hell of a time figuring it out. (He throws the cartilage away).
2ND MAN: I really like this weapon. It's really an amazing piece of equipment.
1ST MAN: It jammed.
2ND MAN: That was because of the bent cartilage.
1ST MAN: I could've been killed. Why didn't you kill me?
2ND MAN: You asked me to stop shooting.
1ST MAN: You stupid asshole, I'm the enemy. We've been enemies for generations. You should have shot me.
2ND MAN: Well, you didn't shoot me when I was re-loading my rifle.

1ST MAN: That was different.
2ND MAN: How was that different?
1ST MAN: It surprised me.
2ND MAN: How do you think I felt when you asked *me* to stop shooting? How do you think I felt when you said I should bring my rifle out here? I could've killed you right then and there, if I'd thought about it. I had a round in the chamber.
1ST MAN: Well, you didn't think about it.
2ND MAN: Yeah, that's really weird, isn't it? It just didn't occur to me.
1ST MAN: I like your rifle better than my rifle.
2ND MAN: Really? Well, it's quite simple to operate.
1ST MAN: That's why I like it.
2ND MAN: I think I like your rifle best. I'm sort of into mechanical stuff. I fooled around with it a bit before they sent me here.
1ST MAN: You told me that already. Well, I'll tell you this, you're not such a hot shot when it comes to history, that's for sure.
2ND MAN: I'll admit I'm pretty ignorant when it comes to that.
1ST MAN: It's history that tells us how we're supposed to live, not your frigging mechanical gadgets.
2ND MAN: How does it do that?
1ST MAN: You learn from the past, idiot! What else?
2ND MAN: Well, we've sure learned to fight better with all this great new stuff.
1ST MAN: Complicated gadgets. Mostly useless crap the way I see it.
2ND MAN: I suppose you'd rather fight with a bow and arrow.
1ST MAN: Quit being a smart ass. You interested in trading?
2ND MAN: Trading?
1ST MAN: The rifles. You interested in trading?
2ND MAN: You mean you take my rifle and I take yours?
1ST MAN: Yes, damn it! Isn't that what trade means?
2ND MAN: You said mine was inferior.
1ST MAN: It is.
2ND MAN: Then why would you want to trade yours for mine?
1ST MAN: I told you — because it's simple.
2ND MAN: But you have to re-load all the time.
1ST MAN: I don't mind re-loading if it's simple.
2ND MAN: Well, it's a lot of trouble. And you'd have to keep asking me to stop firing while you re-load.
1ST MAN: I'd never be that stupid. Besides, I know I can re-load a helluva lot faster than you.
2ND MAN: You don't know that. I just bet this is some kind of trick.
1ST MAN: A trick? What do you mean trick?
2ND MAN: I was just thinking you might know something about the history of war that I don't.

1ST MAN: No, it's you who knows something about these bloody gadgets they're making now that I don't.
2ND MAN: It was just a bent cartilage.
1ST MAN: Yes, but you could get it out and I couldn't. What if there are more bent cartilages? What if the son of a bitch is sitting on the production line and gets a hard on thinking about screwing his girl friend? And all the while all those bent cartilages are flying right by him headed for my rifle?
2ND MAN: Then it's not a trick?
1ST MAN: Trick! What trick? What the hell makes you think it's a trick!?
2ND MAN: You said we learn from the past. I was thinking maybe you learned a trick or two from history that you might pull on me.
1ST MAN: No, no, you dummy! History teaches us a lot about war, but the main thing it teaches us is how to live!
2ND MAN: Oh. If it teaches us how to live, what the hell are we doing out here dying?
1ST MAN: We're not dying, you idiot! We're just fighting each other.
2ND MAN: We could die, though.
1ST MAN: Well, you have to do that sometimes in order to live.
2ND MAN (A beat): That's kind of confusing.
1ST MAN: There's nothing confusing about it, you bloody ignorant runt!
2ND MAN: I'm thinking maybe technology is a lot easier to understand than history.
1ST MAN: The hell it is. Hey, are we trading rifles or not?
2ND MAN: Why not, since your rifle is better than my rifle.
1ST MAN: Here. Take this piece of complicated gadgetry and give me something that's simple to operate. (He hands him his rifle).
2ND MAN: It's obsolete, don't forget that. Here, take it. Now you realize you have to re-load ...
1ST MAN: I know all about that!
2ND MAN: Right. Now that we've done this trading, maybe we could just take a little break. It's really hot behind that barricade. I'm stuck right in the sun. (He walks over to the tree and looks up at it). It's nice under this tree. Is this a palm tree?
1ST MAN: No. Listen, I'm a soldier and I ain't getting paid to just sit around under some damned tree.
2ND MAN: What kind of tree is it?
1ST MAN: How should I know.
2ND MAN: I think maybe it's a palm tree.
1ST MAN: It's not a palm tree. I've seen pictures of palm trees in the south sea islands so I know it's not a palm tree.
2ND MAN: I'm pretty sure we're not there.
1ST MAN: Where?
2ND MAN: The south sea islands.
1ST MAN: No, runt, we ain't there.

2ND MAN (He looks around): I'm just not sure where we are.
1ST MAN: We're in limbo.
2ND MAN: Where?
1ST MAN: There's a hill over there and a valley over here. There's this tree and that's all I know.
2ND MAN: And it's not a palm tree.
1ST MAN: No.

A shell EXPLODES very close to them. They hit the ground. Several beats.

2ND MAN: Wow! That was close.
1ST MAN: Yeah, but it could have been closer.
2ND MAN: That was from your side, wasn't it?
1ST MAN: No because if it were from my side, it would have been closer.
2ND MAN: Why do you say that?
1ST MAN: Because our side has better weapons than your side.
2ND MAN: Well, my side knows I'm here.
1ST MAN: My side knows I'm here. You think that makes any difference?
2ND MAN: Well, we've got a whole battalion over there. (He points off left).
1ST MAN: We got a whole battalion over there. (He points off right).
2ND MAN (A beat): I don't know where that shell came from.
1ST MAN: No. But it was probably from your side.
2ND MAN: Maybe. Everything's so confusing.
1ST MAN: Of course, that's the way war is.
2ND MAN: Is that what history tells us?
1ST MAN: No, idiot, it's what *I'm* telling you.
2ND MAN: Well, you're right. I mean I *think* my battalion is over there, but I haven't seen anybody lately. The Lieutenant said get behind that brick thing and hold that position so that's what I'm doing.
1ST MAN: No you're not.
2ND MAN: What?
1ST MAN: You ninny, you're not holding that position. You're sitting out here with me on your ass under the shade of this tree.
2ND MAN: Well, I notice you're not holding your position either.
1ST MAN: The only reason I'm sitting under this tree is because you're not behind that brick thing holding your position. In my opinion you are some lazy asshole of a soldier. (He flops his back against the trunk of the tree in disgust).
2ND MAN: I'm not lazy either. I'm just taking a break. I don't know if I'll ever get used to sleeping outside on the ground. Boy, that was one thing that used to make my dad really angry. He said I should learn to love sleeping out like he did. You know, being close to nature and all that.
1ST MAN: He was right. You make some lousy soldier if you don't like being cold and wet and miserable. And the bloody insects have gotta eat, too, just like the rest of us. It's nature's way.

2ND MAN: I never really thought about it like that. I mean — you know — that it was nature's way. (A beat). Say, I was wondering — if you don't mind my asking — were you drafted or did you volunteer?
1ST MAN: Drafted. I'm no goddamned fool.
2ND MAN (A beat): I volunteered.
1ST MAN: Volunteered! What a goddamned fool. Why?
2ND MAN: They asked me to.
1ST MAN: They asked you to! Why didn't you say no?
2ND MAN: Oh my dad would have been furious if I had done that, rest his soul. I mean, the men in my family has been volunteering for generations so I felt obligated.
1ST MAN: I didn't feel that way.
2ND MAN: Why not?
1ST MAN: Hells bells, I was making a lot of money off the war. I was working in a pub near an army camp and the tips were great. Even saved up enough money to buy me a new car. Ha! The next week I got drafted. See, all these drunk soldiers were big spenders. They knew that in a week or so they'd be going up to the front and maybe die for their country. Since they were doing it, I couldn't see any reason why I had to. I mean, they had plenty of guys. They didn't need me.
2ND MAN: Well, you haven't died.
1ST MAN: But I could. Fortunately, you're the enemy.
2ND MAN: What does that mean? I should resent that, shouldn't I?
1ST MAN: It's not personal, kid. Your side just has obsolete weapons.
2ND MAN: But you've got my weapon now. We traded, remember?
1ST MAN: I was speaking generally. Generally speaking, your side's got obsolete weapons.
2ND MAN: But you've got my ...
1ST MAN: Never mind that! I was speaking generally. Christ's sake, don't you understand plain English!
2ND MAN (A beat): I suppose we ought to get back to work like you said.
1ST MAN: What's the hurry?
2ND MAN: No hurry. I would like to try out this new weapon, though.
1ST MAN: Why? It won't shoot through a brick wall.
2ND MAN (A beat. He gets up and goes over to stage right and examines the wall): You're right. Geez, I could never get a bullet through this. (He turns and crosses over stage left to his brick wall). Hunh. You can't get a bullet through my wall either. We're just wasting time and the army's ammunition, aren't we?
1ST MAN: No. We're doing our duty. This is what we were told to do and we're doing it. So why don't we have lunch?
2ND MAN: Lunch? I don't know. All I've got left is some canned fruit. I was trying to save it.
1ST MAN: Save it for what?
2ND MAN: (A beat): For lunch, actually.

1ST MAN (He looks up and examines the sky): Well, it's time for lunch. Look, the sun is directly over head. (He opens his backpack and pulls out a can). I'll be damned. Look at this. All I've got left is a can of this shitty tasting meat.
2ND MAN: You've got meat? Your rations are better than mine.
1ST MAN: Well, my country's better than your country in most things.
2ND MAN: I'm just going to ignore that.
1ST MAN: Well, you can't ignore the truth.
2ND MAN: It isn't the truth.
1ST MAN: I won't argue about it since I'm right.
2ND MAN: Me either, since you're wrong and I'm right. This is why we've been fighting each other for generations, isn't it?
1ST MAN: No. We've been fighting for generations because of your stupid religion.
2ND MAN: Our religion isn't stupid. You guys just won't accept it. You guys are not true believers.
1ST MAN: We're the ones who are true believers. The trouble is you guys won't accept the truth of the true believers.
2ND MAN: That's not true. Our ceremonies reflect the true beliefs as taught in the scriptures.
1ST MAN: Your ceremonies are pompous nonsense. All that intricate bullshit. Who can believe in that?
2ND MAN: Truth is never simple.
1ST MAN: Truth is very simple.
2ND MAN: If it's so simple then how come you've got all those complicated gadgets you keep complaining about? Rockets and missiles and these great rifles you've got?
1ST MAN: I thought you liked that stuff. You said you were into all that complicated bullshit. Our religion doesn't have anything to do with that stuff anyway.
2ND MAN: Yes it does because you've got it and we have — some of it. It just proves my point. Truth is never simple.
1ST MAN: That doesn't prove anything. That's not what history tells us.
2ND MAN: Yeah, well just what does history tell us?
1ST MAN (A beat): I thought we were having lunch.
2ND MAN: I forgot about that.
1ST MAN: That's what happens with you religious fanatics. You forget the basics.
2ND MAN: I'm not a religious fanatic. Just a true believer — most of the time. I'd like to know where you learned all this history — in the pub?
1ST MAN: In school, nitwit. Where were you? I thought you said you were voted "Mostly Likely to Succeed"?
2ND MAN (A beat): You want to split lunch?
1ST MAN: Split lunch?
2ND MAN: Yeah, I give you half my fruit and you give me half your meat.
1ST MAN: Oh, I see. I bet you want some of my shitty tasting meat because your side's too cheap to provide good rations for its soldiers.

2ND MAN: Our side thinks fruit is more healthy than chunks of fat meat that could clog up a soldier's arteries.
1ST MAN: You fanatics are all the same. Think you know everything. Now you want to play doctor. What kind of fruit is it?
2ND MAN: It's a cocktail. It's got all kinds of fruits. Cherries and peaches and pears ...
1ST MAN: We could split it. Now that's an idea.
2ND MAN: That was my idea. Half and half.
1ST MAN: Well, I don't know about half and half.
2ND MAN: If we don't do half and half, that's not splitting it.
1ST MAN: I could take two-thirds of your fruit and you take one-third of my meat.
2ND MAN: I say we do it half and half or not at all.
1ST MAN: We could trade like we did with the rifles.
2ND MAN: An even split. I only want half your shitty tasting meat.
1ST MAN: All right, it's a deal. Your army issue canteens?
2ND MAN: Of course, we have canteens.
1ST MAN: I thought maybe they were too cheap to issue canteens.
2ND MAN: They're not obsolete, are they?
1ST MAN: That's true. Let's get them out.

They take off their backpacks and get out their canteens and food packs.

1ST MAN: Your religion doesn't have any restrictions on meat, does it?
2ND MAN: No.
1ST MAN: That's good because no telling what they've put in this can. Back home it's the kind of thing I might feed to my dog.

They portion out the food in their canteens.

1ST MAN: Here's your half the meat.
2ND MAN: And your half the fruit. You've got a dog? I always wanted a dog. (He tastes the meat and grimaces).
1ST MAN: I don't have a dog. I just said this is the kind of thing I would feed my dog if I had a dog. Hey! Your cocktail juice is running all over my meat.
2ND MAN: That's a good thing because this is really shitty tasting meat.
1ST MAN: Hum. You're right. This cocktail juice really helps get it down, doesn't it?
2ND MAN: Surely your country can do better than this! If I weren't hungry I'd puke.
1ST MAN: I've tasted better fruit.
2ND MAN: It makes me wish I hadn't volunteered.
1ST MAN: Ha! It makes me wish I hadn't been drafted.

A shell EXPLODES close to them forcing them to hit the ground. In the process they spill all their food in the ground. They lie there for a moment.

1ST MAN: You're not dead over there, are you?
2ND MAN: No.
1ST MAN: Are you wounded?
2ND MAN: No. Lunch is over though.
1ST MAN: Well, it was a shitty lunch.
2ND MAN: I'm wondering if we should get up.
1ST MAN: I can't think of any reason why we should.
2ND MAN: We could check our rifles. See if they're damaged.
1ST MAN: Why?
2ND MAN: Because—
1ST MAN: Who cares?
2ND MAN (A beat): We might look at the tree. See if it's damaged.
1ST MAN: Who cares?
2ND MAN: Wonder what kind of tree it is.
1ST MAN: It's not a palm tree.
2ND MAN: Right, because you've seen palm trees.
1ST MAN: No, I've seen pictures of palm trees.
2ND MAN: Oh. That's different.
1ST MAN: No it isn't. If you've seen pictures of palm trees, you've seen palm trees.
2ND MAN (A beat): Oh. What's your point?
1ST MAN: Point? What point? There isn't any point, for Christ's sake! I'm getting up.
2ND MAN: Why?
1ST MAN: I may have a cramp. (He sits up and rubs the back of his leg). I'm really tired of this fighting shit. I told them when they drafted me that I was easily fatigued and had flat feet and should be placed in a motor pool. Dumb shits never heard a word I said.
2ND MAN (He sits up): I'd just like a home cooked meal. My mom's a really great cook.
1ST MAN: All mothers are great cooks.
2ND MAN: No, I don't think that's true.
1ST MAN: You don't think all mothers are great cooks?
2ND MAN: No.
1ST MAN: Just how many mothers have you had?
2ND MAN: I'm just going to ignore that.
1ST MAN: Every soldier always says that his mom was a great cook, but you're saying that isn't true.
2ND MAN: Right. They say that because they have to eat all this shitty tasting meat our armies give us.
1ST MAN: Well I have to admit that my own mother, rest her soul, was not a great cook. You know why?

2ND MAN: Why?
1ST MAN: Technology.
2ND MAN: Technology?
1ST MAN: The bloody microwave. If you couldn't put it in the bloody microwave, mother wouldn't cook it, rest her soul.
2ND MAN: Your mother's passed away?
1ST MAN: She didn't pass away. She died.
2ND MAN: Oh. From radiation?
1ST MAN: Radiation?
2ND MAN: The bloody microwave.
1ST MAN: You're trying to be funny, right? I get saddled with a smart ass kid for an enemy. I wish you'd just go ahead and surrender. It would make things a lot easier.
2ND MAN: Surrender?
1ST MAN: Yeah. It's simple enough. If you surrender the war is over and you can go back to mother's cooking.
2ND MAN: Oh, I couldn't do that. I mean it just wouldn't be the manly thing to do. In my country we have a lot of pride.
1ST MAN: We'd like nothing better than to bury your manly pride.
2ND MAN: Now if you surrendered it would be different.
1ST MAN: Different? How would it be different?
2ND MAN: In your country you don't have as much manly pride as we do.
1ST MAN (On his feet): What a thing to say! What do you mean we don't have as much manly pride!? I oughta punch you in the mouth! Listen to me, damnit, we're bigger, stronger, better and prouder in my country.
2ND MAN: You could never prove that to me so I don't see what you're getting all riled up about.
1ST MAN: Pride! That's what I'm getting all riled up about! (He paces about angrily). Insulting! How dare you talk about me or my country like that!
2ND MAN (On his feet): Well, it was you who made the insulting suggestion that I should surrender, all because you're just a little tired of fighting. Our countries have been fighting for generations and just because you finally got drafted you want us to quit and surrender. Well fat chance! We've got plenty of men with manly pride who are ready to fight and die for our country. As a matter of fact, according to the last census, we're over-populated with men.
1ST MAN: We've got plenty of men, too, and more missiles and rockets than your country.
2ND MAN: You can't win the war with your missiles and rockets. It takes men with manly pride to win a war.
1ST MAN: Then why haven't you won it? It's been going on for years.
2ND MAN: Why haven't *you* won it with your missiles and rockets and *your* men with manly pride?
1ST MAN: Well we would win if you'd surrender and give up all that religious hanky-pank.

2ND MAN: It's your bogus religion that's the problem. You aren't true believers and ought to surrender and regain the true faith.
1ST MAN: True faith, my ass. Who wants to watch people traipse around in those hot robes every bloody Sunday and mumble voodoo in some foreign language that nobody understands.

A shell EXPLODES knocking down the 2ND MAN's brick barricade. The two of them have hit the ground again and remain there for the moment.

1ST MAN: Are you dead this time?
2ND MAN: Not yet.
1ST MAN: And not wounded?
2ND MAN: Not yet.
1ST MAN: That's too bad. But it's only a matter of time.
2ND MAN: How about yourself?
1ST MAN: Only a matter of time. (He looks around and sees the barrier is destroyed). Ah ha! Your time before my time.
2ND MAN: Oh yeah. Why do you say that?
1ST MAN (He points at the destroyed barricade): Look around.
2ND MAN (He looks around, then jumps to his feet): Holy cow, look at that! Blown to smithereens!
1ST MAN: I think it's time we went back to work.
2ND MAN: God! If we hadn't stopped for lunch and eaten that shitty tasting meat, I'd have been in there.
1ST MAN: Shooting at me.
2ND MAN: Well, you'd have been shooting at me, too.
1ST MAN: So what happens when I'm shooting at you now?
2ND MAN (A beat): We're taking a break.
1ST MAN: We've had us a bit of lunch, discussed the tree and our mothers' cooking. I think it's time we went back to work, don't you?
2ND MAN: What's the big rush! We've been fighting for generations.
1ST MAN: I thought you were in a hurry to try out my rifle.
2ND MAN: What the use. I can't shoot through a brick wall. (A beat). You've got the advantage now, haven't you?
1ST MAN: Looks that way.
2ND MAN: Maybe if we wait a while a shell will take out your brick wall.
1ST MAN: It's not likely. It's a random thing, you know.
2ND MAN: I thought your weapons were more advanced than ours.
1ST MAN: They are. They can hit the side of a barn but they can't hit a pea in a pod. That brick wall was a pea in a pod.
2ND MAN (A beat): I think I'd just like to look around for a minute. You don't mind if I look around for a minute, do you?
1ST MAN: Take your time. It won't do any good. When you're nowhere you can't go nowhere.

2ND MAN: Look what they did to these nice bricks. Scattered everywhere.
1ST MAN: Yeah, you've really got a mess over there.
2ND MAN: There was a nice little niche where I could stick my rifle.
1ST MAN: I've got one of those. It's probably a relic from the last war, don't you think? Anyway, mine's still there.
2ND MAN: Yeah, I see that. Hey, what if we came to an agreement?
1ST MAN: A what?
2ND MAN: You know, an agreement.
1ST MAN: Our two countries never agree on anything, you know that.
2ND MAN: Didn't we have a treaty once? We had to agree then.
1ST MAN: That's true. We agreed to not agree on the terms of the treaty and went back to war.
2ND MAN: Couldn't we just agree to not agree? Then we could all go home and quit fighting.
1ST MAN: Oh, you couldn't do that. If you don't agree, you have to fight. It's always been that way.
2ND MAN: That's the way it's been down through history?
1ST MAN: More or less. It's traditional. You got to respect tradition.
2ND MAN: Our church has lots of traditions. You guys don't respect them.
1ST MAN: Well, that's different. You've got all this symbolic bullshit nobody can believe in.
2ND MAN: I suppose your church doesn't have any symbolic bullshit.
1ST MAN: We have only a little bit of symbolic bullshit. We keep it simple. How come you guys don't respect that?
2ND MAN: Because it's meaningless to us.
1ST MAN: No, it's your clap-trap that's meaningless.
2ND MAN (A beat): Maybe they're both meaningless.
1ST MAN: Both? Ha! What an idea. (A beat). Well, it's not certain.
2ND MAN: Just remember in the eyes of God, we're all equal.
1ST MAN: Yeah but we don't have the eyes of God.
2ND MAN (A beat): I'm through looking around since there's nothing to see — except the tree, of course.
1ST MAN: It's not a palm tree.
2ND MAN: Right. I was thinking that since there's nothing to see and no one is around, we might just — leave.
1ST MAN: Leave?
2ND MAN: Yeah.
1ST MAN: We can't just leave.
2ND MAN: Why not?
1ST MAN: We can't abandon our post. We're soldiers.
2ND MAN: Yes, but you're tired of fighting. Anyway, you were drafted so you shouldn't feel obligated.
1ST MAN: But you volunteered and so you probably feel more obligated than I do.

2ND MAN: I don't know, I feel I've probably fulfilled my obligation.
1ST MAN: Have you won?
2ND MAN: Won what?
1ST MAN: The war, idiot!
2ND MAN: No one wins the war. It just keeps going on.
1ST MAN: Then you haven't fulfilled your obligation.
2ND MAN: Well, you probably have.
1ST MAN: How do you figure that?
2ND MAN: You were drafted so your time is probably up, right?
1ST MAN: My time's not up. I've still got six months, three days and two hours before the next generation takes over. I'm stuck.
2ND MAN: Oh.
1ST MAN: So I have to do my duty.
2ND MAN (He looks forlornly at his pile of bricks): I wonder if you could give me a couple of minutes to stack those bricks up—what's left of them?
1ST MAN: Oh, I couldn't do that.
2ND MAN: Why not?
1ST MAN: It wouldn't be ethical.
2ND MAN: Ethical?
1ST MAN: Our countries are at war. The object is to kill you people. A soldier can't go around showing mercy to the enemy. For Christ's sake, where's your manly pride?
2ND MAN: That's it, see—if you let me pile up my bricks, I can show you my manly pride. Otherwise, it appears I won't be able to.
1ST MAN: I let you do that, what about my manly pride?
2ND MAN: You'll still have your manly pride because you'll be showing a willingness to be fair.
1ST MAN: But this is war. No one's fair in war. The whole idea is ridiculous!
2ND MAN: What should I do then?
1ST MAN: I already told you. You surrender.
2ND MAN: You know I can't do that. There's my manly pride to consider.
1ST MAN: I think I'm going to go behind my barricade and start shooting. It's getting late.
2ND MAN: Wait! I've an idea. I'll retreat into the woods back there and you can overrun my position.
1ST MAN: I can't overrun your position. My orders are to hold my position. If I overrun your position how can I hold my position?
2ND MAN: You could come back after you overrun my position and hold your position.
1ST MAN: Somebody might take my position while I'm overrunning your position. Then where would I be?
2ND MAN: But there's nobody around.
1ST MAN: If there's nobody around who's firing those shells in here?
2ND MAN: I mean there's nobody around close by.

1ST MAN: How do you know that?
2ND MAN: We had lunch, discussed the tree—and I told you about my mother's cooking and nobody came.
1ST MAN: That was because nobody's interested in your mother's cooking.
2ND MAN: That's not why nobody came. (A beat). I could just disappear in the woods and you'd never see me again.
1ST MAN: It would be just the same if I shot you.
2ND MAN: No it wouldn't. If you shoot me you'd probably never forget it.
1ST MAN: What are you talking about?
2ND MAN: I'd probably appear in your dreams as some horrible apparition. And it would probably weigh on your conscience for the rest of your life that you killed the man who shared lunch with you. You'll remember that shitty tasting meat we had. The whole thing is going to leave a bad taste in your mouth forever.
1ST MAN: What bullshit! Why I'll probably end up bragging to my friends about killing you. People like nothing better than hearing a good war story, especially when you add a little imagination to it. For instance, I could add a little bit and tell them how we fought hand to hand with our bayonets and how …
2ND MAN: I don't have a bayonet.
1ST MAN: What?
2ND MAN: I said I don't have a bayonet.
1ST MAN: Your country doesn't issue its army bayonets?
2ND MAN: In a technological war, bayonets are obsolete.
1ST MAN: But wars are won in the trenches, you know that.
2ND MAN: Right. Hey, do you realize we actually agree on something.
1ST MAN: That may be, but it's clear your army doesn't agree with us.
2ND MAN: That's because in this kind of war bayonets are obsolete.
1ST MAN: But they aren't obsolete, you ninny, because I've got one!
2ND MAN (A beat): I wonder if I could see it?
1ST MAN: You want to see my bayonet?
2ND MAN: Yes.
1ST MAN: Why?
2ND MAN: Because I've never seen one before.
1ST MAN: My God! What kind of backward country do you live in? No wonder you're losing the war.
2ND MAN: We're not losing the war. Of course, we're not winning, but we're not losing either.
1ST MAN: Well, you're not winning, that's certain.
2ND MAN: Well, neither are you. I wonder if I could see that bayonet?
1ST MAN: You want to see my bayonet?
2ND MAN: Don't worry, I'll be very careful with it.
1ST MAN: Boy, you are some pain in the ass. No wonder we hate each other. (He takes out his bayonet from the case at his side). Here. Be careful. It's pretty sharp.
2ND MAN (He examines it): My God! What a barbaric weapon this is.

1ST MAN: Yeah, it's quite a thing, isn't it? You attach it to your rifle.
2ND MAN: Yes, I see that. You mean armies actually use this?
1ST MAN: It's for hand to hand combat.
2ND MAN: You mean they slash each other up with this?
1ST MAN: That's the idea.
2ND MAN (He hands it back): Well, it's obviously obsolete in a civilized technological war.
1ST MAN: If you had one of these I'd show you whether or not it's obsolete.
2ND MAN: Well, I don't have one. So that's one war story you can't tell.
1ST MAN: I ought to use this one on you right now.
2ND MAN: But since I don't have one, that wouldn't be fair—sorry.
1ST MAN: There you go again! It has nothing to do with fairness, damn it! It's a matter of manly pride. It would be cowardly of me to stick this thing in your gut when you're defenseless.
2ND MAN: I'm not defenseless! I have your rifle. (A beat. A thought). Hey—since my barricade is down, what happens if, say, I decide not to pick up your rifle?
1ST MAN: What kind of question is that?
2ND MAN: Wouldn't I be defenseless?
1ST MAN: No, you'd be foolish.
2ND MAN: That's not the point. The point is I'd be defenseless.
1ST MAN: No, you'd be foolish.
2ND MAN: No, damn it! I'd be defenseless and it would be cowardly of you to shoot me if I were defenseless.
1ST MAN (A beat): I hadn't thought of that.
2ND MAN: Well, it's something to consider.
1ST MAN (A beat): I've considered it and now that I've considered it, I don't agree.
2ND MAN: Why not? Isn't it a matter of manly pride, just as you said?
1ST MAN: No, this is different.
2ND MAN: Different? I don't see how it's different?
1ST MAN: You don't have a bayonet.
2ND MAN: That's right. They're obsolete.
1ST MAN: They're *not* obsolete, damn it!
2ND MAN: Well, anyway, I don't have one.
1ST MAN: Right! But you have a rifle. As a matter of fact, you have my rifle. And my rifle is better than your rifle because your rifle is obsolete.
2ND MAN: I can't help that. You were the one who wanted to trade.
1ST MAN: We're not talking about that.
2ND MAN: We aren't?
1ST MAN: No. We're talking about whether or not you are defenseless and whether or not it would be cowardly for me to shoot you.
2ND MAN: Oh right. Because you have to consider your manly pride in a situation where I'm defenseless.
1ST MAN: Exactly. But you're not defenseless so I don't have to consider that.

2ND MAN: But I am defenseless.
1ST MAN: No you're not. All you have to do is go over to that tree and pick up the most advanced fucking technological rifle ever conceived by man.
2ND MAN: Oh. But I can't do that.
1ST MAN: Why not?
2ND MAN: If I do that, then you'll go over and pick up my rifle which you say is obsolete and go behind your barricade and kill me.
1ST MAN: What's wrong with that?
2ND MAN: My barricade is smashed! I'm defenseless! Not even the best fucking technological rifle ever invented can save me!
1ST MAN: I can't do anything about that.
2ND MAN: But I'll die. You'll shoot me and I'll die!
1ST MAN: So what? This is war, man. People have to die in war.
2ND MAN: I'm not people, I'm me. I fixed your rifle, remember that? If it hadn't been for me, you'd be defenseless.
1ST MAN: It's not my rifle, it's your rifle. We traded, remember that?
2ND MAN: I fixed your rifle *before* we traded, remember that? So it was your rifle I fixed before it became my rifle.
1ST MAN: Is that important?
2ND MAN: Hell yes, it's important. I fixed it for you and—and you thanked me. Remember that? You thanked me. So when I fixed it, it was yours.
1ST MAN: What's that got to do with it? That was a long time again. Things have changed.
2ND MAN (A beat): You've tricked me. I knew your giving me your rifle was a trick.
1ST MAN: Trick? What trick?
2ND MAN: You knew all along they were going to blow up my barricade.
1ST MAN: How the hell would I know that?
2ND MAN: I don't know because it was probably some kind of secret operation.
1ST MAN: You ignorant stupid runt! Do I have a fucking radio? Do I know the coordinates for that fucking pile of bricks? Hell, I don't even know where the fuck I am!
2ND MAN: You said we were in limbo.
1ST MAN (A beat): When I shoot you I'm going to aim for your ass.
2ND MAN: I say it was a trick. If you hadn't been so greedy for lunch, I'd be dead right now.
1ST MAN: What the hell are you talking about? It was time for lunch!
2ND MAN: Yeah, but I wanted to wait. I was saving my lunch.
1ST MAN: I saved your life and here you accusing me of a trick.
2ND MAN: You saved me life? How do you get that you saved my life?
1ST MAN: If I hadn't wanted lunch your ass would have been behind that barricade and you'd have been blown to smithereens!
2ND MAN (A beat. He crosses to the barricade and looks at it again): You're right. You saved my life. I don't know how to thank you.

1ST MAN: Just forget it.
2ND MAN: Oh, I could never forget a thing like that. If it were in my power, I'd offer you some kind of medal.
1ST MAN: I'm not interested in any kind of medal. All I want to do is get the fuck out of here and back to the pub and drive my new car.
2ND MAN: That's it. You could put the medal on your car.
1ST MAN: On my car!? You think I want to fuck up my car with some medal? Where the hell would I put it?
2ND MAN: On the front of the hood! Yes sir, if I were President of my country I would see to it that you got some kind of medal for your new car for saving my life.
1ST MAN: Are you crazy? You want me to fuck up the hood of my brand-new car with some kind of cheap medal from your country? I'd never accept a medal from your country in any case.
2ND MAN: Well, I don't see why not.
1ST MAN: Because you're the enemy, nitwit! We've been fighting you bastards for generations!
2ND MAN: Well, I know that. But if we gave you a medal, it might improve relations.
1ST MAN: I don't want your medal! My car doesn't want your medal! I just want to kill you and win the war.
2ND MAN: Oh. I don't think killing me is going to win the war.
1ST MAN: I know that, dummy! We have to kill lots of yous to win the war.
2ND MAN: I see.
1ST MAN: No, you don't see anything. I'm tired talking. Let's get back to work and do our duty.
2ND MAN: I just have one question.
1ST MAN: Oh for Christ's sake, what now!?
2ND MAN: Why did you save my life?
1ST MAN: Because I was hungry and wanted lunch.
2ND MAN: You mean it wasn't a trick?
1ST MAN: A trick? What trick?
2ND MAN: To confuse me. To make me suffer. To make me think that maybe I would live and get back home and see mom and get one of her home-cooked meals.
1ST MAN: What the fuck is this?
2ND MAN: Well, I mean you saved my life. And now you're going to kill me because you know I'm absolutely defenseless since my barricade is smashed. That's why I thought maybe it was a trick.
1ST MAN: I can't believe you said that. I can't believe you could even think a thing like that about me — especially when the whole idea all along was to kill you. You think I meant to save you so I could torture you? That I had some sort of devious, inhumane trick like that in mind? You think I planned that stinking lunch with that awful fruit?

2ND MAN: It was your meat that was awful, not my fruit.
1ST MAN: That's a matter of opinion. Anyway, you can see there was no trick, that my motives were honorable. I was hungry. As a matter of fact, I still am.
2ND MAN: So am I. If we had anything, we could split it.
1ST MAN: Well, we don't have anything. So there's nothing to do but pick up our rifles and get behind our barricades.
2ND MAN: Fine, but as you can see, I don't have a barricade to get behind.
1ST MAN: Well, that's your problem. I can't do anything about that, can I?
2ND MAN: You could save my life again.
1ST MAN: Why would I want to do that? I mean, I already done that once, haven't I?
2ND MAN: Give me a minute and maybe I can think of a reason.
1ST MAN: Well, hurry up, will ya? I'd like to get out of here and join my battalion before dark since I don't know where the fuck I am.
2ND MAN: I've already given you a couple of reasons. You know, some possible options.
1ST MAN: They weren't acceptable. Now if you could get your country to give up its religion, we might settle this in a friendly way.
2ND MAN: I don't know how I could do that. I mean, it would be pretty hard to give up truth for some phony system of values I could never believe in.
1ST MAN: I'm getting my rifle. I don't feel like arguing politics.
2ND MAN: You mean *my* rifle. We traded, remember?
1ST MAN: Of course I remember. Your rifle is my rifle. That's why I called it *my* rifle.
2ND MAN: I just wanted to make sure you remembered. I wouldn't want you to pick up the wrong rifle.
1ST MAN: I don't think my rifle is going to do you much good now.
2ND MAN: Well, I liked it a lot better than my rifle. You ought to practice re-loading my rifle before you use it.
1ST MAN: I don't have to practice re-loading. It's simple.
2ND MAN: Of course it may be obsolete, just as you said.
1ST MAN: It can fire and hit its target, can't it?
2ND MAN: Of course. I told you I was the top marksman in my battalion, didn't I? But there is that re-loading problem.
1ST MAN: I'm not worried about the goddamned re-loading, damn it! (He has picked up the weapon). Why the hell do you care when I'm going to kill you with it?
2ND MAN (A beat): Good question. Perhaps I just haven't come to grips with the idea.
1ST MAN: It's not an idea. It's reality.
2ND MAN: Right.
1ST MAN: Well — aren't you going to get your rifle?
2ND MAN: Why should I? What the use?
1ST MAN: Manly pride, that's why.

2ND MAN: Absolutely, I forgot.
1ST MAN: That's the problem with your country, you forget the important things.
2ND MAN: The important thing is our religion. We're true believers.
1ST MAN: That's right and you're willing to die for it, right?
2ND MAN: I didn't say that. It's the politicians who say that. I wish they'd come out here on the battlefield once in a while.
1ST MAN: Right, they should come visit with us sometime. I've got my rifle.
2ND MAN: Which is really my rifle.
1ST MAN: We've already discussed that, goddamn it!
2ND MAN: There's just no more to say about that, is there? (He goes and picks up the rifle). You're going behind your barricade?
1ST MAN: Of course, you ninny!
2ND MAN: You know you can't see what you're shooting at from behind there.
1ST MAN: No, but I can just spray it all around. I'll find you. You're going over where your barricade was, aren't you?
2ND MAN: I guess so. I might just get behind the tree.
1ST MAN: No, that's no good.
2ND MAN: Why not?
1ST MAN: 'Cause the trunk is too thin, can't you see that, stupid? You think that lousy little tree's gonna protect you from a bullet?
2ND MAN: It's the only one around. You say it's not a palm tree?
1ST MAN: I already told you that.
2ND MAN: And you don't know what kind it is?
1ST MAN: I'm a soldier, not a fucking tree surgeon. Why don't you just get over there where your barricade was?
2ND MAN: There isn't any protection there either.
1ST MAN: Well, there's nothing I can do about that, is there?
2ND MAN: No.
1ST MAN (He goes behind his barricade): Let me know when you're ready.
2ND MAN: Why?
1ST MAN (He looks over the barricade): Why what?
2ND MAN: Why should I let you know if I'm ready?
1ST MAN: Because, goddamn it, it's the manly thing to do!
2ND MAN: Oh. (He crosses to the place where his barricade was and looks at it forlornly. He has a thought and turns toward the other barricade). I just remembered something I should tell you.
1ST MAN (He sticks his head above the barricade): You what?
2ND MAN: I said I just remembered something I should tell you.
1ST MAN: Something you should tell me? What?
2ND MAN: My name.
1ST MAN: Your name? What the fuck do I care what your name is?
2ND MAN: You're not interested in knowing the name of the person you're about to kill?
1ST MAN: What the hell use is that to me?

2ND MAN: For when you tell your war stories.
1ST MAN: What's the matter with you? You don't use people's names when you tell war stories about killing the enemy. I mean, you might call them "those ugly yellow-bellied shit faces" or something like that, but you don't use names, for Christ's sake!
2ND MAN: Is that something else history tells us?
1ST MAN: History? What the fuck does history have to do with it?
2ND MAN: Tradition then, it's probably tradition.
1ST MAN: How the hell should I know? I've never told war stories before.
2ND MAN: That's right, you were drafted—and only a week after you bought your new car.
1ST MAN: Don't mention my new car again.
2ND MAN: But you've heard war stories, right?
1ST MAN: Of course, I've heard war stories! We've been fighting for generations, haven't we? You mean you haven't heard war stories in your country?
2ND MAN: Oh yeah. And you're right, now that I think about it. I don't think anyone ever used the name of any enemy in those stories.
1ST MAN: So you can see why your name isn't of much interest to me.
2ND MAN: Right. It sort of interests me, though.
1ST MAN: Why?
2ND MAN: Because it's me, I guess.
1ST MAN: Well, you're going to be dead so I can't see what the fuck difference it's going to make. Anything else?
2ND MAN: I guess not.
1ST MAN: You better take cover 'cause I'm going to start shooting.
2ND MAN: There isn't any cover.
1ST MAN: That's your problem, not mine. (He ducks behind the barricade and pokes the rifle in the hole).
2ND MAN: It's O'Brien. Timothy O'Brien.
1ST MAN (He pokes his head over the barrier): What was that?
2ND MAN: What was what?
1ST MAN: Your name, idiot!
2ND MAN: Oh. I didn't think you were interested. O'Brien. Timothy O'Brien.
1ST MAN: You wouldn't happen to be kin to a Frankie O'Brien, would you?
2ND MAN: Frankie O'Brien? Sure, I've got a first cousin named Frankie O'Brien. But there are lots of Frankie O'Briens. I mean, it's a common name. I mean, it's like Timothy O'Brien. A common name.
1ST MAN: You've got a cousin named Frankie O'Brien?
2ND MAN: Everybody's got a cousin named Frankie O'Brien.
1ST MAN: That's not what I asked you, runt!
2ND MAN: What did you ask me?
1ST MAN: I asked you if *you* had a cousin named Frankie O'Brien?
2ND MAN: I told you, yes. But it's a common name. Everybody's got ...
1ST MAN: Where does he live?

2ND MAN: Who, Frankie?
1ST MAN: Yes, goddamn it!
2ND MAN: He lives in the capitol.
1ST MAN: Does he happen to live just down the street from that big obscene looking cathedral your country built?
2ND MAN: Hey! I resent that. That's a beautiful cathedral. It celebrates our religion.
1ST MAN: It's a fucking obscenity with all those spirals and arches and snaky-looking curves. I've seen the ugly pictures of it.
2ND MAN (He points the rifle at him angrily): Man, you better get behind that barricade before I lock and load this rifle. I just might do that even though I'm defenseless.
1ST MAN: Just answer the damned question!
2ND MAN: What question?
1ST MAN: Christ! I asked you if Frankie O'Brien lived down the street from that—that place.
2ND MAN: Our beautiful cathedral?
1ST MAN: Oh shit! That—place, right?
2ND MAN: Yeah, that's where Frankie lived. With his mom and dad and three brothers and a sister. A house on the corner across the street from a pub. Very convenient for Frankie. I have to tell you that their house got car-bombed once by terrorists from your country. Fortunately, they weren't at home at the time so nobody got hurt.
1ST MAN: I know about that. Frankie told me.
2ND MAN: What?
1ST MAN: I said I know Frankie O'Brien, your first cousin.
2ND MAN (He crosses center stage): You know Frankie? How do you know Frankie?
1ST MAN: He visited my country.
2ND MAN: Frankie visited your country? Why the hell would Frankie visit your country?
1ST MAN (He moves from behind his barricade): To see his sister. His sister married a guy from my country. I can't remember his name.
2ND MAN: I didn't know that! Why did she do that? I mean, you're the enemy.
1ST MAN: How should I know? Maybe she was in love or something. Probably she thought our country was better than your country.
2ND MAN: She would never think that. Why, that would be treason.
1ST MAN: She might think that.
2ND MAN (Pacing): Boy, this is some news. Here you are about to kill me and you tell me that my cousin Frankie has fraternized with you and, my God, that his sister has married the enemy and gone off to live in the enemy's country. What a downer this is for a guy about to die for his country.
1ST MAN: What a remarkable coincidence this is. Unbelievable, isn't it? I mean, that I should know your first cousin.

2ND MAN (He throws down the rifle): Son of a bitch! Members of my own family actually visiting and living in your damned country!
1ST MAN: Hey, careful, you might break one of them gadgets. Anyway, I got to know Frankie when he visited. Wonderful guy. Came into my pub and drank everybody under the table the first night.
2ND MAN: Frankie always liked his drink.
1ST MAN: Yeah, that was the first thing I noticed about him.
2ND MAN: Frankie refused to volunteer for our army. Now I know why. I never trusted him.
1ST MAN: He's no goddamned fool, that's why.
2ND MAN: They finally drafted him.
1ST MAN (He shakes his head): That's too bad. Frankie's not suited for war. He's a pacifist, you know. Poor damned fool, he doesn't belong in this world.
2ND MAN: He's also an atheist, damn his soul. He's probably going to burn in the fires of Hell.
1ST MAN: Well, I'll say this. He really knows how to enjoy life.
2ND MAN: I guess maybe he's not too worried about the fires of Hell.
1ST MAN: Well, he probably should be.
2ND MAN: I think your Hell is a little more extreme than our Hell, isn't it?
1ST MAN: It may be. I hadn't thought too much about it.
2ND MAN: I've been thinking a lot about it just recently.
1ST MAN: Listen, I don't think I'm going to be able to kill you now even though you're the enemy.
2ND MAN (He stares at him in disbelief): Really!? (He slides down the tree trunk on his backside). Boy, is that a relief. Do you know I had already planned to give myself last rites even though, according to church doctrine, I'd still end up in Hell.
1ST MAN: I don't think I could kill anybody kin to good old Frankie O'Brien.
2ND MAN: Well, we're only cousins.
1ST MAN: I just couldn't face Frankie if I'd killed one of his relatives. Oh, we had some great times together while he was visiting his sister in my country. Hell, I think Frankie spent more time with me than he did with his sister.
2ND MAN (He gets up): Why that traitorous bastard! He's supposed to be your enemy. For all we know, he could be a spying for you right now.
1ST MAN: Not old Frankie, he's a pacifist. He wouldn't spy and I sure couldn't see that guy shooting anybody.
2ND MAN: No, but he could probably drink them under the table.
1ST MAN: That's true. There's a man who enjoys life.
2ND MAN: Of course, if he couldn't shoot anybody, he's surely dead by now.
1ST MAN: Well, if that's true, I could just go ahead and kill you and it wouldn't make any difference.
2ND MAN: But we don't know that, do we? For all we know, Frankie might have become a hero. He might even have gotten a medal or something for bravery from the President.

1ST MAN: Now that's really stretching things a bit, don't you think?
2ND MAN: I guess so. In addition to being an atheist and a pacifist, Frankie always struck me as being somewhat of a coward.
1ST MAN: What makes you say that?
2ND MAN: Well, when we were kids and Frankie and I would have an argument he'd always end up running to his momma. I just found that pretty disgusting.
1ST MAN: Frankie did that? I knew he was a pacifist, but I didn't think he was a coward. That is disgusting.
2ND MAN: He wasn't very manly, when you think about it.
1ST MAN: I didn't know that about Frankie. That makes me kind of angry.
2ND MAN: It made me pretty angry when we were kids and he'd run to his momma like that.
1ST MAN: And here I was thinking the guy was such a manly prince of a fellow.
2ND MAN: Well you know how it is when people get to drinking. It's like war stories. They start exaggerating things a little.
1ST MAN: That makes me think that in good conscience, I can't save your life for Frankie's sake. I would be shirking my duty for the sake of that cowardly son of a bitch.
2ND MAN: Hey, wait! You shouldn't take too seriously what I've said about Frankie. I just never much cared for him myself, so I may have just given you the wrong impression.
1ST MAN: Ran to his momma, did he? That coward.
2ND MAN: That didn't happen every time, you understand. Just once or twice.
1ST MAN: The other times I bet you whipped his ass good, didn't you?
2ND MAN: Actually, Frankie was a little bigger than I was.
1ST MAN: Are you saying that that fucking coward whipped your ass!? Jesus! And I thought you were manly. You're just like all the people from your country. In addition to being religious fanatics, you are all fucking cowards. Get over there. I'm going behind my barricade.
2ND MAN: Now wait a minute …
1ST MAN: There's nothing to wait for.

The SOUND of a screaming shell that seems to be coming closer and the SOUND is getting louder and louder.

2ND MAN: What's that?
1ST MAN: What's what?
2ND MAN: Don't you hear it?
1ST MAN: Oh hell, it's another artillery shell. It sounds like it's coming from your side.
2ND MAN: No, I think it's coming from your side.
1ST MAN: Goddamn it, the sound is coming from your side!
2ND MAN: I better get my rifle in case it's from your side.
1ST MAN: What good is that going to do? Hey! I asked you a …

The SOUND of a horrific explosion. The LIGHTS flicker off, then a tremendous flash of LIGHT. BLACKOUT for two beats, then dim LIGHT. The area is hazy with smoke. The tree is down and so are the 1ST MAN and the 2ND MAN, the 1ST MAN's head and shoulders lie over his partially destroyed barricade. The 2ND MAN lies down left. No one moves for several beats.

2ND MAN (He raises his head): Aren't you going to ask me? ... Aren't you going to ask me if I'm dead? Aren't you going to ask me if I'm wounded? (No answer).

The 2ND MAN gets up, puts his rifle on his shoulder and looks over at the 1ST MAN who does not move. He stares at him for a moment, then crosses to the broken barricade in front of the 1ST MAN and looks at him.

2ND MAN: I think that one came from my side. (A beat. He leans over the barricade to look at the rest of the body of the 1ST MAN. He looks away quickly). Gaw! Gaw! (He leans over, about to throw up, but doesn't, just breathes heavily for several beats, stops, take a deep breath and looks up. He stares out for several beats, then he sees his rifle below the barricade. He crosses down and picks it up, looks at it, opens it, closes it, sees that it works. He stares at it, then turns toward the barricade and crosses to it. He takes the 1st Man's rifle off his shoulder, looks at it for a beat, then sits it down and leans it against the barricade near the 1st Man's body. He backs away, then turns and puts his own rifle on his shoulder and crosses to where his own barricade was. He takes his rifle off his shoulder and sits down and lays the rifle beside him. He sits looking across at the other barricade and does not move).

The LIGHTS fade very slowly to BLACKOUT.

RELATIONSHIPS: WHITE, BLACK AND GAY

Three One-Act Plays

The Lunch Hour

On Beech Street

Metamorphosis

THE LUNCH HOUR

A One-Act Play

CHARACTERS

FREDERICK — in his 30s or 40s
OLIVIA — in her 30s or 40s

SETTING

The bedroom in a downtown apartment house.

The Lunch Hour

FREDERICK in undershorts is sitting on the bed leaning against the head board smoking a cigarette as he watches OLIVIA in panties and bra as she gets into a slip and continues dressing.

FREDERICK: That was delightful. What a nice way to have lunch.
OLIVIA: Yes, it was a nice lunch. (She smiles). And a nice way to stay on a diet.
FREDERICK: I'm not on a diet.
OLIVIA: Well, I am.
FREDERICK: Why?
OLIVIA: So I won't get fat, silly.
FREDERICK: Will I get fat?
OLIVIA: No one cares if you get fat.
FREDERICK: Why does no one care if I get fat?
OLIVIA: I don't know. They just don't.
FREDERICK: You mean women. They wouldn't care.
OLIVIA: Well, they care some — if you're too fat.
FREDERICK: But men care a lot, right — if you're too fat?
OLIVIA: Women care a lot, too.
FREDERICK: Why?
OLIVIA: You like me this way, don't you? (A sexy pose). The way I curve. I have nice boobs. And I curve down to the waist and then I curve again at my rear. It's artistic, is it not?
FREDERICK: It's certainly interesting.
OLIVIA: There you see? But what if I went straight down? Big boobs almost to the waist, then straight down with no curve at the rear.
FREDERICK: (Pause). I'd have to see.
OLIVIA: See what?
FREDERICK: See what it looked like. Straight down.
OLIVIA: You wouldn't like it.
FREDERICK: You don't know that.
OLIVIA: I know.
FREDERICK: Would that mean I wouldn't have lunch with you any more like this?
OLIVIA: Probably.
FREDERICK: Would that mean that nobody would have lunch with you anymore like this?
OLIVIA: We're not talking about anybody.
FREDERICK: We're just talking about me?
OLIVIA: Yes.
FREDERICK: Shouldn't I be offended?

OLIVIA: I don't see why. Shouldn't you be dressing?
FREDERICK: I think I should be offended. For some reason.
OLIVIA: You're too sensitive.
FREDERICK: I?
OLIVIA: About some things.
FREDERICK: Meaning that I'm not sensitive about other things.
OLIVIA: I didn't say that.
FREDERICK: What things am I not sensitive about?
OLIVIA: I don't know. I don't know you well enough yet.
FREDERICK: Well, you know pretty much.
OLIVIA: Do I?
FREDERICK: Obviously, you know some things I'm not very sensitive about.
OLIVIA: Are you worrying about it?
FREDERICK: Not really. I'm just not sure I know what you mean. The way you deliberately qualified what you said.
OLIVIA: "Deliberately qualified." My. Maybe we should simply have lunch together and not talk.
FREDERICK: You mean make love with gags in our mouths.
OLIVIA: (Amused). Now that would be interesting. Of course, there would be certain things we couldn't do.
FREDERICK: Keep things simple.
OLIVIA: Yes. It seems that when people get to talking to each other, that's when it becomes difficult.
FREDERICK: That's when we find out how sensitive you are about your weight. That's when we find out that I'm not so sensitive about "some things," whatever they are.
OLIVIA: (She stops dressing, looks at him and smiles). Okay. For one thing, you bite too much.
FREDERICK: (Pause). I bite too much?
OLIVIA: Yes. Every time I have lunch with you, I have these little welts and bruises. I mean it's quite exciting when it's happening and all that, but …
FREDERICK: But what?
OLIVIA: Well it's just fortunate that you pick places that don't show, otherwise—
FREDERICK: Otherwise, what?
OLIVIA: I might have considerable explaining to do. Fortunately, Roy likes to make love in the dark. I think he likes to fantasize that he's with some young whore in a brothel somewhere.
FREDERICK: Really. Why?
OLIVIA: I don't know. We've been together a long time now. He's like an animal for a while there but, at the same time, detached. If we were to turn on the light he'd be talking about the car or his golf game or whatever.
FREDERICK: Ah, a romantic, is he? But then of course he doesn't bite, does he?
OLIVIA: No. He's really very sweet, but rather pragmatic about things.

FREDERICK: (Pause). I'm practical about things, too. There are salves and lineaments for that sort of thing.
OLIVIA: I'm well aware of that. I thought there might be a better solution.
FREDERICK: Really?
OLIVIA: I thought perhaps you might consider not biting me — so much.
FREDERICK: Oh.
OLIVIA: You might still bite some, of course — just not so much.
FREDERICK: (Pause). I just might have a few complaints of my own, you know.
OLIVIA: Yes?
FREDERICK: Yes, what?
OLIVIA: What are your complaints?
FREDERICK: I'll try and think of one.
OLIVIA: That's very flattering. You're not dressing. What time is it?
FREDERICK: There's one, you're in a hurry. That's my complaint.
OLIVIA: I'm not in a hurry, but lunch hour's over, isn't it? We have to get back to it. Actually, I'd like to take a nap.
FREDERICK: Yes, why don't we?
OLIVIA: Because we have to get dressed and get back to it.
FREDERICK: (He begins dressing). Right. We're not irresponsible types, are we? We always try to do a good job, right? We keep the wheels from squeaking, don't we? We deserve a little illicit fuck now and then, don't we?
OLIVIA: That's a rather crass way of putting it, don't you think?
FREDERICK: You're right, it is. I suppose I deserve a kick in the crotch.
OLIVIA: Well see if you can do it.
FREDERICK: What?
OLIVIA: Kick yourself in the crotch.
FREDERICK: I had in mind your doing it.
OLIVIA: Sorry, I can't manage it. I could provide a little verbal abuse, if you like.
FREDERICK: I see. You don't go in for whips and belts and leather, that kind of thing? There are people who do that sort of thing, you know.
OLIVIA: It doesn't interest me. We torture ourselves enough without going in for that kind of thing.
FREDERICK: Not me. I don't go in for self-flagellation.
OLIVIA: Yes you do. We all do.
FREDERICK: I see. You have a degree in the subject?
OLIVIA: I have an opinion on the matter. I don't believe I need a license to practice in order to have an opinion.
FREDERICK: Based on experience?
OLIVIA: Exactly. I suppose you'd like to limit your experiences to having a good lunch.
FREDERICK: That's not true. But I do offer a good lunch, don't I?
OLIVIA: That's beside the point.
FREDERICK: Oh. I thought having a good lunch was the point. I thought having a good lunch was a pleasant experience, not like some of the others we might have.

OLIVIA: (Pause). You go all out.
FREDERICK: Yes. That's not beside the point either, is it?
OLIVIA: It's all connected, isn't it? Isn't it all connected?
FREDERICK: I don't know. All I know is you don't go all out.
OLIVIA: What does that mean? I thought you had no complaints.
FREDERICK: You hold back.
OLIVIA: Are we on the bed or off the bed at the moment?
FREDERICK: Off and on.
OLIVIA: (She stares at him). I don't give enough, in your opinion?
FREDERICK: You don't take enough.
OLIVIA: I see. I wasn't aware of that. You must have a degree in the subject.
FREDERICK: Just an opinion.
OLIVIA: Based on vast experience, no doubt.
FREDERICK: Thank you.
OLIVIA: For what? It wasn't a compliment.
FREDERICK: I make no such claim to such "vast experience." However, It's nice to be appreciated.
OLIVIA: You don't fool me. I went into this with my eyes open.
FREDERICK: Did you? I'm glad.
OLIVIA: I don't make a habit of this, you know. But I've been around. I see what's going on.
FREDERICK: What's going on?
OLIVIA: Hell, we ought to button up a little. It's frightening, the way we give of ourselves. As though we had to have some sort of adventure just to prove we're alive.
FREDERICK: Is that what we did?
OLIVIA: I don't know. I don't make a habit of this, do you?
FREDERICK: What is this, our fourth lunch together?
OLIVIA: Yes.
FREDERICK: We're really starting to get acquainted, aren't we?
OLIVIA: I don't know what happened. I was just standing in the deli line thinking of lunch. A salami and cheese or a ham on rye—without mayonnaise, of course. Anyway, I couldn't decide. What I should have ordered was a salad.
FREDERICK: Your diet.
OLIVIA: I was hungry, feeling guilty. Thin toast for breakfast. And coffee. A thin sliver of corn oil margarine on the toast. A smidgen of jelly.
FREDERICK: A smidgen?
OLIVIA: What did I finally get at the deli?
FREDERICK: I don't remember.
OLIVIA: You were behind me in the deli line. I could feel your eyes examining me.
FREDERICK: You have a lovely face.
OLIVIA: You weren't examining my face.
FREDERICK: The way you frowned and pondered, trying to come to some

decision. A war was going on between the salami and the ham. Of course, I didn't know the adversaries at the time.
OLIVIA: You weren't looking at my face.
FREDERICK: It was amusing. I didn't know there was a third party—the salad. It was a serious moment for the world. (Pause). All of this was before.
OLIVIA: Before you undressed me in the deli line?
FREDERICK: I saw you before you saw me.
OLIVIA: I hate it when someone undresses me in public. It's disgusting.
FREDERICK: I couldn't help it.
OLIVIA: I was thrilled by it.
FREDERICK: Make up your mind.
OLIVIA: It was you. You. Why was that different?
FREDERICK: I couldn't help it.
OLIVIA: Was that why it was different?
FREDERICK: I don't know.
OLIVIA: If I had been straight from my boobs to my waist, you wouldn't have noticed me.
FREDERICK: You don't know that.
OLIVIA: Yes I do.
FREDERICK: I was looking at your face. The expression on your face.
OLIVIA: I'm fairly certain of it.
FREDERICK: (Pause). You're probably right.
OLIVIA: Yes. What did you say to me?
FREDERICK: I can't remember.
OLIVIA: Neither can I. Oh—when I couldn't decide you passed me in the line.
FREDERICK: Then I must have said, "excuse me" or something like that.
OLIVIA: You were probably annoyed.
FREDERICK: I wasn't annoyed at all.
OLIVIA: I thought you were probably annoyed.
FREDERICK: No. I just had to do something. You were holding up the line. They were getting annoyed behind me.
OLIVIA: We kept looking at each other. Why was that? You undressed me, but it wasn't an intrusion. It felt as if you were searching for something. Is that right?
FREDERICK: I can't remember.
OLIVIA: What were you searching for?
FREDERICK: I don't recall searching for anything.
OLIVIA: Were you hungry?
FREDERICK: I never cared much for lunch. I always eat a big breakfast.
OLIVIA: Were you hungry?
FREDERICK: Should I have been? I mean when you consider all my "vast experience."
OLIVIA: I was hungry. I got the salami on a big roll.

FREDERICK: I thought you didn't remember.
OLIVIA: I remember now. And there were no seats except at your table.
FREDERICK: Ah, there's Fate working, eh?
OLIVIA: That was our first lunch.
FREDERICK: An animated conversation.
OLIVIA: Was it? I wonder what it was about?
FREDERICK: Where you worked, where I worked, all that, I suppose. Names, times, places, all that stuff, I suppose.
OLIVIA: No, that wasn't it.
FREDERICK: No?
OLIVIA: I think I sat across the room from you and you beckoned me with your finger and I came to you and you threw me across the table and made love to me.
FREDERICK: In the deli?
OLIVIA: In the deli. You could have — that day.
FREDERICK: My sense of propriety prevented it, no doubt.
OLIVIA: Some electricity there that day. Some hot line that connected us.
FREDERICK: It was there, all right.
OLIVIA: Still — I might have stopped it. Cut the line, stamped out the fire. Whatever.
FREDERICK: Why didn't you?
OLIVIA: What sort of question is that?
FREDERICK: You mean you weren't — indifferent toward me.
OLIVIA: Indifferent?
FREDERICK: Yes, that's the wrong word, isn' t it?
OLIVIA: Did I call you or did you call me?
FREDERICK: I called you.
OLIVIA: Good. That was proper. The way it's done, or used to be done, at any rate.
FREDERICK: Actually, I came to your building.
OLIVIA: Ah, so you did.
FREDERICK: I couldn't call you because Roy might answer. Or be there.
OLIVIA: I couldn't call you because Jan might answer. Or be there.
FREDERICK: I met you at five o'clock when you were just coming out.
OLIVIA: Do you suppose Roy and Jan might enjoy being together like this? Having lunch?
FREDERICK: (Pause). There was a big crowd coming out of the building at that hour. I almost didn't see you.
OLIVIA: Then ran into me. Is that old Fate again?
FREDERICK: (Pause). I didn't run into you. I ran into some other woman. She was straight down from her tits to her waist.
OLIVIA: I was behind her. I know her, she has a very pretty face.
FREDERICK: I didn't notice.
OLIVIA: You were looking for me, right?

FREDERICK: I was on an errand for my boss.
OLIVIA: But you knew I was there. You knew I'd be coming out at five o'clock.
FREDERICK: I was on an errand for my boss. I didn't think there was any chance of seeing you.
OLIVIA: But you were looking for me.
FREDERICK: No, those kinds of things never work out. Not in a crowd like that.
OLIVIA: That's when you saw me.
FREDERICK: Yes.
OLIVIA: (Pause). If you hadn't seen me you could have gotten someone else.
FREDERICK: Do you think so?
OLIVIA: I'm sure of it.
FREDERICK: I'm not so sure of it.
OLIVIA: You'd have had lunch together.
FREDERICK: Here?
OLIVIA: Probably. But at the deli first, though. You're a man of some propriety.
FREDERICK: (Pause). We're really getting acquainted now, aren't we?
OLIVIA: This is a nice apartment. Everything is so neat and orderly. Everything convenient and in place.
FREDERICK: Are we liking each other less and less or more and more? What would you say?
OLIVIA: It's convenient for you to have this place so near your office. You can come home to lunch.
FREDERICK: (Pause). Yes.
OLIVIA: Then in the evening go home to dinner with Jan.
FREDERICK: (Pause). Hard for you, I suppose. Work all day then have to go home and cook for Roy.
OLIVIA: We take turns.
FREDERICK: Take turns?
OLIVIA: Yes. Roy cooks for me, then I cook for him.
FREDERICK: Very nice. I don't do that.
OLIVIA: What?
FREDERICK: Cook. Never learned how. I wasn't allowed in the kitchen.
OLIVIA: You have a kitchen here.
FREDERICK: She was an old-fashioned mom. No one was allowed in her kitchen.
OLIVIA: (Pause). Then Jan cooks?
FREDERICK: Yes.
OLIVIA: All the time?
FREDERICK: Yes. Sometimes we go out to eat. Especially when we're in town.
OLIVIA: Oh. Seems unfair to me.
FREDERICK: She's never mentioned it.
OLIVIA: Suffers in silence.
FREDERICK: (Pause). Jan likes to cook.
OLIVIA: It's an art, you know. If done properly.
FREDERICK: Is it?

OLIVIA: Jan's not a good cook?
FREDERICK: I didn't say that.
OLIVIA: Oh. Roy's an excellent cook. He likes a fully-equipped kitchen—like the one you have here.
FREDERICK: Good. He's practical, right? (Pause). This isn't my apartment, you know.
OLIVIA: It isn't? I thought it was. I had the impression it was.
FREDERICK: It's never come up.
OLIVIA: What?
FREDERICK: The ownership of the apartment.
OLIVIA: No. He—or she—must be a good friend. You seem to know your way around.
FREDERICK: He is. And I know my way around—except in the kitchen.
OLIVIA: I wonder what he must think of me.
FREDERICK: He doesn't know you.
OLIVIA: I know. I wonder what he must think of me.
FREDERICK: I've explained it.
OLIVIA: Have you?
FREDERICK: Yes.
OLIVIA: Explain it to me, then.
FREDERICK: I'm not sure I know what you mean.
OLIVIA: Explain it to me the way you explained it to him.
FREDERICK: Why?
OLIVIA: I'd just like to know how I've been explained. Or is that man talk.
FREDERICK: Man talk?
OLIVIA: I'm aware of how some men talk about women—in this kind of situation.
FREDERICK: Is that how you think I talked about you?
OLIVIA: (Pause). I really can't imagine how one would do that. You know, make arrangements. It would be awkward for me.
FREDERICK: It was awkward for me.
OLIVIA: Was it? I thought it might be a kind of permanent arrangement. "Bill, old friend, if I should find something nice on the street, or at the deli, would you mind foregoing lunch at your place and let me use it?"
FREDERICK: (Pause). He doesn't come home for lunch.
OLIVIA: Ah.
FREDERICK: I feel guilty, too.
OLIVIA: Do I feel guilty?
FREDERICK: I don't feel dirty or—or anything like—you know.
OLIVIA: Well, you had a good lunch.
FREDERICK: (Pause). We're really getting acquainted now, aren't we?
OLIVIA: I thought you were a sportsman.
FREDERICK: No.
OLIVIA: (She crosses to the door and pulls it back). Then these golf clubs behind the door aren't yours?

FREDERICK: No.
OLIVIA: Good. It's a silly game. Roy loves it. And all those framed baseball pictures in the livingroom?
FREDERICK: He's a sports writer for one of the newspapers.
OLIVIA: Oh? Named Bill?
FREDERICK: Yes, as a matter of fact.
OLIVIA: Got it right the first time, didn't I?
FREDERICK: I wondered about that.
OLIVIA: Did you? Well, the place looked like a Bill to me, not a Frederick. I do have the right name, don't I?
FREDERICK: (A touch of irritation). Of course you have the right name.
OLIVIA: Olivia is nice, don't you think?
FREDERICK: It's very nice.
OLIVIA: Better than Jan, don't you think? More poetic, wouldn't you agree? Ah, but what's in a name? What play is that from? I can't remember, he wrote so many.
FREDERICK: Should I look it up?
OLIVIA: Bill's a sportswriter. He probably wouldn't have it. Does he have a video camera?
FREDERICK: Video camera?
OLIVIA: I'd feel better if he didn't have one.
FREDERICK: He's got one. It's probably hidden in the closet. There's probably a concealed peep-hole and a timer that goes off at noon. He's probably filmed the whole lunch hour and he'll take it to the locker room before the next game and show it.
OLIVIA: (Pause). Very funny. They'd like seeing me, you know. My curves, my boobs, my pub hairs and thighs. The rewards of dieting. Makes me want to keep eating salads for lunch. They probably wouldn't have much interest in you unless there's some closet-fag in the group.
FREDERICK: Oh, I don't know about that. They'd probably like to see how I perform. How big I get. How I use my muscles. My technique when I throw you down and climb on top of you.
OLIVIA: (Pause). You don't throw me down. You're a very tender person when you make love. Even when you bite, so tender. Are you aware of that?
FREDERICK: It probably wouldn't be masculine enough for the group, would it?
OLIVIA: So sweet. It made me shiver at first. I had goose bumps. (Pause). I wonder if you're like that with the others.
FREDERICK: Have I missed something? I don't know what you're talking about.
OLIVIA: The other ones you've brought to Bill's for lunch.
FREDERICK: Did I say I'd brought anyone else here for lunch?
OLIVIA: No.
FREDERICK: But you've made an assumption, right?
OLIVIA: It's quite convenient for lunch, you'll have to admit that.

FREDERICK: Very convenient. It's part of the downtown redevelopment project. The idea is to get people closer to their work. And improve the downtown area.
OLIVIA: Oh, goody. What a nice idea. You like it?
FREDERICK: I hadn't given it much thought. I don't know if it's working.
OLIVIA: It's working for Bill.
FREDERICK: Right.
OLIVIA: It's working for you. For lunch, at least.
FREDERICK: Yes. Is it working for you?
OLIVIA: (Pause). Bill's place — you've been here before — before us.
FREDERICK: Of course. Bill's had me over.
OLIVIA: For lunch?
FREDERICK: Bill doesn't eat lunch here. Except on weekends, I guess.
OLIVIA: For an evening, then?
FREDERICK: Yes, after a show.
OLIVIA: You and Jan?
FREDERICK: Yes. And Bill and his date.
OLIVIA: Did you and Jan stay over night here?
FREDERICK: Occasionally, yes.
OLIVIA: In this room? (No answer). Probably screwed Jan right on this bed, isn't that right?
FREDERICK: (He moves to the dresser mirror to tie his tie). We've really gotten well acquainted now, wouldn't you say?
OLIVIA: Roy doesn't like to come in for shows. It's such a long drive. Maybe you should introduce him to Bill and we could stay over.
FREDERICK: Is that what you'd like me to do?
OLIVIA: I was kidding, you know that. It was just a joke.
FREDERICK: Oh.
OLIVIA: You didn't think it was a joke?
FREDERICK: You're not laughing.
OLIVIA: Wasn't that kind of joke.
FREDERICK: What kind of joke was it?
OLIVIA: Forget it. Do you think it might have been better if we had gotten acquainted before rather than after we made love?
FREDERICK: (He stares in the mirror). I don't know.
OLIVIA: We've behaved irrationally.
FREDERICK: Does that mean you regret coming to lunch with me?
OLIVIA: (Pause). No. But I probably will later.
FREDERICK: I see.
OLIVIA: I'd like it better if we had gotten acquainted first. It's hell letting things get out of control. I was practically at your mercy.
FREDERICK: (He turns to her). At my mercy?
OLIVIA: You were never out of control.
FREDERICK: Wasn't I? I thought the opposite.

OLIVIA: No. It was you who thought everything through. Arranged it all. Talked to Bill. Arranged the lunch date here.
FREDERICK: What would you have us do? Make love on the deli table? In front of your building out in the street? That what you wanted?
OLIVIA: Probably. I was out of control. I was wrapped in a sort of cocoon. I was enchanted like a fairy-tale princess. Nothing could touch me. I have no idea what happened that day from five o'clock to lunch time the next day when we met here. And you tell me you were at the building on an errand for your boss.
FREDERICK: No, I came for you.
OLIVIA: I was looking for you. I was dying. I would have done anything—and did.
FREDERICK: You held back.
OLIVIA: I had to! You thought it all through, that's what I couldn't get. Talked to Bill, made a plan, while I was falling apart.
FREDERICK: I had to. What if I hadn't?
OLIVIA: (Pause). All I know is one can't be so vulnerable.
FREDERICK: One should build a fortress around one's self.
OLIVIA: Is that what's happening? I can't sort it all out. You can't have lunch forever. There's a street out there and our jobs and our—all sorts of things.
FREDERICK: Yes, all sorts of things.
OLIVIA: Some of them very important.
FREDERICK: Yes.
OLIVIA: They occupy your time—your thoughts.
FREDERICK: They're important.
OLIVIA: More important than this.
FREDERICK: What would you like me to say?
OLIVIA: I mean, compared to this? To having lunch together?
FREDERICK: They diminish. They disappear.
OLIVIA: Then they come back. They re-appear.
FREDERICK: You'd like to be rid of them?
OLIVIA: Wouldn't you?
FREDERICK: (Pause). You can't have this all the time. You have the other all the time except when you have this.
OLIVIA: Then is it worth it? I mean if you can't have this all the time.
FREDERICK: You have to decide.
OLIVIA: Have you?
FREDERICK: Yes.
OLIVIA: And?
FREDERICK: What have you decided?
OLIVIA: I asked you first.
FREDERICK: Maybe we should answer at the same time.
OLIVIA: Why? So neither will have an advantage? Like a tennis match. This is deuce, right?

FREDERICK: Sorry. It's this fortress you're building. Brick on brick, so to speak.
OLIVIA: I hold back, right? I'm wide open for you but I'm holding back.
FREDERICK: (Pause). I'm committed to it.
OLIVIA: (Pause). To lunch.
FREDERICK: It's as far as we've gone.
OLIVIA: But we're getting acquainted now, aren't we? And now there's Roy and Jan and Bill and your boss and my boss and we're late for work because lunch was over a long time ago.
FREDERICK: I'm still very hungry.
OLIVIA: But lunch is over now. Anyway, you had a big breakfast, didn't you?
FREDERICK: (Pause). So it's finished, is it?
OLIVIA: (Pause). You won't forget to thank Bill.
FREDERICK: So it's brick on brick now, isn't it?
OLIVIA: (She turns away). No, it's sand on sand.
FREDERICK: (Pause). I might see you again at the deli, you know.
OLIVIA: No, I won't be there. There are too many temptations. I'm dieting, you know. Perhaps you'll make other acquaintances.
FREDERICK: Right. And you?
OLIVIA: No. I have enough friends. Sometimes meeting new people is awkward for me.
FREDERICK: Me, too — especially over lunch.
OLIVIA: You won't forget to thank Bill?
FREDERICK: I'll remember.
OLIVIA: He has a very nice place.
FREDERICK: Yes.
OLIVIA: An enchanting place in a way. In spite of the clubs and the pictures. I thought it was yours until we got acquainted.
FREDERICK: No, it's Bill's place.
OLIVIA: Anyway, I'll always remember it.
FREDERICK: Yes, so will I.
OLIVIA: But you'll see it again. With Jan.
FREDERICK: (Pause). Probably.
OLIVIA: I love that tie. It's a beautiful tie.
FREDERICK: Thank you.
OLIVIA: I loved unknotting it and taking it off.
FREDERICK: You do that so nicely.
OLIVIA: Yes. I didn't want it to twist or wrinkle. I knew you had to go back out there.
FREDERICK: Yes, we do have to back out there, don't we? Both of us.
OLIVIA: (Pause). Thank you for lunch.
FREDERICK: Of course. Oh, I'm sorry — you know — about the biting.
OLIVIA: (She smiles). It's all right. I'm fine. We did get acquainted, didn't we?
FREDERICK: I might see you again, you know. At your building. I might have an errand there for my boss.

OLIVIA: No. The streets are so crowded. You'd probably miss me.
FREDERICK: Yes. (Pause). Well, that's Fate, isn't it?
OLIVIA: Yes. It seems to work that way. Good-bye then. (She looks at him a beat then goes out the door).

FREDERICK stares at the door for a beat. Then he sits and slowly begins to unknot his tie and lets it fall across his knees and looks at it.

The LIGHTS dim slowly to BLACKOUT.

THE END

ON BEECH STREET

A One-Act Play in Three Scenes

CHARACTERS

BIG DAVE — a big strong, good-looking Afro-American man in his early 30's. A former boxer who now lives from day to day.

DENISE — A petite Afro-American woman in her late 20's who serves others as a cleaning woman and who is trying to escape her past life, but whose vision of the future is bleak.

THE SCENES

Scene 1 — The front porch of an old apartment house that has three steps leading to the porch and an old-fashioned railing around the front of the porch. There are two tin pots with geraniums in them on the porch railing. There is a screen door center and two large windows right and left in the back wall. The time is the present.

Scene 2 — The same. A few weeks later.

Scene 3 — The same. Late afternoon, several days later.

On Beech Street

Scene 1

Front porch of a rundown, but neat apartment house. BIG DAVE a strong black man, early 30's, sits in a rocker on the porch. DENISE, a young black girl, late 20's, comes out of the interior door after a beat. She stands thinking, not noticing Big Dave until he speaks.

DAVE: You like the apart-mint, baby?
DENISE: I can afford it.
DAVE: That ain't what I askt you.
DENISE: Ain't none of your business and I ain't your baby.... It's clean. Got some yard out the window. Prob'ly take it.
DAVE: Good.
DENISE: What's good about it?
DAVE: Good that you satisfied.
DENISE: That ain't what I said. I said I could afford it. What street's this anyway? I done forgot.
DAVE: Beech Street. 218.
DENISE: Beach Street? I don't see no beach. Not even a mud puddle.
DAVE: Nah, baby, Beech—like the tree.
DENISE: What tree? I never heard of no beach tree. Beaches got sand, not trees.
DAVE: There's beech trees, they say. Hell, I don't know.
DENISE: How they spell that? (No answer). Too bad it ain't a beach. I'd just run down to that old ocean and jump in and cool myself off. Then I'd lie down on the sand and burn up my skin and make it dark like white folks do.
DAVE (He laughs): You play hell making your skin any darker, baby.
DENISE: I am a real nigger ain't I? The envy of those white folks.
DAVE (He laughs): I wouldn't say that. Nah, I wouldn't say that.
DENISE: You wouldn't, eh? So what's it like 'round here where I gotta live? Which one of them houses is the crack house? I don't see no wild kids runnin' round. Where is everybody?
DAVE: None of that stuff in this neighborhood. People workin'. Kids in school. Ain't a whole lot of them.
DENISE: Well, that's somethin'. People workin'. You ain't.
DAVE: Day off.
DENISE: Mid-week and you got the day off?
DAVE: You could say I'm between things right now.
DENISE: Or you could say you ain't working at all.
DAVE: You could say that if you want to.
DENISE (Pacing the porch, looking all around): Nice porch. Good place to sit in the evening, if it's safe.
DAVE: It's safe.

DENISE: Course if you gonna sit you need more than one chair.
DAVE: This my rocker.
DENISE: These your plants too?
DAVE: Belong to Miz Potts. Live downstairs across the hall from me.
DENISE: Pretty. Geraniums. Always liked geraniums. My momma used to keep 'em in these big old pottery pots. Heavy as hell to carry. Everybody got the grass cut and weeded out.
DAVE: Good neighborhood.
DENISE: Look like it. What makes it good?
DAVE: Right peaceful, usually. Miz Potts get on her old man sometimes and there's some yellin' goes on. But seldom see a lawman. Ain't no gangs or nothin' like that. Lot of white folks still live around.
DENISE: Got white folks in the neighborhood, have you? Is that what make it good? Them white folks living around?
DAVE: Might be.
DENISE: What you mean "might be"?
DAVE: Just said it might be. What you want me to say?
DENISE: I want you to say what you think. What else?
DAVE: I got no opinion on it.
DENISE: Oh yeah? You prob'ly wish I'd not take this apartment. I might fuck up the balance, right? Get them white people upset and they start packin' their duds and movin' out.
DAVE: Never thought about it. None of my business what you do.
DENISE: Well, you just got no opinion on nothin', do you? Ha! I thought I was your "baby."
DAVE: Sound like you got out of bed on the rough side this mornin'.
DENISE: I get out on the rough side every morning. It's why I'm lookin' for a decent place to live where it's safe. Where if I turn 'round and see somebody I don't get goose bumps and sweats all at the same time.
DAVE: It's safe.
DENISE: No lawman, eh? I betcha this — there may not be no lawman around regular, but if one of them white folks wants a lawman, I bet one come running like a bat out of hell.
DAVE: Come when they needed.
DENISE: Bet your sweet ass, they come. You think they'd come if it was just me and you? I see how they operates with black folks.
DAVE: You ain't gonna be easy to get on with, you know that?
DENISE: Well, least I got an opinion on things.
DAVE: I got opinions.
DENISE: Well, I ain't heard one yet. I'm easy. I just know where I stands on things.
DAVE: Well, it ain't on no beach.
DENISE: Ha! Now you have said something true. Sure ain't no beach. Up a tree maybe. You live downstairs?

DAVE: Got this apart-mint right here. (He points to the window beside him).
DENISE: I'd be right above you, if I take it. I ain't noisy. I ain't one to clog around above you in wooden shoes. And got a good thick rug. Name's Denise.
DAVE: I'm Dave. Ever body just call me Big Dave.
DENISE: You big, all right. Been eating them Wheaties, I'd say.
DAVE: Was a boxer at one time. Damned dumb thing to be.
DENISE: Won't argue with you there.
DAVE: That's a fact, not an opinion. Loved it, though — 'til they started making me do things.
DENISE: What things?
DAVE: Lie down for guys I knew I could beat.
DENISE: Why'd you do that?
DAVE: Money. Gotta eat. They kept saying my time would come — that if I didn't take a fall now and then, they wasn't goin' to handle me. Get me fights. So I'd win big couple times, then I'd have to take a fall.
DENISE: Sound pretty stupid to me.
DAVE: Well, you wasn't me in my shoes, baby. Got rid of them guys, but by then I'd took too many falls so nobody had no interest anymore. This eatin' business ruin everything.
DENISE: Gotta breathe, eat and have shelter. When it come right down to it, ain't no time for nothin' else.
DAVE: Seem that way. Maybe a little dancin' now and then.
DENISE: Yeah, little music help.
DAVE: Little courtin' now and then. That help.
DENISE: That don't help. Just usually mean trouble. Gotta be mighty careful with that.
DAVE: Why you say that?
DENISE: 'Cause you gentlemen always figure you can just walk away after you done your business, whatever that business might be.
DAVE: That what happen to you?
DENISE: That's my business. This courtin' stuff you talkin' about happen just the way I said to my sister and my mother and my aunt and my neighbor down the street. Those fine gentlemen just walk away. Got no idea who my daddy is. Never seen hide nor hair of him. Never came 'round. Never sent one dime to my momma to pay for the business he done. That business was me. That's why I become like one of them squirrels. I see a man comin' on I run up one of them beech trees you supposed to have 'round here.
DAVE: Ain't always like that.
DENISE: It mostly like that. Sometimes even squirrels get caught.
DAVE: You talkin' bad luck.
DENISE: If I got lucky I'd rather it be with the lottery or that huckster on the TV who try to sell magazines. Win 10 million dollars. Not some man who's likely to pull some disappearin' act on me.
DAVE: Well, I can see you ain't gonna be easy, but you're close by.

DENISE: Oh, so you already made the plan, have you? I ain't even said for sure I'm taking this place here on your Beech Street where your white folks keep the peace. For sure, I ain't settin' foot in your bedroom and you sure as hell not comin' into mine. You best make another plan, big boy.

DAVE (He laughs): Lawdy me, ain't no jokin' around with you, is there? Hell, baby, I never had a plan in my life. I was gonna box cuz I liked to box. That was the only plan I ever had. Right now I just do what come next.

DENISE: So I'm what come next 'cause I'd be right convenient. Is that it?

DAVE: You're a right pretty girl, baby.

DENISE: Oh Jesus, I put a padlock on that flimsy door you box your way right through it. I ain't movin' here.

DAVE: No sir, no jokin' with you. Lissen, woman, I don't go nowhere less I'm invited. You better believe that.

DENISE: Then you ain't comin' at all 'cause I ain't issuing no invitations.

DAVE: Whatever you say, baby.

DENISE: Quit callin' me that! And why don't you get your big ass out of that rockin' chair and go to work.

DAVE (He stands): You watch how you talk. Now you crossin' my lines.

DENISE: Expect you do your socializin' with some of these white folks in the neighborhood.

DAVE: You funny.

DENISE: You mean to tell me you don't do no socializing with your neighbors? I thought you was the friendly sort. You mean to say you don't call all them white girls in the neighborhood baby?

DAVE (He sits down again and looks away from her): Smile and say "How you doin'." They smiles and say, "How you doin'." Don't nobody care how we doin' either way.

DENISE: So that's how it is? Then you ain't invited to tea? Hey, baby, I'm comin' over to have tea in your livin' room. Get rid of your folks and we'll rub bodies and make some oreo cookies.

DAVE (Angrily stands and shakes his fist at her): You a smart one, ain't you! Come 'round here spittin' fire. Who needs it?

DENISE: Yeah, the truth it hurts, don't it, baby? You think you're the great rooster boy 'til you go down them steps and put your foot on that sidewalk.

DAVE: There ain't no trouble. You smile and say "How you doin'" and you becomes invisible.

DENISE: Hell you say. You ain't invisible. They watching you like hawks, man. Betcha there's somebody behind that curtain over yonder in that house just watching out to see what we gonna do. Step out of line and you'll see.

DAVE: Black preacher live there.

DENISE: Oh?

DAVE: See that big window up yonder on the second floor?

DENISE: Uh huh.

DAVE: That be where the preacher's wife watch from. If she seen you comin' she up there.
DENISE: Oh. Ain't people got better things to do?
DAVE: Which people? White people or black people?
DENISE: Oh go to hell, smart ass.
DAVE: She know everybody's troubles. Anyway, don't nobody serve tea on this block that I know about.
DENISE: Just call me by my name, smart ass. Where is that damned real estate man? I ain't got all day.
DAVE: You got business?
DENISE: Yeah, I clean, I dust, I mop. That my business. I get chewed out if it ain't right. I try to do it right.
DAVE: Take pride in your cleanin' and dustin' and moppin'.
DENISE: Well, there sure ain't nothin' else to take pride in. Everybody I know made dumb choices. Why should I be different?
DAVE: Quit school.
DENISE: Yep.
DAVE: Slung hash. Worked the family dollar store.
DENISE: Yep.
DAVE: Hit the dope.
DENISE: Missed that, but was on the old welfare train for a time.
DAVE: Been there. Got pregnant?
DENISE: Yep. That was afterwards. Wasn't no tea party either. Was doin' pretty good. Then in he come, uninvited. He raided me.
DAVE: Where's the kid?
DENISE: Ain't no kid.
DAVE: You was lucky.
DENISE: I wasn't lucky.
DAVE: Got rid of it, didja?
DENISE: Not the way you think.
DAVE (A beat): I ain't gonna ask.
DENISE (Tears in her eyes): Doesn't matter now. It's gone. Out there buried somewhere—or incinerated. Mixed in with the trash. I made real sure it wouldn't be found by nobody. Keep thinkin' about it. About him. What he would be like. What we'd be doin' together. But that wasn't no way to have him. Torn open like that. Violated! He come bustin' in my room, my own place …
DAVE (Up and beside her now, arm on her shoulder): Hey, take it easy now. Come on over now and sit in this here rocker. (He guides her). This here is one grand rockin' chair. Fits the back and the backside. Could sit here all my life, I could.
DENISE: Course the real truth is, I couldn't take care of him. End up dead anyway and sufferin' all the while. I ain't sorry for what I done. You lookin' at a murderer, Big Dave. I ain't sorry, though.

DAVE: Nah, nah now. You just sit and rock a bit.
DENISE: Wouldn't mean a thing—'cept I keep thinkin' 'bout what we'd be doin'. Say right now, what he'd be sayin' and what I'd be sayin' to him. Oh Jesus, to be torn open like that.
DAVE: Hey, never mind. Don't say no more. Makin' me angry. Like to tear him open and could. I could.
DENISE: What the hell you care? Can't understand why come I told you that anyway. Perfect stranger and all.
DAVE: We was talkin' about livin'. Just come out.
DENISE: Like vomit. Upchucking our lives. That's what it's worth, our lives. To be upchucked.
DAVE: Wisht you wouldn't say that. I don't know. Wisht you wouldn't say that. (He paces to the other end of the porch wringing his hands).
DENISE: It's what's real, ain't it? Gotta look at what's real.
DAVE: Nah, nah, gotta change it, that's all.
DENISE: How!? Answer that one, big man. It's done, man, it's done. It's the way it's gonna be.
DAVE: Figure it out.
DENISE: You all muscle and no brain. What's to figure out?
DAVE: Yeah? And what are you?
DENISE: All soft and stupid.
DAVE: A damned spit-fire. My muscle and your spit. Ought to put these here great talents together.
DENISE: It don't take no talent to know the score.
DAVE: Goose eggs is what we got. That's funny.
DENISE: What's funny about it?
DAVE: Never even thought about it. Then here you come along.
DENISE: Yeah, I've got the bad news, all right.
DAVE: Just sit here and never thought about it.
DENISE: You thought about it. That's why you just been sittin' here wearing your big ass out.
DAVE: Nah, nah, I been out there scrappin'. Like you say, you gotta eat. Ever mornin' I go downtown to that little shoppin' center. You know where I'm talkin' about?
DENISE: Yeah I know where that is.
DAVE: Stand around in front of the likker store there. See, that's where they expect us to be. Figure that's what we lookin' for—money for booze. They come by in their pick up trucks and look us over. I got an advantage 'cause I'm strong and big. Usually get picked. Nobody come by today.
DENISE: What happens you get sick?
DAVE: Stay home and don't go downtown.
DENISE: Nah, I mean real sick. Or hurt, maybe.
DAVE: Never been real sick or hurt.

DENISE: It ain't gonna work. Can't live like that. You ain't always gonna be strong and big.
DAVE: Why not?
DENISE: I don't know. Cause you get old or — or you fall and break somethin'. The man he give you somethin' risky to do and you got to do it and it don't work and you fall or somethin'.
DAVE: Could happen, I guess.
DENISE: Then what you gonna do?
DAVE: What would you do?
DENISE: My work ain't dangerous like yours might be.
DAVE: So you ain't plannin' to get old and sick either?
DENISE: I don't know! How the hell we get on this, anyway? I'm just lookin' for a place to live and you come talkin' this trash.
DAVE: You the one talkin' trash. Fussin' at me for sittin' on my big ass in this here rockin' chair makin' it your business.
DENISE: It ain't none of my business.
DAVE: I know that, but you make it your business askin' dumb questions.
DENISE: They ain't dumb questions.
DAVE: Mindin' my business and takin' over my rockin' chair.
DENISE (She stands): I didn't take no rockin' chair. You put me in this here chair. Here take your damned rockin' chair and see if I care.
DAVE: Think I'll stir around a bit. Walk around the block maybe.
DENISE: Yeah, why don't you do that. Look at them beech trees, why don't you?
DAVE: Yeah. Wisht I knew which ones them beech trees was. (Goes down the steps).
DENISE: What you care? They all got leaves and they shady. It's like music. You don't have to know no music to hear its got a beat.
DAVE: You dances to the beat.
DENISE: That's all you got to know.
DAVE: That's the way I do it ever day. Just dances to the beat.
DENISE: That's different. Ain't no joy in that.
DAVE: Don't know what else to do.
DENISE: Me neither, but it ain't like dancin'. I keep lookin' for a different beat.
DAVE: Like movin' to a new place, maybe?
DENISE: I don't know, maybe. Pretty awful where I was. Had to do somethin'. Right tidy neighborhood here, but I don't feel no changes. The beat is sure the same, it seem like.
DAVE: Well hope that real 'state man come soon so you can get back to your business.
DENISE: I bet so. That way you can get back to this rockin' chair and sit on your big rear all day in peace.
DAVE: Might be a good thing if you not move in that apart-mint after all.
DENISE: Well, that ain't for you to decide, big man. Hope them white folks say "How you doin'" and smiles at you on your walk.

DAVE: Oh don't you worry your pretty black face about that. They got obligations to fulfill, you know. They still in their repentin' stage so long as it don't require nothin' of 'em.
DENISE: That's funny. I thought George Foreman was the only boxer man who was funny.
DAVE: Shouldda been a minstrel man. Born too late and missed my callin'. (Starts walking stage left).
DENISE: Hey! I think I'm gonna take this place on your Beech Street with your white folks and black preacher. Live right on top of you, whether you like it or not. Bring on more bad luck.
DAVE: It figures. Trouble ain't new to me, baby.
DENISE: Hey, I got a name and it ain' t baby! (She looks across the way). She up there. That black preacher woman's up there scoutin' me out.
DAVE: Well that ain't no surprise. (Goes off stage left).
DENISE: Up there rustlin' them curtains. I seen you, woman, in your big house doin' your good works for the neighborhood. Got you a new neighbor and what you don't know ain't gonna hurt you. (She sits back down in the rocking chair and begins rocking vigorously). I watch out for you and you better watch out for me. You better go get you a chair, too, 'cause you know well as I that white man is gonna keep me waitin' here 'cause he couldn't care less that I got business to do. And there ain't nothin' you or me can do about that. (She rocks vigorously).

BLACKOUT.

Scene 2

It is evening, a few weeks later. DENISE is sitting still in the rocker on the porch. After a beat, BIG DAVE comes up the steps. He sees her and stops.

DAVE: Got my chair.
DENISE: Ain't your chair.
DAVE: It's mine. Done your business and loafin' around, are you?
DENISE: My feet was tired.
DAVE: Dustin' and moppin' done wore you out, eh?
DENISE: Done three houses today.
DAVE: Done made a pile of money.
DENISE: Old smart ass. (Nonetheless, she is amused). Why come you so dirty?
DAVE: Done made a pile of money.
DENISE: You ain't workin'? You must of set two weeks in this chair watchin' me go out and slave.
DAVE: Then got me a big desk down at the bottom of that gravel pit.

DENISE: Lawdy mercy, ain't you important.
DAVE: Tomorrow I movin' my desk up to a roof top. Gonna rap a few shingles on.
DENISE: Lawdy, what has caused all this sudden trouble?
DAVE: Eatin'. Beans and soup was gettin' old. And rent comin' up due.
DENISE: You is motivated. You goin' to make the big time.
DAVE: I was gonna make my rockin' chair.
DENISE: You come too late.
DAVE: I could pick you up and throw you out in the yard, if I'd a mind to.
DENISE: That preacher man's wife'll fix you good if you do.
DAVE: She up there?
DENISE: She might be.
DAVE: If she didn't mean well, one of these days I might just bust that window for her.
DENISE: "One of these days, one of these days." One of these days I'll fly to the moon and back.
DAVE: You as likable as ever this evening. If I can't sit I'll shower. (He starts to go in, then stops). How you makin' out up there?
DENISE: I'm settled in, I guess. Got enough to pay the rent.
DAVE: Wasn't for creaky floors, I wouldn't know you was there.
DENISE: I be there all right.
DAVE: Ain't heard no music.
DENISE: Ain't got nothin' but the radio. All they want to do is blab about things they don't know nothing about and sell stuff.
DAVE: How you know they don't know nothin'?
DENISE: 'Cause I'm stupid smart. I know they don't know what they talkin' about, but I don't know what to do about it either. If'n I did I'd be livin' in the preacher's house.
DAVE: Well, just don't ask me.
DENISE: Oh I wasn't goin' to. Needn't worry about that.
DAVE: So you happy in your new place?
DENISE: What you want? What you fishin' for?
DAVE: Just seein' if things was all right.
DENISE: What are you, the host around here or somethin'? You ain't gettin' this chair, if that's what you after.
DAVE: Don't want the chair.
DENISE: The hell you don't.
DAVE: No use tryin' to be friendly with you, I can see that.
DENISE: Depends on what you mean by "use."
DAVE: You willin' to think the worst, ain't ya?
DENISE: It's just what happens, that's all. I ain't mean.
DAVE: Well you sure fooled me. (He starts to go).
DENISE: Damned sore-head.

DAVE: Lissen here, baby, you want a pleasure trip, you go to some other planet. You just sit there and stew in your juice, ain't nobody gonna care. You want some fun come sit down at my desk in the gravel pit. Come up to that roof top tomorrow, I give you some fun. I do your dustin' and moppin' you do my roofin'.

DENISE (She laughs): Old Big Dave got his dander up. 'Stead of takin' it, he's dishin' it out now. Well that's all right.

DAVE: Now what you sayin'?

DENISE: I ain't sayin' nothin' that you don't understand in the pit of your belly.

DAVE: Get this dust off. Take me a shower. You a waste of time.

DENISE: That's so. Hey! You handy with a screw driver?

DAVE: What?

DENISE: A damned screw driver. You know what I'm talkin' about.

DAVE: What about it?

DENISE: Been hangin' my towels on the shower rod 'cause I can't get that screw driver to work right. And need some rods in the kitchen for dish towels and things.

DAVE: What you want?

DENISE: I want you to put the damned things up, that's what I want.

DAVE: You want me to come up to your place?

DENISE: Where else would I want them rods except my place? Don't get any ideas, it ain't no invitation. I'm payin'.

DAVE: Payin'? Ain't nothin' to puttin' couple rods up.

DENISE: I'm payin'. Can't do a thing, you have to pay to get it done. Got two holes in the plaster and a broken screw driver. If I keep it up I'll lose my damage deposit.

DAVE: And the floor'll be falling on my head.

DENISE: I knew you'd say somethin' smart like that. Just remember I'm payin' so I don't have to hire you. Get me somebody else to do it, if I have to.

DAVE: Well, what you payin'?

DENISE: What you chargin'?

DAVE: It ain't worth nothin'. Couple towel racks ain't worth nothin'.

DENISE: Worth a good supper, ain't it? A supper that don't have no canned beans and soup?

DAVE: That an invitation?

DENISE: I told you, it's wages. Payment for work done.

DAVE: Said you wasn't gonna let me in your place.

DENISE: This be different. This is business.

DAVE: Eatin' supper ain't business.

DENISE: Lissen, big man, you bring up your hammer and your screw driver and your empty belly. You work, you eat, you leave and there ain't nothin' more to it, so quit fishin' around.

DAVE: Then it ain't no invitation.

DENISE: No, damnit, it ain't no invitation. Jesus! I shouldn't have asked.

DAVE (He laughs): Just tryin' to keep things straight.
DENISE: Well, you got it. It's "no" and I don't mean "yes." It's business, Big Dave, small business.
DAVE: I be up for supper after while.
DENISE: You be up to work, then you have supper.
DAVE: That's what I meant.
DENISE: That ain't what you said.
DAVE: Do that work in two minutes. That's what I meant.
DENISE: Well, took me two hours to put them holes in the plaster.
DAVE: You ain't too handy with tools, are you?
DENISE: No shit. I 'spect you ain't too handy with a mop either.
DAVE: We specialists in our fields, right?
DENISE: Yeah, real artists. Born and reared in it.
DAVE: You best get out of my rocker and start your cookin'.
DENISE: It ain't got your name on it.
DAVE: Well, it belong to me.
DENISE: I don't see no proof of it. Things change, you know.
DAVE: Well they ain't for the better.
DENISE: I didn't say they was for the better, I said they changed.
DAVE: Well then things'll change again and maybe then for the better.
DENISE: Don't count no chickens on it. Speaking of which, we eatin' fried chicken tonight. If you don't like chicken, you out of luck.
DAVE: Like winning "Pick 3" on the lottery. But it ain't no invitation—just business.
DENISE: That's right. When it come time to eat, you get a fork, knife and spoon and I get the hammer.
DAVE: And ain't no finger-lickin' allowed.
DENISE: You just you keep it up, big man, and you'll end up on soup and beans.
DAVE: Gonna be soup and beans anyway cuz I can't do it tonight.
DENISE: What you mean, you can't do it tonight? You just foolin' around with me again?
DAVE: Gotta go downtown. Didn't mean to kid around like that. I'll do them rods tomorrow.
DENISE: Somethin' happen?
DAVE: Yeah, kid brother in jail.
DENISE: Oh Jesus, what'd he do? He ain't no doper, is he?
DAVE: Saw him a pair of shoes he liked. Trouble was he didn't have no money to pay.
DENISE: Shopliftin'.
DAVE: That's what it was. Gotta go down and talk 'em in to lettin' me pay for 'em or get him on probation or somethin'.
DENISE: I expect you ain't goin' to have any luck.
DAVE: Why you say that?

DENISE: He ain't no white middle class rich boy. You think they gonna trust you bein' black and without no regular job?
DAVE: I got no record with them. Anyway, I'm gonna pay.
DENISE: What kinda shoes he steal?
DAVE: Rodney a basketball player. Prob'ly them kind of shoes.
DENISE: How much you think them kind of shoes cost?
DAVE: I don't know that.
DENISE: How much money you takin' to buy them shoes?
DAVE: Figure 50 dollars be enough.
DENISE: Lawd me, they gonna laugh in your face.
DAVE: That ain't enough?
DENISE: That ain't gonna be near enough, if it the kind of shoe I'm thinkin' about. I hear the white folks where I work complainin' about it. They had a kid tryin' out for the team last fall. Shoes he got cost over 100 dollars.
DAVE: Rodney ain't taken no shoes like that.
DENISE: Why not? If you ain't payin' might as well try to go first class.
DAVE: Can't pay that. I ain't got it. Maybe they take back the shoes, eh?
DENISE: They done taken back the shoes. Your kid brother is goin' to jail.
DAVE: You always got to look at the bad side, ain't ya? We'll work somethin' out. They ain't gonna send no 14-year-old kid to prison.
DENISE: Why ain't they?
DAVE: They just ain't, that's all.
DENISE: Your daddy goin' down with you?
DAVE: Daddy ain't livin'. And mama's had a bad sick spell. Can't look out for him no more. I'll have to bring the boy here. He can sleep on the couch. Ain't much room but we can manage. Get him straightened out. Show them cops I can do it. Get him here on Beech Street where there ain't no trouble. Save up and buy him them shoes. He ain't a bad kid, just wanted to play the game is all.
DENISE: They all want to play the goddamned game, but they don't go out and steal shoes to do it! Wake up, Big Dave, you got you a problem.
DAVE: That's you, all right. You always make things badder than they are.
DENISE: You got a suit and tie to wear?
DAVE: What I need that for?
DENISE: Do you got one?
DAVE: Got an old one in there somewhere.
DENISE: Got a tie?
DAVE: Got ties.
DENISE: What about a white shirt? You got a white shirt?
DAVE: Somewhere. From church days. What about it? What you doin' now?
DENISE: A suit, a tie, a white shirt, that's what you got to wear to the jail.
DAVE: To the jail?
DENISE: Yeah, to the jail.
DAVE: Why you say that?

DENISE: 'Cause if you go down there any other way, they ain't gonna give you the time of day. Prob'ly ain't gonna give you the time of day anyway, but that the chance you gotta take.
DAVE: You think I don't dress like that, they ain't gonna talk to me.
DENISE: That's right. If you want them middle class white folks to look beyond your skin, then you dress like they dress. You dress like them lawyers dress.
DAVE: I seen how they dress. Hell, they got money.
DENISE: Well, you got to look like you got money even if it look like less money.
DAVE: I got ya. It ain't me that speaks, it's money.
DENISE: It ain't money, you gotta *look* like money. Like you got some. Like you can pay your own way. You can't look like you down to beans and soup. Ain't none of those folks interested in anybody down to beans and soup. That's who they got in their damned jail so you might as well be in there with 'em, for all they care.
DAVE: I gotta be a chicken-eater, right?
DENISE: Well, you got my drift anyway.
DAVE: So you think maybe I'll get a better deal that way?
DENISE: I don't think no such thing. I think you get to *talk* to 'em that way and they *might* listen that way. Otherwise, you might as well not be there.
DAVE: Yeah, I see that. Well, the suit's all right. It hung up somewhere in the closet. Got a little hole in it, but no place you can notice it. Gotta tie that'll do all right. The shirt be a problem. It's all balled up somewhere in a drawer, I think.
DENISE: Ain't no problem with that. You go find it and you iron it smooth again.
DAVE (A beat): Iron it?
DENISE: Yeah... . What's the matter now?
DAVE: Nothin'.
DENISE: Uh huh. Never ironed nothin' in your life, have you?
DAVE: Can't say I have.
DENISE: And don't own no iron and don't have no ironin' board, right?
DAVE: Nah, don't have those things.
DENISE: So what you goin' to do? You goin' to wear a wrinkled up white shirt down to the jail, that what you goin' to do? (No answer). And you talk about my work bein' easy. (Mimics him). You come up on that roof and rap shingles for a day. You come down that gravel pit and sweat with me a day. Shit! You come over to my place of business and iron for me a day where it got to be perfect or my ass is chewed out.
DAVE: So what you want me to say, smart baby?
DENISE: I want you to say, "Denise, I pay you two dollars to iron that shirt for me."
DAVE: Two dollar!
DENISE: This is business, man, and my business day done ended. This be overtime.
DAVE: How 'bout them towel racks you want up. That gonna be two dollars 'cause my business day done ended, baby, and that is a fact.

DENISE: How much you reckon a chicken dinner's gonna cost you in one of them fast-food places? And how good you think it's gonna taste when put up against mine?

DAVE: You just think you got me comin' and goin', doncha?

DENISE: I don't think it, I know it.

DAVE: By damned that real estate man made the biggest mistake in the world lettin' you have that apart-mint. Ever thing goin' mighty smooth around here 'til you come along with all your big ideas.

DENISE: Yeah, I seen how smooth things was goin'. Your great boxin' career, for instance. And I seen how you finally got your ass out of that rockin' chair and done gone to work.

DAVE: You didn't have nothin' to do with that.

DENISE: Fine! So what's those big ideas I done come along with?

DAVE: Nothin', just forget it.

DENISE: Didn't do nothin' except stir up that pea brain of yours a little bit. That's what's botherin' you.

DAVE: Goddamn, woman, just leave me alone! And get out of my chair! That chair belong to me, understand!?

DENISE (She gets up): Take your damned chair, Big Dave. I got chicken to fry. You want that shirt ironed, you bring it and the two dollars upstairs to me. And you better move fast before I change my mind. (She goes in and slams the screen door).

DAVE (He stares after her, then slowly moves to the chair. He rocks): Crazy damned woman. Thinks she know ever thing. I gotta make a plan. (He stops rocking and pulls his wallet from his back pocket and pulls out two dollars). Two dollar! Damn-a-nation! Rodney, I'm gonna whip your ass! ... . No I ain't either. I ain't wearin' no suit and no tie and no white shirt to no jail house. (He puts the two dollars back in his pocket and begins rocking again). Ain't no woman gonna run Big Dave's life. Big Dave knows what to do cuz Big Dave's been doin' all this time. (He stops rocking and looks across the street at the upstairs window). You hear that, woman? You can quit watchin' behind that curtain. Big Dave is in charge of Big Dave and that's that.

BLACKOUT.

Scene 3

The scene is the same. Late afternoon several days later. DAVE is sitting in the rocking chair quite still looking out vacantly as though in a trance. After a beat or two DENISE appears and turns toward the house and up the porch steps. She moves very slowly, slumped over, very tired and discouraged. Neither one looks at the other. It is obvious that their relationship has cooled. DENISE goes inside the screen door, shutting it softly, unlike before. She disappears for a beat, then returns to the screen door and stands.

DENISE: Help me. (No answer). I need help. (A beat. She comes out the screen door). I need to talk to somebody.
DAVE: Don't see nobody else around but me.
DENISE: Well, you the somebody I need to talk to.
DAVE: Why's that?
DENISE: I don't know. Does it matter?
DAVE: Well, you've not spoke to me in some days now.
DENISE: No, it's you that's not spoke to me.
DAVE: Seem to me it was the other way around.
DENISE: Nah, you was mad about the two dollars I was goin' to charge you for ironin' that shirt.
DAVE: Wasn't mad.
DENISE: Yeah, you was.
DAVE: Said I wasn't mad.
DENISE: Well, you was.
DAVE: That what you want to talk to me about? Come out here to argue over that?
DENISE: Nah, that ain't it.
DAVE: Well, seem like it.
DENISE: Ain't seen him around. What was the boy's name? Rodney?
DAVE: That's right.
DENISE: Didn't come to stay with you, eh?
DAVE: Nah, went some place else to stay.
DENISE: Good. I'm glad he found him a place.
DAVE: Oh yeah.
DENISE (A beat): I done got myself fired from my best job today.
DAVE: Fired?
DENISE: Yeah.
DAVE: What did you do?
DENISE: Didn't do nothin'.
DAVE: Nothin'? Must've done somethin'.
DENISE (Tearing up): It was a accident.
DAVE: Acci-dint? What you talkin' about?
DENISE: Oh God!
DAVE: He didn't have nothin' to do with it.
DENISE: This ain't no time to be funny.
DAVE: No. You go ahead.
DENISE: Was cleanin' up the livin' room with the vacuum cleaner.
DAVE: Uh huh.
DENISE: You know the cord they got on them things, always gettin' tangled up, always where you don't want it to be.
DAVE: Yeah, they can be a mess. Don't own one myself.

DENISE: Well, I was doin' this big rug and got myself over to the corner by this end table. Well, this end table had this nice vase on it. Understand, I done vacuumed this rug, I done been in this same corner a hundred or two times. But this time that cord, it looped itself up on that end table and somehow got itself wrapped around that vase.
DAVE: That ain't good.
DENISE: Pulled that thing off and it smashed into a hundred pieces I bet.
DAVE: Well, what could you do? Couldn't be helped.
DENISE: That vase been in the family over a hundred years, they say. Go back before the Civil War.
DAVE: Back in slave time, eh?
DENISE: Back then. She say it priceless. Over 500 hundred dollars.
DAVE: Who she?
DENISE: Miz Braxton, the lady I works for. Used to work for.
DAVE: If it be priceless, how come it got a price on it?
DENISE: That be the price I got to pay.
DAVE: Price you got to pay?
DENISE (Tears begin to come): Yeah, to keep my job I gotta pay them five hundred dollars for breakin' that vase.
DAVE: You ain't got five hundred dollars.
DENISE: Nah, I ain't got five hundred dollars. They was gonna take some out of my pay each week.
DAVE: It was a acci-dint.
DENISE: Nah, they say I was careless. They say I wasn't payin' attention to what I was doin'. I was payin' attention. I was cleanin' that damned rug. I was doin' what I paid to do and was doin' it right. And that old cord just up and flipped around that vase. A heirloom, they called it.
DAVE: I don't know what that is.
DENISE: Means it's valuable. Means it's been in the family for all them years.
DAVE: All the way back to slave time.
DENISE: Yeah, and I wouldn't be surprised if they had some the way they treats me. But they pays well. It's my best job. The rest of 'em just piddlin' jobs when you put it up against this one. Lawd, I don't know what to do now, Big Dave.
DAVE: You say you fired?
DENISE: Told 'em I couldn't afford to pay them no five hundred dollars. They say either pay the five hundred dollars or get out. Didn't even pay me for what I done today.
DAVE: What you gonna do?
DENISE: I don't know.
DAVE: You can find you some other place to work.
DENISE: You wanna work for rich folks like them, they gotta know all about you. Gotta show your whole history. Miz Braxton ain't gonna give me no reference. Hell, she gonna pass the word along to all her rich friends that I careless and sassy.

DAVE: Sassy?
DENISE: I got mad when she told me what I had to do for breakin' that vase.
DAVE: You got a sharp tongue.
DENISE: Well, I used it, damnit. Wisht I could cut it out.
DAVE: Nah you don't.
DENISE: Yes I do. Ain't nothin' to do now but go sling hash for the minimum now. Can't keep this place on your Beech Street if I have to do that.
DAVE: You could clean my place.
DENISE: Oh boy, big deal. And how much you gonna pay me for it?
DAVE: Two dollar.
DENISE: You a funny man, Big Dave. You know just what to say.
DAVE: You'll do okay. Tomorrow morning you'll just pick yourself up and get on out there.
DENISE: Will I? Just how many more days and years have I got to be doing that? Just spinnin' my wheels, Big Dave, and ain't goin' nowhere.
DAVE: You is discouraged.
DENISE: Tell me about it.
DAVE: Gotta keep goin'.
DENISE: Who says?
DAVE: Don't nobody say, you just do.
DENISE: And what if you don't do? What if you decide you ain't goin' to do no more?
DAVE: I don't have no answer for that.
DENISE: You die, that's what. And maybe that ain't a bad idea.
DAVE (He gets up): What you talkin' about, girl?
DENISE: What you callin' me "girl"? Ain't I your baby anymore?
DAVE: You done lost your senses.
DENISE: I ain't lost my senses. I lost my job, my income, my hope for nothin'. I work hard, Big Dave, and try to do it good and what's to show for it?
DAVE: You no different from anybody else.
DENISE: You mean I ain't no different from you and people like you. How about them Braxtons? How come they got it all and we got nothin'? How come you ain't heavy weight champion of the world? Somebody's got to be.
DAVE: I would like to be.
DENISE: But you ain't.
DAVE: You don't get ever thing you want.
DENISE: What about anything? Do you get anything you want that's really worth anything?
DAVE: Ain't we talked enuff for one time?
DENISE: I done worn you out with my troubles. Worn myself out. I'm just gonna sit down on these steps and have a good cry.
DAVE: You ain't gonna cry.
DENISE: Who says I ain't?
DAVE: You too tough.

DENISE: Soft and stupid. (She sits on the steps).
DAVE (He gets up from chair and joins her on the steps): Didn't tell you ever thing.
DENISE: Didn't tell me everything about what? What you talkin' about?
DAVE: Talkin' about the boy.
DENISE: What boy?
DAVE: Rodney. He ain't stayin' no other place. He in jail.
DENISE (A beat): That don't surprise me.
DAVE: Wasn't no white ironed shirt gonna help neither.
DENISE: Didn't say it would. Said it might.
DAVE: That judge out to skin that boy's ass. Give him two year in detention center.
DENISE: He stole. He got to be made an example of.
DAVE: For sure he ain't to be playin' no basketball for a time.
DENISE: He be worse when he come out.
DAVE: He a good boy. Just made a mistake. Rodney be all right.
DENISE: He be worse.
DAVE: Why you say that, woman? Always look at the bad side.
DENISE: Cuz I seen it. I seen what they become cooped up with riff-raff all that time. Some smart ass who become a leader telling 'em how he done stashed his wad on the outside and all he's got to do to git it is serve a bit of time. You come out and you see me and I git you your stash. Course he don't tell 'em that to get that stash they gonna get caught and serve a little bit more time and a little bit more until there ain't no time left.
DAVE: Rodney too smart for that.
DENISE: It ain't got nothin' to do with bein' smart. It's the riff-raff. They in charge, so you do one thing, then that lead to another and you theirs.
DAVE: How you know all this?
DENISE: Cuz I seen 'em when they come out. They call those places correction schools. They ain't nothing but misdirection places. I swear, Big Dave, you done lived on Beech Street too long. Been watching trees and squirrels too long. Oughta get yourself over to my old street and live there for a while. That's the world, not these trees and squirrels. Lawd, Lawd, it is peaceful, though.
DAVE: What can I do?
DENISE: Do? About what?
DAVE: 'Bout Rodney. He my kid brother. Made a mistake.
DENISE: Made a mistake, that sounds familiar. If it ain't shoes, it's vacuum cords.
DAVE: I'll go talk to the boy.
DENISE: Riff-raff got six days of talking to your one. Who you think is gonna win that one?
DAVE: You sayin' it ain't no use.
DENISE: Just givin' you the odds.
DAVE: Forget about him. Just put him on the garbage heap, like you done.
DENISE: That was real ugly, Dave. I never shouldda told you how all that happened. (She moves to the far end of the porch). Told you why I done that.

DAVE (He follows her): I gotta have some hopes, ain't I!? Ever thing I say, you put down. I trapped. I never been trapped before. Even the boxing thing, I just pick up my duds and go on. Since you come, ever where I turn it's a trap.
DENISE: Who says you gotta listen to me, eh? I ain't obligated to put no sugar in your tea, big boy. I just lost my good payin' job today and here you want me to be the good news lady for you. Boy, you somethin' else.
DAVE (Frustrated, he yells at her): I got to tell the boy to do what he gotta do!
DENISE (She yells back): How he gonna do what he got to do when he ain't got nothin' to do it with!
DAVE (He slams into the rocking chair his fists tight against its arms): Somethin' inside. There gotta be somethin' inside that tell him.
DENISE (A beat): We ain't all like you, Big Dave. Come a time when we just gives up.
DAVE: That ain't you, sister.
DENISE: You the ugly bastard that just brought up the time that I did.
DAVE: That survivin', that ain't givin' up.
DENISE: That what it was? How come I didn't know that? How come it never come into my mind? It was bein' smooth, it was bein' clever. It was gettin' revenge on what the law won't touch. I never thought about nothin' else—'til later. I was cool on every move—not like little brother, Mr. Hot-Shot shoes. See, they gets away with that shit all the time—only sometimes they don't. They gets careless, not cool. Do stuff like that you got to be terrified—like me. But don't nobody know 'cept me, so I settle my panic and turn cool and clever and get it all done. Then I lie down and gives up. (She sits down on the steps).
DAVE: But you didn't. You come to Beech Street lookin' for better.
DENISE: Didn't find it.
DAVE (A beat): Want the rocker?
DENISE: Your rocker. You always tellin' me that.
DAVE: Willin' to give it up—for a time.
DENISE: Ain't good enough. I want it forever.
DAVE: Well, you ain't gettin' it forever. You gettin' it for a time. (He stands).
DENISE: Sit down. I don't want your damned rocker. You act like it medicine or somethin'.
DAVE: It is. For my back, for my legs, for my arms, for my head.
DENISE (A beat): Maybe that be a good idea.
DAVE: What idea? What you talkin' about now?
DENISE: You talkin' to the boy.
DAVE: It like you said. I can't run up with the riff-raff. They got six days to my one.
DENISE: Yeah, but you bigger than them. He seen you box?
DAVE: Sure he seen me. Seen my best fight.
DENISE: There you go.
DAVE: Seen me take a dive, too. He come after me after that. You know cryin' and all and beatin' his fist in my belly.

DENISE: He knew.
DAVE: Couldda beat that fella with one arm behind me.
DENISE: He see how big you are and what you are inside. Won't take him long.
DAVE: Won't take him long to what?
DENISE: To start puttin' you up side that small-time riff-raff.
DAVE: He'd see I'm bigger.
DENISE: He'd see you're better.
DAVE: Seen me box.
DENISE (She stands): Ah, c'mon, Big Dave, that ain't the reason. You better than them. You walk in to see that boy and he look up to you and he see better.
DAVE (A beat): You want this chair or not?
DENISE: I'll take it now.
DAVE (He gets up): Remember now, it ain't forever.
DENISE: Ain't nothin' for forever.
DAVE: Yours 'til you find the next job.
DENISE: That might be forever. (She sits in the rocker).
DAVE: Ain't gonna be forever.
DENISE (She leans forward in the chair): You like me in spite of everything, don't you, Big Dave?
DAVE: Never said that.
DENISE: Then I guess I ain't your baby — ain't what you call me.
DAVE: Call lotsa women that.
DENISE: Do you now? Just one of them Don Juan fellows you hear about.
DAVE: It just an expression. Don't have no meaning to it.
DENISE: I get you. All us women is babies, that what you mean?
DAVE: See, there you go. Ain't nobody gonna put you down. Tears a minute ago, now you already fixin' to pick another fight.
DENISE: Maybe I shouldda been the boxer, 'stead of you.
DAVE (He chuckles): Maybe you right.
DENISE: But can't no *baby* be a boxer. Babies is weak and soft and triflin', ain't that right?
DAVE: Done told you it an expression. Call a fella "man", call a girl "baby." Just the way it's done.
DENISE: Well, the way it's done ain't pleasin' to this girl's ears, boy. You hear me talkin', boy?
DAVE (A beat): This "boy" got the message.
DENISE: You is a bright fella. (She rocks). You never did answer my question.
DAVE: What question? I don't remember no question. You so busy with your games about who to call what, I done forgot.
DENISE: You ain't forgot.
DAVE: Ain't decided.
DENISE: Give me your rocker.
DAVE: Done told you, it ain't forever.

DENISE (She rocks. A beat): Gonna be a pretty sunset this day.
DAVE: Look like it.
DENISE: Preacher's wife up there.
DAVE: She usually there this time of day when I'm sittin'.
DENISE: Watchin' over us. Soon be dark, though. Then she can't see nothin'. Won't know what happened. Me and you be the only ones that know.
DAVE: Do what we want.
DENISE: Yeah. Then tomorrow come and we do what they want.
DAVE: Well, tomorrow ain't here yet.
DENISE: No, it sure ain't. (She rocks). This here is a fine rockin' chair, I must say. Could prob'ly rock here forever.
DAVE: Well, it ain't forever, you remember that.
DENISE (She laughs): I hear ya, Big Dave. Got a rhythm to it. You know, like a dance.
DAVE: Like a dance. Never thought of it that way. You right, like a dance.
DENISE: You ever danced all night, Big Dave? I mean 'til the sun come out?
DAVE: Yeah. But it been a while. A long while.
DENISE: That's so.
DAVE: I know a place, though.
DENISE: Do you?
DAVE: Wanna go there sometime?
DENISE: Nah, I'd just be another one of your babies.
DAVE: I'd jus' be another of your boys, I reckon.

They both laugh. She stops rocking and points out. The SUN sets.

DENISE (She points up). There it go.
DAVE: Preacher's wife ain't gonna know nothin' now. Jus' me and you.
DENISE: That's right, just me and you. (She rocks slowly).

They watch as the LIGHTS slowly dim to darkness.

METAMORPHOSIS

A Play in One-Act

CHARACTERS

MARTY WILLIAMS — a fine actress in her 20's, boyish in attitude and movement, in love with Beth

BETH LEONARD — A teacher in her 20's, beautiful, feminine, vulnerable, in love with Marty

KEVIN LOCKRIDGE — coach and teacher in his late 20's, handsome, virile, but gentle and perceptive, in love with Beth

THE SETTING

A box set of a living area in a small modern apartment in a suburban Virginia city. A large curtained window is in the stage right wall and a hallway is up stage right leading to an unseen room. The kitchen is up center right. The kitchen appliances are not seen — only the back wall of cabinets through a high open counter that overlooks the living area. Up left is Marty's bookcase and a coat closet in the back wall. The entrance to the apartment is upstage in the left wall and Beth's bookcase is down left of the door. Most of the decoration in the living area is pretty and delicate reflecting Beth's taste. The time is the present.

Metamorphosis

The large window stage right in the apartment has a lovely bright white curtain that is closed now. Below it is a window seat with a delicate flower cover over it. MARTY's bookcase up left in the back wall is cluttered with acting versions of plays and stage pictures of MARTY, both on the shelves and the wall above: MARTY as Hedda Gabler, as Medea, as a very old lady bent over a cane, as Ophelia, as St. Joan. There is also one framed play poster from college, advertising MEDEA, starring MARTY WILLIAMS.

Downstage left below the door is another bookcase, dominated by history books, novels, books of poetry and decorating books. Above the bookcase on the wall are prints of a variety of flowers, very delicate, very tasteful and colorful. This is BETH's corner of the room, very pretty, neat and tidy.

Downstage left of center is a sofa, the cover—like the window seat—representing BETH's delicate touch and design. In front of the sofa is a trunk-like box, nicely finished in brown stain, which serves as a coffee table. The coffee table is cluttered at the moment with MARTY's scripts, notepads, cigarettes, filled ashtray, etc. Center and right is an armchair that matches the sofa cover, again tastefully done.

When the LIGHTS come up MARTY is seated on the sofa with pages of manuscript spread out in her lap, on the sofa and coffee table. Some have spilled over on to the floor. MARTY WILLIAMS, in her early 20s, is tall, rather thin with virtually no bosom. She describes herself as a "fence post" and the description is nearly accurate. She wears faded jeans and shirt with an old pull-over sweater over the shirt. She wears either sneakers or loafers. Her hair is cut very short. Her movements are boyish and unfeminine, but seem natural for her. She is an addicted smoker and a careless one, aiming her ashes for the ashtray but often missing. At present, the ashtray is almost overflowing with cigarette butts. MARTY is attempting to concentrate on some pages from a looseleaf notebook (her promptbook), but her mind is elsewhere.

BETH enters at the apartment door in an exuberant rush. She deposits books and papers on the bookcase by the door. While talking, she will take off her light spring coat and hang it in the coat closet. The dress she is wearing is very professional looking, but also very feminine and colorful. She is a teacher just home from school and clearly in high spirits. She is a very beautiful woman in her early 20s.

BETH (As she enters): Oh wow, what a day! What a fantastic day! Almost spring out there. I can't wait!
MARTY (Without looking up): It is, is it?

BETH (Hanging her coat in the closet): You should see! Birds singing, daffodils, dandelions, wild onions, all the good spring stuff.

MARTY: Haven't been out.

BETH (She crosses to the window right): There are even a couple of fat, fuzzy dandelions peeking through the cracks in the sidewalk in front of the apartment. (She opens the window curtains fully, depositing her handbag on the window seat). How can you stand to keep this closed?

MARTY: Your dandelions won't survive. Charlie's got a weed-eater. He's very proud of his weed-eater.

BETH (She laughs): Oh, I know. He's going to go insane trying to catch them all. I think he must hate nature. Do you suppose all grounds-keepers secretly hate nature?

MARTY: Better to have him just the way he is.

BETH: Yeah, just look across the street at that other place. Charlie's a neat keeper, all right. What do you say we take a walk later? (She crosses to the kitchen area). Right now I've got to have a tea with lots of lemon and ice. It's almost that warm. I'll just pretend it is. You want a tea?

MARTY: I want a bourbon and water, you know that. And I want a kiss.

BETH (Preparing her water for tea): Those kids today! Honestly, so restless! Oh, it's definitely in the air. And it's going to get worse before it gets better. We'll need air-conditioning before it's over except that there isn't any.

MARTY: One must suffer while learning, my dear, you know that.

BETH: That's old Aeschylus, right? Well, the problem here is that the tax-payers are just too cheap when it comes to schools. They all talk about the big need for education and then leave everything for the teachers to do.

MARTY: Everything from testing to toilet training to bus duty, right? Just hush, you love it.

BETH: Well, I'll have to think of something soon before the weather gets too hot. Hey, maybe I'll do a little creative dramatics. What do you think?

MARTY: Yes, do that. Take them out in a thunderstorm and show them how Ben Franklin discovered lightning.

BETH (She laughs delighted, then feigns a gruffy voice): You mean — "Exterminate the brutes!" What an idea! No, actually, I'd just like something upbeat for the end of the year. Maybe we could do a bit from *1776*. The constitutional debate or something.

MARTY: What are you going to do, teach them to be radicals like the founding fathers?

BETH: Oh boy, the parents would love that. Telling Virginia kids that Thomas Jefferson was a radical. Their parents would have a fit. Ha, I wouldn't dare. Anyway, he wasn't really a radical, you know.

MARTY: No, you wouldn't dare. Are you telling me it's nearly May and you've only gotten to the constitutional convention?

BETH: You know better than that. You know I've been reading all this stuff about the

Vietnam war. Boy, that is one helluva way to end their second half of American History. But I got behind. Maybe the last day I'll just skip to the millennium.
MARTY: Well, there's not much Yankee Doodle stuff you can teach when it comes to that war.
BETH: I know. And I want them to leave the course with some positive feelings about their country. You know, that things can be done and that they can help do them.
MARTY: But think of all the juicy roles they could play from that period. Lyndon Johnson showing the press his scar from the operation.
BETH: Oh, Marty.
MARTY: You could show them all those naked and bloody pictures of children running down the road.
BETH: You're being dreadful.
MARTY: Isn't that what Professor Ramsey showed us in class?
BETH: Now there's your radical. He marched in the sixties when he was a student.
MARTY: I remember one day he played the music from *Hair*. Hey, there's an idea. You could get your kids to do something from *Hair*.
BETH: What are you trying to do, get me fired?
MARTY: Well, it's theatrical. Oh well, I guess things have changed, haven't they?
BETH: Yes, they have. Quite a bit.
MARTY: Well, I was just trying to be helpful. Dear me, what ever happened to the old Bill of Rights and Freedom of Speech. The good old American way.
BETH: You're being very sarcastic today. And you're not being very helpful. I'm sorry I brought it up.
MARTY: Well, it might help if I got a kiss in the good old American way.
BETH: In a minute. I'm boiling water. You must be working on rehearsal for tonight.
MARTY: Yes, I've made quite a mess, haven't I? Sorry about that.
BETH: Okay, next you'll be calling me a neat freak, right? Some mood you're in today, I can tell.
MARTY: Really? The truth is I'm speculating as to whether or not Leslie Markham has a soul as well as a body.
BETH: She's still doing her wiggle, is she? (Kidding her). She just wants you to admire her curves.
MARTY: She doesn't care a shit for me. But you can bet she wants Joe Bostic to admire her. And she's succeeding. That's fine with me outside the play, but now he's starting to develop an on-stage stutter. Last night Leslie wore shorts for the first time. I'm certain the cheeks of her ass were frostbitten. As for Joe, he couldn't keep his eyes off her. *He* was sweating.
BETH: Maybe you need to establish some sort of dress code for rehearsal — at least for her.
MARTY: This isn't your public schools, Beth. At least, not quite. It's hard enough getting everybody to rehearsal at the same time and on time. Presumably these are supposed to be mature people.

BETH: Then you're not the least bit jealous of Leslie?
MARTY: Are you trying to make me throw up? I could use that drink.
BETH: In a minute.
MARTY (She stands and crosses downstage left): Good God, how did I get into this damned community theatre thing anyway? Leslie belongs in a magazine centerfold, not on stage. And that damnable Board of Directors, they want me to cut out every single four-letter word in the script.
BETH: These days if you did that, you wouldn't have much script left.
MARTY: Please, no good old phony American puritanism this afternoon. How come you dragged me into this concrete shopping mall suburbia anyway?
BETH: It was quite simple, wasn't it? You didn't have a job and I did.
MARTY: Yeah, simple. I didn't have you in the city. Without you my acting career was a bust.
BETH: Listen, with or without me, your acting career was a bust. You didn't stay up there long enough to give it a chance. It's going to take time, Marty, you know that. And you can't get discouraged. You're a super actress and you know it.
MARTY: I'm an out-of-work actress, I know that.
BETH: Well, that's nothing new, is it? You just keep looking for opportunities, just as you've been doing here. You'll know when to make your move this time. And one day—New York, here I am! (This last accompanied by an elaborate gesture).
MARTY: Only if you are with me.
BETH (She stops her fixing and looks at her): You mustn't say that. You must never hold back because of me. You can't allow that to happen.
MARTY: But when the time comes, we'll make the decision, won't we?
BETH: It's *your* decision and neither love or money or circumstances or—anything or person must hold you back.
MARTY: I'll remember that. Not trying to get rid of me, are you?
BETH: Mar-ty! You drive me up the wall when you say things like that.
MARTY: You mean when I wallow. (She slumps down on the sofa).
BETH: Yes, when you wallow, as you put it. Sometimes your moods ...
MARTY: A good drink would likely bring me up, among other things.
BETH: Give me a break, will ya? I just got in. This burner, I'm not sure the water will ever boil!
MARTY: If I need a drink, why don't I get up and get it myself? Same with a kiss.
BETH: Because I always get it—and love doing it.
MARTY: You do it right, too. If I fix it I make it so strong I get myself stewed, trashed. Everything to the extreme, that's me. Seems like God and I are at war all the time.
BETH (Fixing her drink): Ha, what about the devil?
MARTY: How many times must I tell you, the devil doesn't exist except as an excuse. No, it's God who is always putting the pressure on—tempting you to greatness year to year, or day to day, or moment to moment. Wears you out. How I resist Him! Always too afraid to take a real risk. Or too dull inside to see

a shining promise. There are moments when He reaches me, though—tempts me mightily to get off my rear-end and resume the struggle. Good times, those. Don't last very long, though.
BETH (She hands her her drink): Shall we drink to God and those all-encompassing moments?
MARTY: Don't laugh at me.
BETH: You know I'm not.
MARTY: You've the wrong potion there. God requires strong drink. You will, however, kiss me, won't you—now that I've finally got you close to me.
BETH: Of course.

They kiss. MARTY's kiss is fervent; BETH's much more restrained.

MARTY: My sun's out now.
BETH: Well, if you'd open the curtains …
MARTY: It has nothing to do with curtains. I've been brooding all day. Something unsettling within me and I can't find out what it is. Do you suppose you could help me find out what it is?
BETH: Well, you've certainly smoked enough. Look at this ashtray, and you taste and smell of rancid tobacco. (She takes the ashtray and crosses to the kitchen area and empties it).
MARTY: I've always smoked. I've always tasted whatever way I taste. You must have noticed before.
BETH (Back with the ashtray): It seems stronger today.
MARTY: As compared to whom?
BETH: As compared to you.
MARTY: I suppose others smell minty and medicinal.
BETH (She sets the ashtray on the coffee table): I wouldn't know. What difference does it make?
MARTY: Well, it was you who made the criticism. Just trying to respond. You were spring air to me.
BETH: I was *not* spring air. No one is. It's why we have all those—concoctions.
MARTY: Minty and medicinal. From now on I'm gargling with bourbon first thing in the morning. (She takes her drink and begins gargling).
BETH (She laughs): Marty! That's awful! You're certainly making a big deal of this, really!
MARTY: Now I am neither minty, medicinal or rancid. You can kiss me.
BETH (She laughs again): Hell no. I never get drunk in the afternoon.
MARTY: Criticism, love, creates self-awareness. As you can see, I have endeavored to correct my error. Is this my reward?
BETH: You're ignoring the real problem—smoking.
MARTY: Is that the real problem?
BETH: Brood, brood, brood, no matter what anybody might do, you'd brood. There's no way anyone could make you happy.

MARTY: Happy?
BETH (She sighs): Right. Oh dear me—let us just say—contented, then.
MARTY: You make me contented, Beth. Make no mistake about that. I guess smoking does, too—occasionally. And it's a lot easier to gargle with bourbon than to kick certain kinds of addictions. (She takes her hand).
BETH (She pulls her hand away): I don't know what to do with you and your beastly moods.
MARTY: Something unsettling within me.
BETH: All right. We can at least take that walk, can't we? Let's get out of here and get some fresh air. A quick trip around the block.
MARTY: You're just all spring-time today, aren't you? A spring in your step, a spring in your heart, eh? Loving your restless kids in school and what else? Experiencing joy—right?
BETH: You carry things too far, as usual. But yes, I do feel good. Spring is a very good time, is it not?
MARTY: I said experiencing joy.
BETH: Okay, sure, why not? Happens to me every spring.
MARTY: Does it?
BETH: I think so. I have no way of measuring it.
MARTY: I do because I'm in love with you. Don't you measure me? My moods. My mood today, for instance?
BETH: I usually can, but not always.
MARTY: I can always measure you. But measure isn't the right word, is it? It's much too precise.
BETH: You're setting one of your little traps, aren't you? It's to prove to me that you love me more than I love you.
MARTY: Is that what I'm doing? Not very clever, am I?
BETH: That's the thing—why would you want to be clever with me?
MARTY: Will you be coming with me to rehearsal tonight?
BETH: I've got to do my homeroom attendance forms for April, else the principal's office will be all over me tomorrow. Forms, forms! I'm sick of forms. I just want to teach.
MARTY: You haven't been in over a week now. You've lost the thread of it.
BETH: Ha! And missed all the wiggles, too.
MARTY: The director needs her best critic.
BETH: You put too much stock in that. You're the one who has the instinct for it, not I. I'm just your sounding board.
MARTY: Yes, and that's why I need you there.
BETH: I know. I got behind in my preparations and papers. And there's so much to read about the damned Vietnam war.
MARTY: You went out last night.
BETH (A half-beat as she looks at her): Yes. For a while. How did you know that? You were at rehearsal.
MARTY: I forgot the music tapes for the show. I brought them here night before

last to listen to. You haven't heard them yet. Would you like to hear the music I've chosen for the show?

BETH: What time did you come back?

MARTY: Does it matter?

BETH: No, not really.

MARTY: Maybe you should ask, how long did I stay?

BETH: What are you suggesting?

MARTY: Nothing. It's your business. If it had anything to do with me, you'd tell me because you love me. Am I right about that?

BETH (She takes her hands in her own): You know I love you. You know I do.

MARTY (She looks at her hands, then at her): So lovely. You're so lovely—inside and out.

BETH: You, too.

MARTY: Not like you. I'm not soft like you. I'm all bone. A fence post. Practically no boobs at all. Old Chuck-face had to pad me for every role I played.

BETH: He loved you, too.

MARTY: Yes, because I was tough. I'd be willing to jump through all his hoops, accept any challenge.

BETH: It wasn't toughness. It was what you were, what you could do and what you were willing to try.

MARTY: We did all of that good work on a shoestring. How did we manage it?

BETH: We killed ourselves, that's how. With Chuck cracking the old whip, of course.

MARTY: Those shitheads gave him nothing and we'd go out and create miracles for them. What a college. How in God's name did we end up there?

BETH: I don't know. All I know is that we were happy there.

MARTY: Yes. Not contented—happy. You know I don't think Chuck had any idea about us until the night we put on those matching tuxedos for that cast party.

BETH: Oh, I'm pretty sure he knew. He just didn't care. He knew that in you he had a real actress to work with. That was what he cared about.

MARTY: Oh, don't think you weren't a part of it. I saw how he looked at you. Why, you broke his heart. Beautiful Beth would have no man to love her, only a fence post.

BETH: You're making that up. You were the one who interested him. You were the one with the talent.

MARTY: Oh come on, Beth, I saw how he looked at you. There is the business of the world and then there are dreams. You made his heart ache, his pants itch, but of course he knew he couldn't have you at 20 or at 40 years.

BETH: So you're saying that when it came to me old Chuck had a dirty mind.

MARTY: Not at all. I'm saying he dreamed. Maybe you would have liked what he dreamed.

BETH: None of this ever occurred to me. I know I liked him. And I noticed that whenever you needed anything, he was there. I thought that in his mind I was kind of like a parenthesis mark.

MARTY: He knew that whatever he did for me, it was for you as well.

BETH: I don't believe that. He was devoted to you.

MARTY: Believe what you wish. If there was any doubt about us those matching tux we wore to the cast party brought us out of the closet. Remember how they looked at us? Or rather—how they didn't look at us, averting their eyes as they talked and danced.

BETH: What difference could it make? They all knew anyway.

MARTY: I suppose they did. But this was a graphic presentation of what they knew. There were others, you know, not so brave as we were.

BETH: No, I didn't know. I remember that night for other reasons.

MARTY: Yes, yes, the little blond. What *was* her name?

BETH: You slipped out with her, and when she came back to the party her hair was all mussed and she was confused and breathless.

MARTY: She was like a child. She hardly knew what was happening. It was a mistake for both of us. I'm glad it happened, though. It made me appreciate you as never before.

BETH: Believe me, I wasn't glad it happened.

MARTY: The worst thing was not telling you—even though I knew you knew. To try to go on as if nothing had happened. And you did the same. It wasn't right, was it?

BETH: No. (She moves away from her upstage). Let's just not talk about it anymore, okay?

MARTY: A lack of honesty. A lack of trust. Thank God we managed to get through it. I think we learned our lesson, don't you?

BETH (Her back to her): Yes.

MARTY (Watching her): Do you think old Dr. Chuck knew about her, too?

BETH: I don't know. What difference does it make?

MARTY: I suspect that he did. Some of the kids thought him one of those egghead intellectuals. But I knew better—I saw him intimately from the stage. Oh, he was dying to have one of you girls in his bed.

BETH (Angrily): How can you say that about him? He wasn't like that at all—about me or anyone else. And he loved you dearly and he was so good to you.

MARTY: He was a man, Beth, not a damned god. He never wanted that from me, certainly. Other things he wanted from me. We were in another realm. I was his star. I could play his old lady from my gut. I could be her. I am still her. She is a part of me forever.

BETH (She is at the book case now looking at the picture of Marty as the old lady): He made you be her by telling you that you couldn't do it.

MARTY: Yes. Another hoop to jump through. He knew my insides. Oh, I knew he was a man, all right, but for me he *was* a damned god, always picking at me, searching for a touch of greatness. It would have been easier if he had been after me with his prick. That way I could have kicked him in the balls and that would have been it.

BETH (She sinks into the chair unhappily): Oh Marty, what a thing to say. How demeaning to him—to you. He adored you.
MARTY: Right. I'm being nasty, a trifle excessive, eh, love?
BETH: Yes!
MARTY: It's because everything was so great then. Our problems were small ones, no matter how big they looked at the time. Why must we grow up, Beth? To taste such joy and grow up to this. You in your classroom and me in my damned community theatre. How empty it all seems in comparison.
BETH: You seem to forget, I was your props person, your wardrobe mistress, your—whatever. That wasn't particularly thrilling or rewarding—except, of course, watching how you used what I had made or put there for you. That was the joy of it for me.
MARTY: After the show you'd come back flushed with tears. I thought it meant a great deal to you.
BETH: It did, because it was you.
MARTY: And how we made love then. That wasn't fulfillment? That wasn't thrilling?
BETH: Yes. Yes! But don't you see, it all came from you—what you had done. I had done nothing really but share a little of your light. Now I have something, too, my kids. That comes from me. I'm their star.
MARTY (She turns away): That's not the same.
BETH (She stands): Why not the same?
MARTY: You know why not.
BETH: It isn't like theatre, Marty. It's not the same kind of emotional high.
MARTY (She looks at her): Oh bullshit! Are you in love or not? That's the high. The light, as you put it, doesn't come from you or me, but from that.
BETH: All right, we could make love right now. But would it be the same as it was after one of your performances? Are you that charged up now? Am I flushed with tears?
MARTY: We're quarreling.
BETH: We're not quarreling. I'm simply trying to show you that there is a difference now. I'm in a work-a-day world, not an imagined act. You can't be a star every minute of the day, nine months out of the year.
MARTY: You're being defensive.
BETH: No, you just don't want to hear what I'm saying. It's one of your days and you just want to brood.
MARTY: It's like my smoking you complain about. You can't look at the real problem either.
BETH: Oh, I'm going to take a walk around the block. Do you want to come along?
MARTY: I've work to do. (She crosses to the sofa and sits).
BETH (She looks at her a beat, about to say something, but thinks better of it): All right. (She picks up her glass and crosses to the kitchen area and puts it down and starts for the door).
MARTY (Looking straight out): Aren't you going to take a coat or sweater?

BETH: It's not that cold.
MARTY: You wore a coat this morning. You know you catch cold easily. Last fall you were in bed a week and—you're a very delicate person, you know. You're—a kind of butterfly. A beautiful multi-colored butterfly that flits before my eyes moment to moment—whether you're here or not.
BETH (Very moved, she speaks gently): Oh Marty ...
MARTY (Half turning toward her, but not looking at her): I couldn't bear it, you know, if something came along and crushed you—or—or metamorphosed you. That happens to all butterflies—but only once. I metamorphosed you. Helped, I hope, make you the beautiful thing you are today. Made a place for you by my side.
BETH (She has moved downstage near her at the end of the sofa): I know that, Marty.
MARTY (She looks at her): We were freshman, remember?
BETH (She kneels beside her): How could I forget?
MARTY (She smiles as she remembers): Little babes who knew almost nothing. We just flew into each other's arms without really knowing why that first time. Both of us just out of the nest, lonely and lost. My, how we cried with remorse that first time, hovering together in our shame. But it was so lovely, so spontaneous—and we were warm inside and wanted each other. How could such joy be sin?
BETH: It wasn't, Marty, it wasn't.
MARTY: Who else was reaching out to us? Who else wanted us? All your boys getting in line to try and feel you up with their clumsy hands. And of course no one for this fence post of a body. Ha! Who wants a girl with no boobs? No beer-breathed kid thrust his tongue down my throat, thank God. You poor dear, what you had to go through. I found a butterfly about to be crushed and saved her. I saved you, love, isn't that what you said?
BETH (She throws her arms around her and holds her tightly): Oh Marty! Oh God! Oh God!
MARTY: What is it, butterfly, tell me what it is?
BETH: Nothing, nothing! I just love you so.
MARTY (She breaks the embrace): Sin, all sin. Just barely tolerated, you know. My tongue between your lovely thighs that first time. Nasty business.
BETH (She jumps to her feet): Stop that! Oh God, how dare you treat us that way! (She moves to the bookcase down left, leaning against it). How could you? There was no sin! I won't have you destroy what we've had together. (Weeping, she sinks to her knees). How could you? Why? Why!
MARTY (She stares at her a half-beat, then goes to her): I'm sorry, butterfly. That was ugly of me.
BETH: Yes! How could you do that!?
MARTY: It just came out. For some reason, I had to remind myself of what we've meant to each other—in spite of everything. The abuse, the—never mind. Are you all right?
BETH: I'm humiliated! ... I'm too—I'll be all right, yes.

MARTY (She helps her up, her arm around her): Please forgive me. Am I forgiven?
BETH: I shouldn't be — blubbering like this. I should be able to — you shouldn't have said something like that. I ...
MARTY: Right, I know, love. Go for that walk. The fresh air will do you good.
BETH: No, I have to stay here with you now.
MARTY: No, no, I'll just go with you, if you like. Around the block. But only if you promise to wear a sweater.
BETH (She sinks down on the sofa): I don't feel like it now.
MARTY: Oh damn me. I've ruined your spring day, haven't I? You were so happy when you came in.
BETH: Let's just not talk about it anymore. Where are the damned tissues?
MARTY: The bedroom. I'll get some for you. (She goes off upstage right at the hall).

BETH cannot control her tears. She puts her face in her hands and weeps. MARTY returns with a handful of tissues, stops a beat above the sofa to observe her, then brings the tissues to her. She pulls BETH's hands from her face and gently places the tissues in them.

MARTY: Just blow away, dear. Quickly now, just blow it all away.
BETH: Yes. (She blows her nose vigorously with resolution, trying to gain control).
MARTY: Hmm, a nice little fog horn we have here.
BETH: Oh hush.
MARTY: To hell with your attendance log, why don't you come with me to rehearsal tonight?
BETH (She looks at her a beat, forgetting the tissues): Marty. (She suddenly throws her arms around her).
MARTY (She holds her tightly): Yes, love. I'm waiting.
BETH: You know, don't you.
MARTY: Yes, love, I know. You've been so restless at night. You seem half with me, half not there at all these past weeks. Love *can* measure things, Beth. The spring of the step, the spring of the year. Now an actress can play games with passion.
BETH: But I'm not an actress.
MARTY: No, and you've drifted away.
BETH: I love you.
MARTY: All right.
BETH: I never wanted this to happen. Please believe that, Marty.
MARTY: Spare me that, Beth. (She turns away). That's pity, not love.
BETH: No, you're wrong.
MARTY (She faces her): No, I'm not wrong. You reminded me a while ago about the little blond. It may have been wrong and dishonest not to 'fess up to you about that, but it meant nothing to us and you knew it. You could measure that, couldn't you?
BETH: Yes, I guess I did.

MARTY: You know you did. It was momentary self-gratification, it was oat-sowing, or it was helping the handicapped—whatever. It had no meaning and you knew that.

BETH: It could have, though. You didn't know that at the time. And you did it deliberately. I saw you going after her, in the corner—away from the music and dancing.

MARTY: Yes, deliberately. With presence of mind and the authority of my fence post body. You know very well you weren't the very first—just the first and only one I ever loved. At any rate, that little engagement was all calculated. I processed each blush, the quickness of breath, my eye a stethoscope measuring each beat of her breast until I knew. That's not what happened with you, is it? (No answer). No, I thought not. You're not an actress.

BETH: I've fought this. It was totally unexpected. I fought it because I love you. I—am still fighting it.

MARTY: Why?

BETH: Why! I just told you why.

MARTY: Right. (She begins pacing, agitated). We lovers are a jealous lot, you know. We are compelled to probe the circumstances, the whos, the wheres, the hows, the whys. The chemistry, the physiognomy, first throb, pulse beat, first words, all the forms of self-torture.

BETH: This is demeaning, Marty.

MARTY: Exactly.

BETH: This is not what we are to each other.

MARTY: No, love, but things have changed. Ha! Metamorphosis. Ah, life and the theatre. The essential ephemeral nature of it all, isn't that how Dr. Chuck described it for us?

BETH: It's not true. Our love isn't like that at all!

MARTY: Well, who is she?

BETH: What?

MARTY: Who is she?

BETH: She?

MARTY: Yes, she. What is she like? Do I know her? Have I met her?

BETH: Oh no, Marty, never.

MARTY (A beat): Don't tell me it's a man. Are you telling me it's a man?

BETH: I could never love another woman. Somehow I thought you'd know that.

MARTY: Mind-boggling. And I actually thought I understood you. (Pacing again). Ha! What a day! (She stops and looks at her). Why I may decide to sprout boobs before the sun sets. Freud where are you now that I need you? No, he wouldn't do, would he? To hear you tell it, I thought you had fought enough battles during adolescence to last a life time.

BETH: This is different. He's a very gentle kind of person.

MARTY: Ah, been touching and feeling, has he?

BETH: Don't do that.

MARTY (Trying to keep control): How can I help doing it! We lovers are a jealous lot, I tell you. We *will* demean ourselves in spite of all. (She finds a chair and sits, an anchor for her emotions at the moment). You know as well as I that I don't hate these—these roosters, these cocks.

BETH (She has heard this before): Yes, children, I know. They're all just like children.

MARTY: Well, they are. They need our love so desperately and we give it to them. They require all things from us—to be their mothers, their whores, their girls-next-door, their pals. Whatever they want—we can fill the mold. Hens in their barnyard. They love the sweet between our thighs and we nurture them to greatness—or failure. Whatever. Ha! In return they have practically written us out of their history.

BETH: I've made you bitter.

MARTY (She stands): Not at all. I'm not a part of all that. Those are roles I can't play. I saw my mother play them and it disgusted me watching her preen for him. It was Chuck who taught me how to be feminine and coy. How to attract the appropriate man-child so I could play the lead roles. (She transforms herself even as she speaks. It is not a parody). I can do it, too. You know I can. All I need is a pair of falsies and I can hold my own, can't I? The curve of my hip is just right. I devastate them with my eyes. I can know too much, and then not enough. Whatever is required. I can play the love-game, darling. (The performance is over). I thought the big game didn't interest you either, though I knew they would be after you.

BETH: All of a sudden you've got a neat pigeon-hole for every member of the human race, haven't you? This is my fault, Marty. Forgive me. I'm tearing you up inside.

MARTY: Don't talk to me of pigeon-holes. There's only one—where the candy sticks of the world go for their sweetness.

BETH (She covers her ears with her hands): Please stop! Just don't say anymore.

MARTY: Sorry. But I warned you about jealous lovers. We're a nasty lot. Well, go on. There's more you have to tell me, isn't there?

BETH (A beat): His name is Kevin.

MARTY: Kevin. Sweet. A sweet name, don't you think?

BETH: Marty I.... I didn't know this was going to happen. I've done a terrible thing, but I didn't know.

MARTY: What do you mean? What could be worse than this?

BETH: He's—he's supposed to come over this afternoon.

MARTY (A beat): Here? He's coming here? Today? You invited him to come here?

BETH: No, I—he just wanted to borrow a book I have.

MARTY: A book. To borrow a book! What a simple-minded child-like strategy this is.

BETH: No! Oh God, I left that book in the car! It's been there all the time. I could've given it to him at school.

MARTY: Oh, this is wonderful—and getting more simple-minded all the time. We were to have a casual meeting, he and I—then off to snatch a few minutes alone with him in the car garage.

BETH (Her hands over her ears): I'm not listening to you! I won't hear this!
MARTY (The actress mimicking Beth): "Oh my, I forgot and left the book in the car, Kevin, dear. I'll just run get it." (She mimics Kevin in a pseudo-bass voice). "Quite all right, my dear, I'll run down and get it with you. That way I can sneak a little pinch of your lovely ass when you bend over."
BETH (She runs at her, her arms flailing at her): Don't do this! To yourself—to me!
MARTY (She grabs her arms and pins them to her side): Why the hell not? I'm having fun. How many people can say they're having fun while drowning in self-pity?
BETH: What, God, can I say?
MARTY (She releases her): God won't answer that.
BETH (She turns away): No.
MARTY: Who knows, maybe what's-his-name and I will become pals. How sweet. Maybe we'll become a threesome.
BETH: I think I should leave.
MARTY: No. Who would greet what's-his-name at the door? (A beat). Would you fix me another drink?
BETH: No.
MARTY: Please! I need another drink. (She falls down on the sofa, her body shaking).
BETH: Yes, all right. (She crosses to the kitchen area to fix the drink).
MARTY (She speaks calmly): Don't worry. I will compose myself. I'll play my role when what's-his-name comes to complete "Operation Devastation."
BETH: Kevin! His name is Kevin.
MARTY: Right, thank you. (She stands and turns to her). We jealous lovers may end up grovelling before you, but before others we intend to maintain a shred of dignity—(we think). After all, we know that it is just so much fury that, in the end, is going to signify—nothing.
BETH: Just sit down. Don't say anymore.
MARTY: That was a poor paraphrase, wasn't it? Is that from old Shaky-speare, I can't remember? My mind's a blank. I'll just ask old Chucky next time I see him. If I ever see him.
BETH (She steels herself as she brings the drink to her): This time I made this like you make it.
MARTY: That's the idea, get me stewed, trashed.
BETH: Yes, that's the idea. Now sit down.
MARTY: Right. A tall drink and a tall tale coming I would imagine.
BETH: It's just as you said, there's more to tell and I must tell it, mustn't I. Ready?
MARTY: You're so cool. But this is going to be hard, isn't it?
BETH: Very hard.
MARTY (She takes a big drink): Ready.
BETH: We met at school, while eating in the lunchroom.
MARTY: Gaw! What prose.
BETH: Yes, exactly. He's the basketball coach.

MARTY: Christ, already this is almost too much to bear.
BETH: Yes, isn't it.
MARTY: And highly improbable.
BETH: Yes.
MARTY: Badly plotted. Not a shred of poetry, it would seem. No doubt he caught you with your defenses down.
BETH: No question about that.
MARTY: Coaches the girls' team.
BETH: No, the boys.
MARTY: Ha! I don't know what to say. Nothing seems to fit.
BETH: Then why don't you say nothing and let me tell it?
MARTY: Of course. You said you met at lunch.
BETH: Yes.
MARTY: I thought you said the food was terrible?
BETH: It was. It is. I've been carrying a lunch for months. You haven't noticed?
MARTY: I'm not usually up at that hour. Late rehearsals, you know.
BETH: Anyway, one day I started brown bagging lunch and, coincidentally, he did, too.
MARTY: The same day?
BETH: Yes.
MARTY: Amazing. It just proves that all geniuses think alike.
BETH: I'm trying to tell this.
MARTY: Sorry. It's just hard for me to understand how love could bloom between slices of wheat bread. Does he like wheat bread, too?
BETH: No. He began sitting across from me each day. We would exchange things.
MARTY: Things? You mean your sweet brownies, no doubt.
BETH: Yes, and other things.
MARTY: Of course. Spare me the details.
BETH: As you say, it was quite prosaic—and unintended.
MARTY: It was the same way with us.
BETH: Not at all. We weren't in a public place listening to the clamor of three hundred kids without a single moment of privacy—or intimacy. You and I were alone with every opportunity to know each other and become close.
MARTY: I meant the unintended part. But you're right, of course, we were very much alone. And we had our music—and it all seemed like poetry. All of it.
BETH: But you understand how different this was.
MARTY (No longer listening to her): Just sitting in the dormitory room on the floor cross-legged. I brought the rug, you, the curtains. Miraculously, they matched. We were delighted. It was a chance thing—like us. Room-mates by the luck of the draw and we came with matching rug and curtains.
BETH (Caught up in the memory): You brought a little bottle of wine which I couldn't drink.
MARTY: I had thought of hooking a bottle of my dad's champagne, but figured it would be too much. Had I known it was going to be you, I would have done it.

BETH: I still probably couldn't have drunk it. One drink and I swim.
MARTY: Well, I got you to take a sip or two and we were sitting there so pleased with ourselves, thinking how lucky we were.
BETH: Yes.
MARTY: What were we talking about?
BETH: Summer clothes, don't you remember?
MARTY: Right. It was nasty hot. Fortunately, you brought a fan and we hooked it up and put it in the window.
BETH: Neither of us had brought enough summer clothes.
MARTY: Ah, and decided to share until we could get home for a weekend.
BETH: Yes, that was it. Then we sort of looked at each other and knew that would never work.
MARTY: We had quite a laugh.
BETH: Especially after you tried to slip one of my dresses on over your clothes.
MARTY: I drooped like a scarecrow in the mirror.
BETH: Then I tried on one of yours and almost strangled myself.
MARTY: You nearly ripped a seam.
BETH: Hilarious. I thought I'd never get out of that thing. What kids we were.
MARTY: I was laughing and crying all at the same time. It was one of my best dresses and I thought you were going to ruin it. I didn't know then that I'd be wearing grubby jeans for the next four years.
BETH: You were laughing, not crying. Tears of laughter.
MARTY: I guess so. What a time. Then we sat there exhausted and just looked at each other.
BETH: I just couldn't think of anything to say.
MARTY: I just wanted to look at you.
BETH: Then we tried not to look at each other.
MARTY: Right then, we knew we were in love.
BETH: No. I was confused. I didn't know what was happening.
MARTY: I just knew I had to have my arms around you. You tried to resist me at first.
BETH: I was frightened—but you were so gentle. God, so gentle. It was so different from anything before. I had always felt like I was being invaded, not loved. This was so different.
MARTY: I was simply overcome with love. Perhaps I haven't been so gentle since.
BETH: Oh, but you have. You are always gentle.
MARTY: Am I? Perhaps I won't be now—now that the invader has returned.
BETH: He's not like that.
MARTY: Isn't he? How do you know that? You haven't slept with him. Oh yes, I know that. You can be sure, I would know if you had.
BETH (The spell of the last moments is broken now): Yes, I suppose you would. Because you measure things, don't you. The quickness of breath, the beat of the breast, and so on.

MARTY: Ah, you see? You remember what a jealous lover feels like. Too bad this wasn't calculated.
BETH: I — didn't mean that the way it sounded.
MARTY: Of course not. What you meant was you felt chained to me. That now I'm an obstacle, something to get around or overcome.
BETH: That's not true!
MARTY (She stares at her a beat): I guess we'd both like to believe that. But, you see, I came back last night to get the music tapes. You, with your loads of school preparations, were out. (A half-beat). I didn't go back to rehearsal. I stayed here and waited.
BETH: You were here?
MARTY: Yes. With the lights out. For two hours. Until I saw your car turn the corner and go down into the parking garage. Then I left.
BETH: Then you were — spying on me. I could have been anywhere, you know. Shopping — or anywhere.
MARTY: You told me you would be here.
BETH: And you told me you would be at rehearsal.
MARTY: I was here by accident — not design. What about you? (No answer. She stands before her). Suddenly, it's all very trashy, isn't it? You deceive me, and I, the jealous lover, spy on you. Mutual love becomes mutual distrust.
BETH: Oh no, Marty, we can't let that happen to us. We mustn't allow that to happen.
MARTY (She slaps her hard across the face): How dare you plead with *me* to save our love! How dare you!
BETH (A beat. She is stunned by the blow): Yes. You're right, of course. Forgive me.
MARTY: Oh my God, I can't believe I did that. (She falls to her knees before her). Oh my God, oh my Beth, it's you who must forgive me. How could I do that!? How could I!?
BETH: It's what you should have done.
MARTY: Never. Never!
BETH: I've done this to us. I've been such a fool. Why, I could have destroyed all we have together. (She lifts her up from her knees). Marty, I want to kiss you — really kiss you.
MARTY (She pulls away abruptly and moves away from her): No! ... Not now. Let's just let things — settle for a moment. I haven't eaten anything today and the drink has made me dizzy. I've been riding one helluva emotional roller-coaster. I'll be all right in a moment.
BETH: I've put you through Hell. Myself as well.
MARTY: No. You were happy.
BETH: No, just thoughtless and selfish — and dumb, not to realize what was happening.
MARTY (A beat): Does he know about us?
BETH: Yes. No — not everything.

MARTY: Not that we're lovers?
BETH: No.
MARTY: What would he say if he knew that?
BETH: I don't know.
MARTY: Maybe you were afraid to find out.
BETH: Things haven't gone that far.
MARTY: Just how far have "things" gone?
BETH: We both teach History. There's a lot to talk about.
MARTY: And much that goes unsaid.
BETH: I suppose that's true.
MARTY: You know it's true. Last night, for instance?
BETH: We had coffee at that restaurant down the street where you and I used to go sometimes.
MARTY: And afterwards?
BETH: We sat in his car for a while before I came home.
MARTY: That all? No kissing, no fondling of your beautiful breasts? What do you suppose is wrong with him?
BETH: Marty, this is difficult enough. I've told you I've been foolish. I know this won't be easy to forget, but could we just drop the whole subject for a while?
MARTY: We can't. He's coming over. You're attracted to him.
BETH: To borrow a book. It was all a mistake, I see that now.
MARTY: And he's attracted to you.
BETH: I don't know that.
MARTY: What the hell do you mean you don't know that!? Quit fooling yourself—and me! He's not coming to borrow any goddamned book. He's coming to see you.
BETH: He's coming to borrow a book! Maybe he was coming for something else, as you say, but now he's coming to borrow a book! Period!
MARTY (A beat): Whatever you say.
BETH: Hell's bells, let's just get out of this apartment for a while.
MARTY: We can't now. What if he comes while we're gone?
BETH: I can give him the book tomorrow.
MARTY: No. It's better if we play this little scene today. I don't want to go through another day like this one.
BETH (She has moved by the window): I'm sorry, Marty.
MARTY: I'm sorry, too. I don't normally slap beautiful butterflies. Why don't you let me fix you a drink for a change? It might help.
BETH: Are you crazy? One drink and I'm flying, you know that.
MARTY: Well, maybe that's what you should do for once, fly.
BETH: How about out this window?
MARTY: It's too high. You're a butterfly, not a bird. Shows how different we are. I can drink a birdbath of drinks and never feel a thing.
BETH (She turns to her): That is the most absurd thing you ever said in your life. Three drinks and you start re-living every role you ever played.

MARTY: Well, it's tiresome being myself all the time.
BETH: I never know who you're going to be. It's a little disconcerting to go out with someone and come back with an entirely different person.
MARTY: Nonsense, you love it.
BETH: I'll admit the comic roles are a trip, but some of the others ...
MARTY: I suppose you're referring to Medea.
BETH: Last time you were Medea you found a Jason to pick on. We almost got arrested.
MARTY: The barkeep, you mean. Yes, that was a bad choice.
BETH (She can't hide her amusement): All I can say is, it's a good thing there weren't any children around.
MARTY (She makes little karate chops with her hands): Chop-chop-chop-chop!

BETH begins laughing hysterically, a release.

MARTY: Am I right? The barkeep disappeared under the counter?
BETH (Through her laughter): What did you expect—the way you were flailing your arms and—and standing on—on the—stool!
MARTY: It started twirling around, you know. I could have been killed.
BETH: The guy next to you ...
MARTY: That slob.
BETH (Mimics her): The BIG gesture ...
MARTY: Right in his fat face.
BETH: He didn't deserve that.
MARTY: Oh yes he did. He was bending all over me trying to get a look up your dress.
BETH: What thunder when he fell!
MARTY: Yes, a colossus crumbling.
BETH: Hilarious!
MARTY: No, satisfying! I demolished him!

They are both laughing hysterically, a great relief, but the underlying tension is triggered instantly by the SOUND of a knock at the door. The knock catches them at the peak of their laughter and stops them at a high pitch. Silence as they freeze. Two beats, then MARTY crosses to the sofa and sits.

MARTY (Flatly): We have a guest ... . Well, go to the door, damn it!
BETH: I'm going! ... . I'm going. (She crosses to the door, looks back at Marty, then opens it).

KEVIN LOCKRIDGE stands there. He meets the expectations of a coach: handsome, tall, muscular, virile-looking. Still, there is a soft, unassertive quality about him. He looks the shy young man courting a lady, tugging awkwardly at his tie and offering to Beth a gentle smile.

KEVIN: Hi. Came for that book.

BETH: Oh yes, hi. I—(Not said: "left the book in my car"). Come in, I'll have to get it.

KEVIN: Thanks. I hope I haven't come at a bad time, interrupted anything.

BETH: No, no, it's fine. Fine—oh eh, I'd like you to meet someone. (She looks to the sofa where Marty sits straight and has not turned. There is a frenetic quality in Beth's voice and movement as she guides him to the sofa). This—this is my—friend, Marty. Kevin Lockridge, the coach at the school, Marty. This is Marty—Marty Williams.

KEVIN: Hey, you could mention that I teach a little History, too. After all, it's why I'm here. Nice to meet ...

MARTY (She does not get up): History lover, are you?

KEVIN: Yeah, Beth teaches American and I teach World History.

MARTY: I know what Beth teaches. So you teach the whole world, eh?

KEVIN (He smiles): Oh, it's a big chunk, all right. Beth has two hundred years in two semesters and I have three thousand.

MARTY: Either way it's a scandal.

KEVIN: You're absolutely right about that.

MARTY: Like teaching *The Reader's Digest*.

KEVIN: Sometimes it does seem like that. I'm really glad for a chance to meet you. Beth says you're an extraordinary actress.

MARTY: Yes I am. That's why I'm directing community theatre.

KEVIN: Well, it's a very good community theatre.

MARTY: Yes, I know.

KEVIN: I have a friend who played in one of your shows ...

MARTY: Would you like a drink? Tea? Coffee? Bourbon?

KEVIN: He mentioned how professional and demanding you were. You might remember him even though he had only a small role. His name ...

MARTY (She stands): I asked if you wanted a drink. Tea? Coffee? Bourbon? No. Beer, that's it. You'd probably want beer. We don't have any beer.

KEVIN: Beer. Why would I probably want beer? Let me see if I can think of a reason.

MARTY (She sits): Don't trouble yourself too much.

KEVIN: Actually, I just came to borrow a book. Beth's got a western civilization book I haven't seen and I ...

MARTY: Beth, he came to borrow a book.

BETH: What?

MARTY: The book! The damned book! Aren't you listening?

BETH: Well, I know that! Why do you think he's here?

MARTY: I don't know. You tell me.

A beat of tense silence as KEVIN looks from one to another.

KEVIN: I'm sorry, I must have interrupted something. I couldn't help but hear the laughter when I came to the door. Sounded like fun. But when I knocked everything seemed to get real quiet.
MARTY: That's true, everything seemed to stop right there.
BETH: That was just—we were into old times. A couple of months ago, Marty and I were out for a drink and ...
MARTY: Marty drinks like a damned fish, you see. Marty often gets trashed. It's really disgraceful how trashed Marty can get. You ever do that?
KEVIN: Sometimes when my team plays a particularly rotten game, I've been known to over-indulge a bit.
MARTY: I never "over-indulge," I get trashed. There's a big difference you know. Getting trashed is much more serious, don't you agree? You understand, I'm not trying to be critical.
KEVIN: Right. Clearly your drunks are far more fulfilling than mine.
MARTY: Yes, because there's a difference between re-playing some damned game and spilling your guts out.
KEVIN (A beat): You're right. It's the difference between fooling around and going straight for the jugular.
MARTY (She stands pushing her hands up and down and yelling in his face): T-E-A-M! T-E-A-M! TEAM! TEAM! TEAM!
BETH (She pulls him away from her by his coat sleeve): I left the book in my car, I'm sorry. I put it there—oh sometime—I can't remember—to bring it to school and—oh I don't know—it's down there. I mean it's in my car.

MARTY sits and pretends to work.

KEVIN (He has been stunned by Marty's outburst and looks from one to the other in confusion. Finally, he looks at Beth and sees she is upset. He takes her hand): Listen, it's okay. I've come at a bad time anyway. Why don't you just bring it to school tomorrow?
BETH: No, I'm going to get it now!
KEVIN: I'll remind you tomorrow. There's really no rush.
BETH: I'm going to get it for you now. You come with me.
KEVIN: I can just wait ...
BETH: But the car's in the apartment garage.
KEVIN: Oh. (He glances at Marty). It's okay, you go ahead. I don't mind waiting. Maybe I could just sit and talk to Marty.
MARTY (Not looking up): Marty's busy.
KEVIN: Right. Then I'll just sit and wait.
BETH: Kevin! (Flustered). I—my keys. I don't know where my keys are. (She looks around confused).
MARTY: They're right there in your bag.
BETH: What?

MARTY: In your bag. On the window seat!
BETH: Oh. Oh yes. (She crosses quickly to the window seat and fumbles in her bag. She finds the keys then immediately drops them on the rug). Oh!
MARTY: Your hands are shaking. Get control of yourself.
BETH: I'm in control of myself, thank you!
KEVIN: Beth?
BETH: What!?
KEVIN: You're sure you're all right?
BETH: I am fine! I just dropped my keys. That's not much of a big deal, is it? (She goes quickly to the door and exits, slamming it).
MARTY (She pretends to work. After a half-beat): That was a disgusting display, wasn't it? What do you suppose is wrong with her?
KEVIN: I have no idea. Do you? (Of course, he does have an idea).
MARTY (Pause): She given to moods, you see. She's not a very strong person. Much too fragile.
KEVIN: I see. But you're different?
MARTY: That's presumptuous, you know. You're in a place five minutes and you've already analyzed all the characters.
KEVIN: That makes two of us, right?
MARTY: You don't have to stand there. You can sit down.
KEVIN: Thanks. I wasn't quite sure.
MARTY: Well, it's going to take a few minutes. The elevator to the parking garage wouldn't win a race with a turtle.
KEVIN: Right.
MARTY: You'll have to forgive me If I don't talk to you, I have work to do. Preparations for the rehearsal tonight. If I don't line things up one-two-three, it's all chaos with these amateurs.
KEVIN: You go right ahead.
MARTY (Pause): Nothing to drink then?
KEVIN: No thanks. Not even a beer.
MARTY: Well, we don't have Gatorade.
KEVIN (A slight smile): That's too bad. I'm fond of Gatorade.
MARTY (Pause): I hope you won't dehydrate while waiting.
KEVIN: You're a very caring hostess.
MARTY: I'm not a hostess. (Pause). You're trying to top me. Isn't that what you're playing?
KEVIN: Oh, I'm not playing anything.
MARTY: Really? (Pause. Pretending to work). How's the team?
KEVIN: Fine. The season is over.
MARTY: Then it was not a good season.
KEVIN: Yes, it was. We built a lot of character.
MARTY: You mean all that bullshit.
KEVIN: Yes, all that bullshit. It's winning that counts, isn't it? That's the thing.

MARTY: I wouldn't know. I'm not like you.
KEVIN: Oh, I suspect we might have a thing or two in common.
MARTY: I doubt that. At any rate, let's not try and find out. It might take a very long time and I have work to do.
KEVIN: Sure. I guess all that laughter I heard outside the door must have broken your concentration.
MARTY (She looks at him): Some drunken escapade of mine she thought of.
KEVIN: Was it one in which you tore your guts out?
MARTY: Fuck you, Kevin what-ever-your-name-is.
KEVIN: It's Lockridge, Mary what-ever-your-name-is.
MARTY: It's Marty. You know that.
KEVIN: Yes, Perhaps I confused you with somebody else.
MARTY (Pointedly): You know who I am.
KEVIN: Yes. (Pause). This isn't much fun, is it?
MARTY: I've been better entertained.
KEVIN: As for me, I have an English ancestry. We Lockridges go back pretty far. Very undistinguished record, I must admit.
MARTY: Too bad. You've earned my sympathy.
KEVIN: Yes, I can see that. What of you?
MARTY: What of me what?
KEVIN: I was inquiring about your ancestry.
MARTY: My, we're being chatty.
KEVIN: Well, I just happen to have a passing interest in genealogy.
MARTY: Let's hope it passes quickly. But you'd like to hear all about me, wouldn't you? That would interest you at the moment and you'll find I'm much more interesting than those dreadful family tree things.
KEVIN: I'm certain you are. Yes, I'd like to hear about you.
MARTY: Yes, I knew you would. It was a breach birth. My mother hated me as a child. My father raped me at thirteen. My sister cut off my tits and my brother ate them in a covered dish. Finally, I left home and wandered the earth as a penniless orphan only to be adopted by a step-father who beat and starved me.
KEVIN (He laughs): You're wonderful.
MARTY: What did you say?
KEVIN: I said, you're wonderful.
MARTY: You really are an asshole, aren't you?
KEVIN (He leans forward): Yes. To have hurt someone so badly.
MARTY (She gets up abruptly and crosses the room): I don't know what you're talking about. You seem to have gone adrift.
KEVIN (He stands): Why yes, that's it exactly. Gone adrift. And been so unfulfilled. Perhaps you can understand how that feels.
MARTY (She looks at him): No, I wouldn't understand.
KEVIN: Mind if I tell you about it?
MARTY: I haven't the time ...

KEVIN: Good, I appreciate your interest. You see, my whole life until recently has been tied to games and to winning—and to whatever else would get me to the place where I could play those games. Then I come to find out that I'm really not good enough to play. That happens to thousands like me every year. It's nothing new. The real problem came when games weren't good enough for me. That's what I meant by building character—theirs and mine. Actually, my team just won the state double-A championship. But that isn't good enough anymore. It just doesn't do it.

MARTY (Angrily): And she will, is that what you think? She'll—fulfill you. Well, what about her? What will it do for her? Have you thought of that?

KEVIN: She has to decide that.

MARTY: How commendable. Simple as that, is it? Love can't do everything, Coach.

KEVIN: I'm well aware of that.

MARTY (Hurting inside): Are you aware of the commitments involved? The times when you long to be fulfilled and are not? The compromises one makes to hold on to what is precious to you?

KEVIN: And the others involved who love her just as much.

MARTY: Love her as much? Hardly. Hardly. (Bitterly). So sorry I've interfered with your game plan, Coach.

KEVIN: I knew this was different. I just couldn't figure out what it was.

MARTY: Different as in unnatural. Different as in abnormal, isn't that what you think?

KEVIN: Different as in relationship. Well, it is different, isn't it? You're not a room-mate or a friend, you're her lover and that's different.

MARTY: It's not different to us. It's been perfectly natural.

KEVIN: Whatever it is I can't do anything about it.

MARTY (She crosses to him): You damned fool, you already have! It'll never be the same again. Well, take her if you can, man. Take my life, my love, but you'll never get the white flag from me. I wish you dead—even if you walk out of here and never see her again. Because of you it will never be the same again. (She starts up to the hall to the bedroom).

KEVIN: She won't leave you.

MARTY (She stops and looks at him): Is this more of your instant character analysis?

KEVIN: I've just known from the beginning that something—or someone was holding her back.

MARTY: She's a proper girl, Coach. She wouldn't screw on the first date.

KEVIN: It's my turn. Fuck you Marty what-ever-your-name-is.

MARTY (A beat): Well, I'm listening.

KEVIN: When we talk or occasionally when we've touched—I can sense a—holding back, a fear of giving way. She seems so strong in many ways—yet such a fragile, gentle person. She reminds me of a butterfly.

MARTY (Surprised): What?

KEVIN: Yes, a butterfly. So strong in flight, yet so fragile. Over and over I have asked myself, what could be the matter here? I sensed it wasn't me. No, just the opposite. She is drawn to me, I can feel her wanting me, and yet—now I understand it.

MARTY: She loves me and I love her. Isn't that enough for you? I'm sure a handsome champ like you has had his share of women. This is nothing to you. You can walk out of here and another will parade by you and tempt you with her sweets.

KEVIN: You think you're the only one who knows how to love.

MARTY: All I know is she's the only one who ever loved me—and the only one I ever loved. Now it will never be the same again.

KEVIN: But she'll choose you.

MARTY: You want me to let her go, don't you? That's why you're here. You didn't come for any book.

KEVIN: Not true. It was just a chance to see her again today—away from that school. The book was the best excuse I could think of. I'm in love with her. That ought to be easy for you to understand.

MARTY: She's committed to me.

KEVIN: I know that.

MARTY: Even though you think she loves you.

KEVIN (Gently): Yes, Marty, I do think that.

MARTY: You pig! Do you know what you're asking of me?

KEVIN: She's committed to you, just as you said. She'll always be holding back from me.

MARTY: Well, she never held back from me! Not once, Coach, not from the very beginning. She has given herself to me completely and I to her. Do you think for a moment you're capable of understanding or feeling that kind of thing?

KEVIN: How can I if she is with you and not me? (A half-beat). You've won. You get her and I get a textbook.

MARTY (She strikes out at him): Is this what you call winning? Is this what you teach your jock-heads? You come in here and you ruin everything and then you say I win. Ha! Is this your idea of character building? Oh, if I had a weapon, if I had a ...

BETH enters at the door with the book. She closes the door and leans against it, the book wrapped in her arms. MARTY and KEVIN look at her a beat, then MARTY crosses up to the kitchen area and pours herself a stiff drink and downs it. BETH watches her. Finally, MARTY speaks.

MARTY (A jovial attempt that immediately turns bitter): Well, it took you long enough. It's been quite a burden entertaining what's-his-name all this time. We did manage to have a delightful and informative conversation, though, didn't we, what's-your-name?

KEVIN does not reply. His eyes are on Beth.

MARTY: Well, we've chatted so long he's been reduced to silence. He's all puffed out, it seems. I don't know quite what we should do with him, do you?
KEVIN: Beth, I love you.
MARTY: Ah, now he's getting his second wind.
KEVIN (He moves a step toward Beth): I didn't just come here for that book, Beth. I had to see you. I just wanted to be with you. I—wanted to take you with me. But—you have to take me first.

BETH can say nothing. She trembles and presses herself against the door, hugging the book in her arms.

MARTY (To Kevin): Now look what you've done. She's tied in knots. Very heavy stuff, Coach, for someone who was going to settle for a book.
KEVIN: I can't help it! I love her!
MARTY: Hear that, love? Coach won't give up. (Bitterly). These jocks they all want to be winners, you know.
BETH (She straightens up and speaks strongly): I won't leave you, Marty.

KEVIN looks at Beth, but her eyes are on Marty. Finally, he turns to Marty.

KEVIN: You see? It's just as I said. I'll be going now. (He crosses to Beth). I'd still like to have that book.

BETH looks at him, then averts her eyes from him as she releases the book to him. She crosses quickly downstage by the bookcase away from the door.

KEVIN: Thank you. I—Good-bye, Beth. (To Marty). You're a worthy opponent, Marty. I'm glad I met you. Good-bye. (He exits the apartment).

A long silence. MARTY stares at BETH who continues to look away.

MARTY (Gently): You want tea?
BETH: No. Not right now, thank you.
MARTY: No—it's I who thank you.
BETH (She looks at her): For what? All I've done is make you miserable.
MARTY: What about yourself?
BETH: Yes, I'm miserable, too.
MARTY (Pause): It's a shame you held back.
BETH: What?
MARTY: That you couldn't give him what you wanted to give him.
BETH: I don't understand.
MARTY: Well, you wanted to love him, didn't you? But you really couldn't because you loved me.

BETH (She turns away): I don't know what I wanted. Please, let's just not talk about it anymore right now.
MARTY: When you wanted me, you didn't hold back.
BETH: What are you saying?
MARTY (A beat): Nothing. Maybe we've changed.
BETH (She moves toward her): You haven't changed. I'm the one who did this to us.
MARTY: If one of us changes, then the other does, too.
BETH: Oh God, have I ruined everything for us?
MARTY: No. We've always given all we could give to each other. What more can be asked of two people?
BETH (She crosses to her): Marty, you've given me everything.
MARTY: And you've given me everything.
BETH: I never want to leave you, Marty.

They embrace tenderly, BETH holds on for dear life as though it were for the last time.

MARTY: I think now's the time you could use that walk. A little of that fresh spring air will clear your head.
BETH: No.
MARTY: Yes. It's been one helluva a day for both of us. I'll get your coat for you. (She is moving toward the closet). You'll have to hurry. There isn't much daylight left. (She gets the coat and helps her into it).
BETH: You're coming too, aren't you?
MARTY: You forget, I've still got a rehearsal to plan. Someone came by to borrow a book and interrupted me.
BETH: The damned coach.
MARTY: Well, he wasn't exactly a royal prince. Jesus, Beth, love between two slices of wheat bread and a brownie is almost too much to bear.
BETH: Marty ...
MARTY: Just walk, will ya? They say if you exercise enough you can avoid flabby boobs. I always have.
BETH (She smiles): You're crazy.
MARTY: True. There's the door. (She points the way and then moves to the sofa and pretends to go to work).

BETH watches her a beat, smiles, and is about to open the door.

MARTY (Not looking at her): Beth.
BETH: Yes?
MARTY: I think you ought to call the damned coach.
BETH: Marty! (She moves a few steps toward the sofa).

MARTY: Yes, I think you really ought to do that.
BETH: I can't.
MARTY (She stands and turns to her): Yes you can. You must. Listen, it's the only way we can keep what we've had together. Otherwise, we'll lose it. I think you know that.
BETH (Just a hint of a smile): Are you trying to get rid of me?
MARTY: No. I'm trying to hold on to you.
BETH (A beat as she searches her face and understands): All right, darling, I will. I'll — call him.
MARTY (She looks at her a half-beat, then must turn away. She sits on the sofa and picks up her promptbook and stares out rigidly): Good. That's good.

BETH looks at her lovingly, then turns and moves slowly out the door, closing it gently.

MARTY (Still staring out): So what do you think Dr. Chuck? Was that a performance or wasn't it? I'm a fine actress. Hell, I'm a great actress! (She puts her head in her hands, close to breaking down, but holding on. Then she lifts her head and looks to the heavens). So where's the applause? What's the award? (She stands, her arms out pleading). You expect me to go on like this? Well, I'm not that fucking talented. (Her arms at her side). Yes, yes, I know. Settle for less. (She raises her right fist). Well, dear God, if I've got to endure you, you'll have to endure me! (She lowers her fist and looks out menacingly). I hope Leslie Markham throws her goddamned ass out of joint tonight!

The LIGHTS fade to BLACKOUT.